ROCK-A-BYE BABY

ROCK-A-BYE BABY

A Death Behind Bars

Anne Kershaw

and Mary Lasovich

Canadian Cataloguing in Publication Data

Kershaw, Anne, 1952–
  Rock-a-bye baby : a death behind bars

ISBN 0-7710-4521-2

1. Moore, Marlene, d. 1988. 2. Prison for Women
(Kingston, Ont.) – Biography. 3. Female offenders –
Canada – Biography. 4. Women prisoners – Ontario –
Kingston – Biography. 5. Women prisoners –
Ontario – Kingston – Suicidal behavior.
I. Lasovich, Mary, 1952–   . II. Title.

HV9505.M6K47 1991   365'.43'092   C91-093306-5

Printed and bound in Canada. The paper used in this book is acid free.

McClelland & Stewart Inc.
The Canadian Publishers
481 University Avenue
Toronto, Ontario
M5G 2E9

To the memory of Marlene

CONTENTS

These chapter titles are taken verbatim from a sentence-completion test Marlene wrote for a psychologist in 1985.

PREFACE

The eleven federal penitentiaries in the Ontario region house close to 3,200 of the country's 13,000 federal offenders, so it is not surprising that, as reporters for *The Whig-Standard* newspaper in Kingston, Mary Lasovich and I developed a particular and intense interest in covering prisons. In the course of this work we heard persistent and frequent reports from inside these institutions about self-mutilation by inmates and about suicide attempts, successful and unsuccessful.

Mary and I found ourselves increasingly frustrated by the difficulty of conveying anything meaningful about prison conditions and the complex workings of the criminal justice system within the limitations and deadlines of a small daily newspaper. Rather than continuing to cover these tragic suicides as isolated and unrelated events, we wanted to find out in depth what it is about our institutions that drives inmates to such despair. When we learned of Marlene's death in December 1988, we were determined that it not pass largely unnoticed. Marlene, who throughout her life hurt no one as much as she hurt herself, came to symbolize for us the failure of our mental-health and penal institutions to respond to the pain of those in their custody. We asked Neil Reynolds, editor of *The Whig-Standard*, to excuse us temporarily from our regular reporting duties so that we could devote ourselves fully to researching and writing Marlene's story. Eleven months later, on 25 November, 1989, *The Whig-Standard* published "Rock-A-Bye Baby: The Life and Death of Marlene Moore" in a special forty-six-page edition of its Saturday magazine.

For the most part, Marlene's family chose not to participate in the telling of her story. Marlene's mother did not respond to our overtures, made through other members of the family, and her father is no longer alive. Her oldest brother, Curry Moore, did grant an extensive interview, and we made contact with another brother, Tom, and two sisters, Arlene and Maureen. All of them were reluctant to contribute, saying distortion and inaccuracies in previous media stories had misrepresented Marlene's childhood and had caused severe distress to some family members.

After Marlene's story was published by *The Whig-Standard*, at the urging of many readers who wanted to see "Rock-A-Bye Baby" in a more permanent form, we started to think about revising it and making it into a book. Based on the original text, this book incorporates much new information throughout. As well, it continues Marlene's story through the inquest into her death and sets it in the broader context of conditions at the Prison for Women. The book represents the achievement of our goal to make Marlene's story available to all those Canadians who care enough to read about her pain and to learn something about ourselves, our institutions, and our response to the most damaged among us.

It is extremely gratifying now to have an opportunity to thank those people whose expertise helped shape both the article and the book and whose friendship and faith sustained its authors. Mary Lasovich, my co-author on the original article, was unable to work with me in the same manner on the book. But she contributed to the chapter on the coroner's inquest and made valuable suggestions for improving the final manuscript.

Both of us are especially grateful to those people who loved Marlene and trusted us enough to share their memories – particularly June Callwood and Janis Cole. Special thanks go to Barb Dennis, Daryl Dollan, Brenda Hope, Gayle Horii, Patricia, and Corry – the "survivors." They cared enough about the women now fighting for their lives in the Prison for Women to relive and recount their own past horrors. We feel great respect and admiration for their efforts.

Thanks also to Neil Reynolds for believing in this project and for suggesting the title "Rock-A-Bye Baby," which so poignantly captures all that we came to feel about Marlene. And thanks to all our friends and colleagues at *The Whig-Standard* for their enthusiastic support and encouragement.

We would also like to express gratitude to our literary agent Jan Whitford, who deftly and serenely guided us through the legal intricacies of publishing, and to Dinah Forbes of McClelland & Stewart, whose tremendous editing skills and sensitive vision helped shape the book. Thanks also to Robert Clarke for his careful copy editing, and to the photographers who donated their work for use in this book.

I would like to thank my parents, Marjorie and John, and the friends whom I leaned on when my confidence wavered. Thank you Sylvia Barrett, Pam Benson, Jane Derby, Suki Falkner, Maureen Garvie, Sharron Kusiar, and Larry Scanlan. My most heartfelt thanks go to Richard Peterson.

Anne Kershaw
Kingston, Ontario

PROLOGUE

"I'm looking for some answers. I want to know how she could have killed herself.

"I mean I'm not saying they out and out murdered her. I can't believe that. But when I was a kid I remember the time my puppy dog was frothing at the mouth and my dad said it had distemper and told me he wanted to shoot him in the morning. Of course I didn't know or understand anything about distemper and so I took the puppy dog and I went over in a field, Snively's field, and I built myself a lean-to, right by the lake, which was only fifteen or twenty feet away.

"We were country kids. We'd stay out all night and it wouldn't bother us. And I slept with the puppy dog all night. But when I woke up in the morning the puppy dog was gone. Well, I walk over to the lake and there's the puppy dog. It's alive but its head's under the water and it's swimming in little tiny circles – little wee tiny circles – and I realized, of course, that the puppy dog was deathly sick. There was something wrong with it and I didn't know how to deal with that, so I took a stick and I held him under until he was dead, and I let that puppy dog drown.

"And I think I did that because I didn't understand how to take care of it, and I think that's what they done to Marlene. They didn't know how to deal with her and they let her hang herself."

Curry "Sonny" Moore
Marlene's oldest brother

1

When I was a child
I could never defend myself

Around four in the afternoon on Friday, December 2, 1988, senior prison administrator Therese Decaire escorted Marlene Moore on the short walk from the segregation unit at Kingston's Prison for Women to the institution's infirmary. They stopped several times along the way so the frail prisoner could catch her breath. Marlene, only thirty-one years old, moved at the stooped, shuffling pace of an old woman.

Against her short, copper-blonde hair, Marlene's pale skin was nearly translucent. Her face, drawn and sunken under high cheekbones, was haunted with fear. Eyes that once sparkled with mischief now flashed with pain. A grisly gridwork of scars covered her upper and lower arms, upper thighs, chest, and stomach.

Since arriving at the federal women's prison eight months earlier, prisoner No. 739186A had been a frequent patient at the second-floor infirmary. Her body was ravaged by self-mutilation and the intense pain of a chronic bladder disorder. Since April she had been admitted to the hospital for days or weeks at a stretch, sometimes at her own request and sometimes on orders from medical personnel.

Although the infirmary is quieter than other parts of the prison, it is just as bleak. Plumbing pipes painted the same smoky blue as the walls run from floor to ceiling. The furnishings are stark: three steel, adjustable beds, each with its own portable food tray and night table; a tiny refrigerator; a television perched high on a multi-tiered stand; and in one corner a tall, rusted metal cabinet for storing linens. A large bank of fluorescent tubes, slung about three feet from the ceiling, accentuates the harsh atmosphere. Beneath a worn, mustard-coloured spread and blue blanket, Marlene's bed was specially fitted with two blue, disposable pads, a humiliation forced on her by her bed-wetting. Seated in front of one of three large, cathedral-style windows, Marlene could see southward past the prison's massive, grey heating plant to a blue expanse of Lake Ontario.

A few hours after her transfer to the prison hospital on December 2, Warden Mary Cassidy gave Marlene permission to make a long-distance phone call to Sue Kemsley. Marlene and Sue had been lovers, sharing an apartment in Toronto until Marlene's conviction for robbery the previous April. On the phone Marlene told Sue she had agreed to surgery for her bladder condition and that she had "flushed" the piece of glass she usually kept tucked inside her cheek in case she felt the need to cut herself. She sounded calm, kind of distant, but there was no sense of finality, nothing extraordinary in their reluctant goodbyes.

Marlene wasn't alone on the ward. In the next bed was Brenda Blondell, who had been rushed by ambulance to Kingston General Hospital the week before after trying to hang herself in her segregation cell. Blondell, thirty-nine years old, was still weak with a sore throat and congested lungs. The two prisoners traded stories. Marlene was despondent about her future with Sue and pointedly curious about Blondell's brush with death. "Did it hurt? How long were you out?" she asked.

That night Marlene slept fitfully, as usual. She woke up late Saturday morning and ate a light meal of soup and pudding. Later that day, duty nurse Leanne Greene heard a knock on the door of the nurse's station. She found Marlene squatting against the wall, bent over in pain. Greene gave her patient an analgesic and suggested a warm soak in the tub. In the inmate bathroom two doors down the hall Blondell helped with a bubble bath, and when Marlene returned to the ward she was wearing fresh, blue floral pyjamas, a white T-shirt, and white ankle socks.

Before her shift ended Greene removed sutures from Marlene's right leg and right wrist, where she had deliberately cut herself with a razor blade while still in segregation. Throughout the procedure Marlene chatted openly with the nurse. Afterwards Marlene poured herself a cup of coffee and returned to her bed in the ward.

At 3 p.m. nurse Marsha Brown reported for her eight-hour shift. Scanning the shift changeover report, Brown read nothing to suggest that the evening ahead would be anything but routine. The part-time nurse had come to know Marlene well over the summer of 1988. On several occasions Brown had tended to Marlene's self-inflicted injuries.

About fifteen minutes after arriving at her post that December afternoon, Brown heard pounding on the curtained glass wall that separates the nurses' quarters from the hospital ward. It was Brenda Blondell, distraught because Marlene was in trouble once again, with severe pain.

Brown found Marlene curled tightly in a ball in the middle of her narrow bed, rocking back and forth. Marlene managed to tell the nurse that she had stabbing pains in her pubic area. And she said: "If it doesn't go away, I'll have to cut it out, or slash it out, or hang myself." Her anguished words didn't overly alarm Marsha Brown; she had heard similar threats from Marlene many times before. She gave Marlene two Tylenol tablets, one with codeine and one extra-strength. It was a combination recommended by the prison doctor to control

17

the young woman's pain without flooding her system with codeine.

At about 3:45 p.m. an inmate named Adele Gruenke arrived on the hospital ward with dinner trays. Gruenke heard Marlene crying and decided to leave the trays in the hallway outside the room. Marlene's pain soon subsided but she told Brown she was still feeling "uptight." Brown offered her a Gravol pill to help her relax.

During the next hour the nurse spent all her time in the hospital room with her two patients, occasionally perched on the end of Marlene's bed, talking and joking. Marlene seemed to be in better spirits. She nibbled at a tomato sandwich and sipped tea, provoking a round of teasing from the nurse, who knew Marlene as someone who never drank tea.

A few minutes before 5 p.m. Brown left the locked hospital ward unattended and set out to dispense medication to prisoners in the segregation wing. At the same time Brenda Blondell prepared to take a shower in the inmate bathroom two doors down the hall. Blondell deliberately decided to take a shower instead of a bath so she wouldn't be away from Marlene too long. Before leaving she stashed away some plastic knives left from dinner and made her room-mate promise not to harm herself.

In recent weeks, because the segregation area was full, the daily medication run had taken as long as forty-five minutes. This time Marsha Brown was on her way back to the hospital after only fifteen minutes. But even that short absence was too long to avert tragedy.

Just outside Room 202, the door to the hospital, the nurse heard banging sounds and Blondell's urgent screams. The hysterical prisoner, wearing a soaked flannel nightgown, gestured frantically toward Marlene's bed.

The nurse peered past Blondell into the room. She saw Marlene sprawled across her bed, her head and shoulders hanging only a few inches from the floor. There was a pool of blood underneath her head and a length of ripped sheet fashioned in a noose around her neck.

At Kingston General Hospital at 5:43 p.m., Marlene Moore was officially pronounced dead.

Marlene Moore was born in Toronto on October 29, 1957, the tenth child of Edith Elizabeth and John (Jack) Curry Moore. She was just six months old when her parents moved their large family out of Toronto to a small rural community about thirty kilometres straight north on Yonge Street. In spring 1958 the Moores purchased a three-bedroom bungalow of one and a half storeys fronting on what was then called Elgin Grove Avenue, later North Lake Road. They put $500 down and took out a $4,500 mortgage. The small frame house stood a few hundred yards from the north shore of Lake Wilcox near what is now called Sunset Beach, in the middle of a residential grid of streets that surrounded Lake Wilcox Public School. It wasn't long before they added three more children to their new home, and they all had to eat in shifts and sleep four or five to a room. At night Marlene would rock herself to sleep, a childhood habit she never broke; her way, perhaps, of establishing an internal rhythm amidst the chaos. As an adult, her chronic rocking became so intense she once broke the little finger on her left hand.

Today Lake Wilcox bears little resemblance to the place where Marlene spent the first twelve years of her life. Now it's getaway country for Torontonians with money to invest in designer lakefront homes; then it was a poor, struggling community. Long-time residents still bitterly remember how outsiders disparaged Lake Wilcox as a rough-hewn welfare community. Mike Deering, who grew up less than a mile from the Moores, says that compared to the prosperity of Oak Ridges – located about a mile due west, on the other side of the paved highway that separates the two communities – Lake Wilcox was "the bad side of town." He says, "It was always like that. Everybody from Lake Wilcox was second-class citizens." Those sentiments outlasted the introduction of regional government in the early 1970s, when Lake Wilcox was amalgamated into the political jurisdiction of nearby Richmond Hill. In 1975 the editorial page of *The Liberal*, the local weekly newspaper, ran a cartoon depicting a pile of discarded outhouses labelled "authentic Canadiana from the Lake Wilcox area."

When the Moores lived there the community had few amenities other than the requisite public school, grocery, and post office. But at least Lake Wilcox was blessed with the natural beauty of the 143-acre body of water that lends its name to the cluster of homes on its shoreline. Long-time resident Ken Blyth says that for years many residents drank their water straight from the pristine lake.

As soon as she was old enough to keep up, Marlene tagged after her older brothers and sisters. Lake Wilcox offered recreational riches but little else. In the winter they tobogganed and skated on the lake. During long summer days they swam at Sunset Beach. They spent summers fishing, camping, and roaming the area's fields or simply languishing for hours in front of Comfort's grocery or Marie's snackbar stand. The kids of the neighbourhood ran in packs, haunting favourite hangouts whose names – Deer Valley, Banana Ranch, the Hole – held significance only for them. When tourists invaded the area at the height of the summer, the Moore kids headed north across a field and through a stretch of bush to what they called Snively's Lake (St. George Lake on the map) after a local landowner. It was their special hideaway: a tiny lake filled with pike, bass, and blue gill. "Marlene would go. She loved to fish," her oldest brother Curry Moore says.

Marlene was a pretty child with hazel-green eyes, a sideways grin, and straight blond hair that fell in wild tangles down her back – the source of the nickname "Shaggie" that she carried through adulthood. Her fine-boned features gave her a delicate beauty. She was also, Curry Moore says, a live wire – "electric" and always eager to command attention. Moore says, "She would try anything to impress. When you're stuck way down on this list of kids, you want to look as big as you can."

Marlene's rank at the lower end of the sibling pecking order may account for her often perilous lifelong habit of leaping to the defence of others. She had five older sisters and four older brothers. Three more sisters came after her.

Bryan Cousineau, who patrolled Lake Wilcox as a young police cadet on the Whitchurch Township force in the 1960s and early 1970s, remembers Marlene as "very naive and heavily dominated in the family by her older brothers." Marlene herself once said, "I came out backwards. I should have been a boy. I was always brought up to be a boy. I dug trenches. I dug wells. I never did dishes or played with dolls."

By the mid-1960s the population of Lake Wilcox was about fifteen hundred and the Moores ranked among the four biggest families in the community. The Goods, who for years ran the local post office, had ten children, including two who were adopted. The Szelers had eleven. The busiest of all were the Needhams, said to have produced twenty-one children.

Marlene's mother, still in her teens when she married a man in his thirties, always had the last word when it came to running the household. "There was always bickering about whose turn it was to do what, but Mom would just overrule whatever decision or whatever deals were made between the kids," Curry Moore says. Cloistered in the house, her time and energy consumed by the incessant demands of her children, Edith Moore seems to have become an insular, brittle woman. Former Lake Wilcox resident Rita Szeler vividly recalls one brief moment from many years ago: "It's one thing I remember about Mrs. Moore. I was walking by, and I was a bit low myself that day and for some reason the words my Mom said to me – 'Hold your head up high and walk straight' – came to mind. I guess I must have shaken myself and was walking with my nose in the air, and I heard this voice say, 'You snob,' and I turned around and it was her."

Poverty was a common bond in the community. Many parents struggled desperately to feed and clothe their families, but neighbours still looked out for one another. Szeler's daughter, Marlene Newman, remembers delivering food baskets prepared by her mother to the Moore household. "She used to send me there. She'd feel bad for Mrs. Moore. Even though my Mom had a rough life, too, she would send me with things."

Jack Moore, an ex-navy engineer, had steady work in the boiler room at Sterling Drugs Limited, a pharmaceutical plant a few miles away in Aurora. Even so the needs of the Moore household often stretched the budget to its limit. But Jack Moore, the son of an Irish Presbyterian minister, was a proud man who shunned welfare. Curry Moore remembers the time a welfare worker came by to offer financial assistance when his father was off work with a broken leg. Jack Moore threw him out on his ear. "It didn't matter if it was thirteen kids or thirty kids, they'd feed us one way or another," Curry Moore says.

The Lake Wilcox community had its own social ladder, and there was a stigma attached to being a Moore or a Needham. Whenever there was trouble the community would automatically blame the kids from one of these families. The reputations were, for the most part, well-earned. The Needhams, who lived on Bayview Avenue just around the corner from the Moores, terrorized local children by charging a nickel or a dime just to walk by their front door. Those who failed to comply risked being beaten up.

Among other things, the Moore children were accused of bullying and stealing. They also made it clear they weren't fond of the police. Bryan Cousineau, now deputy chief for the York Regional Police force, says that when he drove past the Moore place, especially in the summertime, the kids would be out front, yelling at him to fuck off. "Marlene would have been right in there like a dirty shirt," he says.

At times the Moore boys showed a disregard for the law that was utterly unsophisticated. Deputy Chief Cousineau remembers with some amusement one long-ago investigation into a reported theft at Lake Wilcox. "They broke into a winterized cottage just south of where they lived on the North Road. A lady came home and found her television stolen, a floor-model television, and said they went out the back door. So I went out the back and there were these damn toboggan tracks. It was a beautiful day and it hadn't snowed since, so you could follow the tracks through a couple of backyards and up to North Road.

"Across the street it picked up again on the west side of the Moore house right through their backyard and on the east side to the back door. It didn't take a Sherlock Holmes to figure out where the TV was. I think it was Tommy and Wayne who came to the door. They said no one had been outside. But sitting there inside the door were their old black rubber boots with the red toes, folded down with their names on them, all wet and covered with snow."

Lake Wilcox had entered a rough and troubled time when Marlene was just a young child. On Saturday nights in summer Lake Wilcox teens would flock to the pavilion at Sunset Beach to dance to a jukebox. But that ended in the summer of 1965 amidst mounting concern about the rowdy and sometimes violent behaviour of local teenagers and the threat posed by gangs of bikers who invaded the community on weekends. On June 4, Whitchurch Township Police set up road blocks on the north and south roads leading to Lake Wilcox and checked all incoming cars. "We're trying to stop any trouble before it starts," Police Chief Fred Mason told *The Liberal*.

Six days later the newspaper reported on a meeting of concerned citizens who expressed alarm about the spread of drinking, fighting, and general property damage. *The Liberal* observed: "A fight involving four youths and a police officer, and stoning of a police car, and smashing of windows are a few of the activities indulged in by youths from the area. These, added to the recent beating of a police officer and setting of fires that led to charges against certain youths, leave no doubt that this is the time for action."

Soon after the meeting, the community launched an ambitious campaign to build a youth centre in Lake Wilcox. The first fundraising event, a carnival held at Sunset Beach Park, attracted five hundred people. But five days later, Chief Mason announced that Sunset Beach Pavilion would be closed down permanently in the wake of the visit of two hundred members of a Toronto motorcycle gang. That same summer police jailed eighteen-year-old Curry Moore and three other Lake Wilcox youths for two months for beating two Willowdale youths unconscious outside the Sunset Beach Pavilion. The two victims had been sitting near the pavilion having a snack when a carload of youths jumped them. They said they had never met their attackers before.

Confrontations between police and youth escalated in the early 1970s when the hometown cops were replaced by the York Regional Police, who moved in with a mandate to clean up Lake Wilcox. Curry Moore, the second-born of the Moore clan, was running with a wild gang of local outlaws who took perverse pride in their ability to sabotage cruisers and harass police. "We set some pretty dandy traps where the whole car would fall right in holes in the ground," Moore says. "Shotguns were set up so they would blow the red light out of the car. We'd leap on the police officers, take their badges, and run like hell. We had two-by-fours dug into the ground with a bunch of nails sticking out to flatten all four tires. We set up swinging beams that would come at their cars, and smash the back windshields."

While area police strived to bring law and order to the Lake Wilcox community, no one seemed concerned about the turmoil in Marlene Moore's life. She grew up at a time when the family unit was considered inviolate – a private domain outside the purview of the state. Spousal and child abuse went unnoticed or ignored, and unreported. There were early and unmistakable signals, however, that something was terribly wrong in Marlene's life. Public school teachers and other education officials still harbour sharp recollections of a deeply disturbed child.

On February 14, 1969, a fire of unknown origin swept through Lake Wilcox Public School, destroying all clerical files and reducing to ashes the formal records that might have offered insight into Marlene's earliest school years. But the next year, at age twelve, she transferred to King City Senior Public School, the central school for all Grade 7 and 8 students in the area. There her bizarre behaviour caught the attention of teachers and the school principal. Jan Laughlin, a gym teacher at King City in the early 1970s, remembers Marlene as glum and withdrawn in the classroom. "She would answer questions or reply to conversation but she would never come up to volunteer something that had happened on the weekend, or something that she was happy about."

In the schoolyard and on the school bus it was another story. Laughlin recalls Marlene as a bully who intimidated other children when she didn't get her way. "She was very strong. She would take on bigger kids than herself and she seemed to always get the better of them."

But it was the self-destructive behaviour – "seeking out attention always in a negative way" and "always doing harm to herself" – that caused Laughlin's deepest concerns. "One day I remember her running down the gym from one end to the other with her head down and she would ram the walls, and we're talking a concrete brick wall. She would do things like that."

On another occasion Laughlin was horrified to find Marlene curled up in a corner of the gym toying with a razor blade. "She was sitting very quietly on the stage waiting to start gym class, and she was brushing her hand alongside of her leg, and by the time I had got her to stop she had scratched herself. It was a very light touch. She was just barely touching herself, and she had scratched it, not sliced it, but scratched it. She behaved masochistically."

Carol Cameron, long-time attendance counsellor for the York Region Board of Education, had the most intimate dealings with Marlene and her family. The no-nonsense truant officer was repeatedly summoned to the family home by Edith Moore to extricate Marlene from a locked bedroom or bathroom, where she had barricaded herself, refusing to go to school. Cameron describes the Marlene of that period as a belligerent, aggressive girl who was running wild. But Cameron was not unduly suspicious about the circumstances of Marlene's up-bringing. "The house inside was quite normal. I react when houses are very dirty, very smelly, or they have no furniture. My memory of this house is that it was just a house, not bad one way or another." She has a lasting image of the father as a decent, hardworking guy and of a mother exhausted and trying to do her best.

With few exceptions, throughout her life Marlene remained resolutely silent about her early years. But later on she did reveal glimpses of her childhood. It became clear that Jack Moore, a burly man almost six feet tall, ruled over his children with an iron fist. Family rules were strict and corporal punishment was not unusual for misbehaviour or breaking curfew.

Incensed by Marlene's chronic bed-wetting, her father frequently beat her with the buckle end of his belt, raising welts on her face, legs, back, and arms. "Nothing hurt worse than those beatings," she once said. Jack Moore's disciplinary methods were, at times, more akin to terrorism. He once hung Marlene by her feet out of a second-storey window, swinging and banging her body against the house. When she began menstruating at age twelve, Marlene didn't know what was happening at first and was terrified that her unwilled blood would provoke further violence from her father. She so feared him that, after going through a plate-glass window during a wrestling match with one of her brothers, she stitched herself up with a needle and thread to avoid the risk of her father finding out what had happened.

Later, as an adult, Marlene's relationship with her mother was strained and volatile. At times she spoke fondly about her, and with great sympathy. Friends once saw her, as a grown woman, sitting on her mother's lap, embracing and weeping joyously over their reunion. At other times her hostility and anger toward Edith Moore was unmasked. "I sent her a Mother's Day card to spoil her day. It's been a slice. I'll go to her funeral," she once said.

Edith Moore was no single-minded tyrant. She struggled to shield her children from her husband's rage and from outside interference by the law. When police officers came knocking at the door, the children could usually count on their mother to

26

conceal their whereabouts or concoct a story to get them off the hook. But unschooled and heavily dominated by Jack Moore, she, too, was capable of crude and often cruel methods of punishment. At times she whipped Marlene. For the most part, however, she deferred to her husband in matters of discipline. "Ma would stick up for you if she thought you were innocent, but if you were guilty and getting an ass-kicking, she didn't say nothing. I believe my mother grew up in a fairly strict family too," Curry Moore says.

A long-time friend named Patricia, who first met Marlene in a girls' training school, says that as an adult Marlene rarely talked about family. "It was almost like it was dirty. It was a taboo subject." When Marlene did talk to Patricia about what her father did to her, it seemed she felt a tremendous guilt. "It's like she absolutely didn't want anybody to know about her childhood," Patricia says. "It was almost like she didn't want anybody to know because she didn't want anyone to pity her. Her childhood must have been a scary, scary place to live for a little kid."

The trauma that Marlene experienced as a child went beyond physical and emotional abuse. She also lived in a private hell of sexual abuse involving one or more of her brothers. In a confidential psychiatric report presented to prison officials in December 1982, Dr. Philip Haden cites evidence of "sibling incest that was extremely distressing." That finding was echoed by Dr. Graham Turrall, a Toronto psychologist who had a therapeutic relationship with Marlene for close to a year. Though Marlene was reticent about details of her childhood, Turrall says, "I'm under the very good impression that not only was there physical abuse, corporal punishment, but sexual incest that lasted years, sometimes with one [brother], sometimes with several. This kid was abused."

Marlene was mortified when references to her childhood sexual history turned up in newspaper accounts of a criminal trial. Curry Moore remains incensed that all four Moore brothers were implicated. In a 1985 interview with a Toronto newspaper he commented, "I know which brothers did it. I was in prison when Marlene finally told me the entire story." More recently he said, "I may have said there were two brothers involved. I can't remember. But I did talk to Marlene. We did discuss it, and it was one brother involved in some sort of sexual assault, and it wasn't even indicated whether it was even rape. It could have been rubbing bellies for all I know." Maureen Sutton, one of Marlene's older sisters, says simply, "I don't believe it happened."

In conversations with a few close friends and front-line correctional staff who got to know her, Marlene did speak about forced intercourse with her brothers as a child. Toronto writer June Callwood says Marlene talked about sibling incest, including an incident involving "at least two, perhaps three" of her brothers. The memories always surfaced when Marlene "was upset and she'd cry and she'd say that she kept asking her brothers why they did that to her." Mary Morissette, for many years a guard at Kingston's Prison for Women, says Marlene once talked about sexual abuse by her brothers during a late-night conversation in her cell. "It was more like disappointment, more like a feeling of betrayal that they had turned on her," Morissette says. "It was not just the act itself but that they had used her in that way instead of being her friends."

As a child, though, Marlene kept silent about her dark secret. The trauma of being sexually abused came out not in words but in seething anger and self-hatred, causing considerable trouble, especially at school. Barry Wadman, the principal of King City Public School until 1973, organized numerous meetings with Marlene's teachers to explore ways of dealing with Marlene. More than once, Edith Moore was called in to discuss her daughter's behaviour. But school officials quickly became exasperated and wrote Marlene off as a bad seed. As a child, she encountered no one willing or able to investigate the reason for her troubled behaviour. The response of the school attendance counsellor and other education officials set a pattern that would be repeated throughout her life: authority figures around her seemed more concerned about controlling her disruptive, rebellious behaviour than exploring the reasons for her anger.

One day, when Edith Moore called Carol Cameron to North Lake Road to deal with her daughter, Marlene lashed out at the truant officer. "She wasn't prepared to let anyone help," Cameron says. "She was one of the few kids that have tried to assault me in all the years I've been in this business. She tried to take me on. She just got so angry, she would take on the whole world. She was one of the most aggressive kids I've ever handled, a very angry young lady."

For Cameron, that assault was the final straw. She promptly charged Marlene under the old Juvenile Delinquents Act as a child in need of care and protection. She left no doubt about who in her mind was responsible for Marlene's behaviour. "I can charge either the child or the parent, depending on who I think is being least co-operative, and in this case it was the child." It was Cameron's practice to explore other less radical alternatives first, and she recalls many other occasions when Marlene was taken to court for skipping school or picking fights in the schoolyard. Eventually, she says, she ran out of options. "There was no way you could place her in a foster home or a treatment centre. She wouldn't stay."

Before the 1970–71 school year ended, a weary and defeated Edith Moore stood in the York Region's juvenile and family court in Newmarket and surrendered her thirteen-year-old daughter into the care of the province's juvenile corrections system.

2

If I were young again

never wish I was young again

The sign at the entrance off Highway 24 at Cambridge, Ontario, with its curlicue welcome to the School for Girls, offered no hint of the penal environment inside. Passersby often mistook the well-kept grounds and functional buildings of the training school for the local high school. Its benign appearance was deceptive: the province acknowledged Grandview School to be the last resort for delinquent girls between the ages of twelve and seventeen.

At the time Marlene was committed to Grandview School for Girls on indeterminate sentence – by order of a family-court judge at the Newmarket provincial courthouse – the authorities were not obliged to prove she had committed a crime. In those days you could end up at one of the province's thirteen training schools simply by being ruled "incorrigible," the umbrella term applied to behaviour that somehow transgressed adult authority. Like two of every three girls sent to Ontario training schools in the early 1970s, Marlene was admitted to Grandview under Section 8 of the Training

Schools Act, which allowed committal of any child under age sixteen for so-called "status offences." These included truancy, running away from home, staying out overnight, swearing, disobedience to parents, temper tantrums, and undesirable associations.

Within two years of Marlene's release from training school, Section 8 was declared an intolerable affront to children's rights; the Ontario legislature repealed it on May 5, 1975. Some three years before Marlene's committal order was issued, the province had replaced the old "training school" designation with euphemisms designed to eliminate the stigma of juvenile incarceration.

Grandview School owed its name to a rolling, grassy tract in southwestern Ontario, about a mile or so north of the Grand River at Cambridge. For nearly forty years – since the Ontario Training School for Girls had opened its doors on the five-acre site on September 7, 1933 – the institution had specialized in handling "problem girls" in their early teens. Many of the residents arrived with the label of troublemakers, already veterans of juvenile corrections or other community settings. They brought along histories of truancy, drug and alcohol abuse, vandalism, prostitution, and assault.

The renaming of the girls' institution in March 1967 also introduced the first phase of major structural renovations to the barrack-style buildings, the visible manifestation of an official commitment to a treatment model for juvenile corrections across Ontario. "We are no longer a penal institution," announced Grandview superintendent Rev. Kenneth J. Mac-Donald.

School authorities led local newspaper reporters on a tour of the girls' residences, where walls newly painted in pink and blue pastels had replaced the stark, penal environment of the past. The late 1960s brought a brand new look – and the promise of a new era of rehabilitation. For thirty-five years, the facility had operated as an authoritarian prison for children.

"It had a distinct and persistent military ambience," wrote criminologists Robert Robertson Ross and Hugh Bryan McKay, co-authors of a 1979 study of Grandview. "Discipline, we were told, was of paramount concern and second only to custody. We were appalled at what we saw: the drab uniforms that the girls wore, the dull battleship grey or institutional green of the interior walls, the sterility and barrenness of the girls' rooms, and teenage girls forced to march from place to place. The adolescents spent their evenings sitting around a large common room, in alphabetical order, in silence, knitting or crocheting or staring off into space, or simply chewing their nails or screwing up their faces trying not to cry, or just hanging their heads in boredom or depression."

Just five years before Marlene's arrival at the Cambridge site, there was not one social worker or psychologist on staff. Marlene was greeted by a battery of specialists, the authors of behavioural programs regulated by a strictly enforced token system. Grandview residents had to earn all privileges, including access to a mattress and blankets and the right to their own roll of toilet paper. Staff handed out demerits for infractions ranging from verbal abuse of staff to fist fights to self-injurious behaviour. Freedom hinged on a girl's ability to accumulate a set number of points.

When the Training Schools Act was invoked against Marlene, no one knew for how long she would lose her freedom. All that was required to launch the legal process that led to Grandview was a formal expression of adult concern about a child's conduct. In Marlene's case, this critical step was taken in late 1970; that same year her parents sold the family home in Lake Wilcox and moved north to Queensville. By law a parent or guardian received prior notification of juvenile court proceedings, and the bearer of the news was most often a police constable or probation officer. Though trouble often knocked at the door of the Moore household, this particular occasion most likely caused both foreboding and relief for Marlene and her mother.

Edith Moore may have thought benevolent custody was the answer to the problems of her troubled daughter. According to her oldest son, Curry Moore, "She lost control so she was hoping that whoever was in control could give Marlene what she needed." He says, "Little did she know that a prison system is just that, a prison system." Attendance counsellor Carol Cameron says flatly that the matter was out of Edith Moore's hands: "The judge would have asked her feelings on it and I didn't see any mother happy to see her kid sent away. But if she was being honest, she would have had to say the kid was out of her control."

There is no public record of what was said in the Newmarket courtroom. Nor is there a paper trail to document Marlene's repeat admissions to Grandview over the next two years. It was the practice of Ontario courts to seal official files when the child turned sixteen, and public agencies routinely destroyed old records. Federal and provincial privacy laws reinforce those protective seals by prohibiting access to archival materials until thirty years after a person's death. It's no secret, however, that society's fragmented response to children in need of intervention, coupled with traditional reluctance to enter the sanctum of the family home, meant that cries for help were too often ignored or met with punitive sanctions. Despite the remodelling of Ontario training schools in the late 1960s, Grandview was hardly the sanctuary that Marlene would have chosen – even to escape an abusive environment.

Her first few weeks away from home were spent at Unit 1 of the Reception and Diagnostic Centre, a facility separate from the training school. At the centre new arrivals underwent a complete medical examination and a battery of mental, educational, aptitude, interest, and personality tests. A psychiatrist was on hand to explore any special problems, and corrections staff gleaned additional information from the reports of juvenile court, the family, probation services, and education officials.

A friend who was on Marlene's floor in the residence known as Beatty House remembers her as an easy target for some of the older, mean-spirited girls. "She was very tiny," Patricia says. "There were a few girls who really picked on the younger ones. They weren't very nice. They would come up and stick pins into you."

Marlene stood her ground, often with her fists, or tried to run away from the institution. As a result she was confined for months in Churchill House, a residence built to house the most severe cases. The building's four cell blocks had names befitting a children's summer camp: Olympus, Orion, Cameron, and Pioneer. Outside, a child's swing-set sat incongruously in an exercise yard surrounded by towering barbed-wired fencing. But, as criminologists Ross and McKay observed, "All attempts to have this structure blend into the otherwise gentle surrounds were to prove futile. This was the maximum-security unit which confined 32 intractable 12- to 16-year-old girls in an oppressive atmosphere of locked doors, wire-mesh grilled windows, steel bars, and cells." In response to the harsh indifference of their physical environment, the girls often decorated their cells with plastic flowers.

Marlene and the other residents of Churchill House were kept to a rigid routine. Every day at 7 a.m. sharp, staff entered the corridors, rattling huge rings of brass keys to rouse the girls from sleep and turning up the lights – only slightly dimmed during the night. By the time a staff member had made one round of the cell block, the girls had to be standing at attention by their cell doors. Cells remained locked until each girl had dutifully flipped her mattress. The staff then sent their young charges to fetch buckets of soapy water and scrub-brushes for the gruelling morning ritual of scouring cells from top to bottom. By 8 a.m. the girls were lined up at the back door of the building for breakfast.

Superintendent Thomas J. Loker had recently moved toward greater integration of Churchill House residents, allowing most of the girls to take meals and classes outside the building. They still got vocational training in classrooms in the basement of the maximum-security unit, but attendance was not restricted to building residents. By 1970 integration had expanded the educational plan for Grandview: the academic curriculum now included basic courses up to the Grade 10 level, and students followed an "ungraded system" on individual timetables. For the majority of residents the school built educational programs around female-ascribed occupational training, such as restaurant services, home economics, hairdressing, business machine use, and nurses' aides. Teachers assigned to small groups of problem students were instructed beforehand on security procedures, for their own safety. An English instructor who taught a class of four students – "and that was too many" – remembers being advised never to turn her back on the girls. "You were always to be within reach of the phone in each classroom, and if you couldn't get to it, to yell for help and to kick the phone off the stand."

Because Marlene and the others at Churchill House were considered high runaway risks, they were bused the short distance to the communal dining room for breakfast. After school, which ran from 9 a.m. until 4 p.m., assigned chores had to be completed before the evening meal. At night the residents gathered in the common room to watch television, play cards, or knit until 8 p.m. Then it was lock-up time again until the next morning. On Sundays the girls were allowed to sleep late and enjoyed the luxury of a leisurely breakfast of coffee and rolls in the common room.

It was mainly Marlene's rage and her recurring fist fights with classmates that led to her confinement in the secure unit. In time staff and other residents came to recognize the signs of an impending explosion. "There was a lot of tension and her way of alleviating it was to rock violently, and then they knew she was going to spin out because she would start pacing and you couldn't talk to her," Patricia says. "It was just like a blank wall. She was so detached, and she could pull into herself so far and it was like nothing else was around."

Twice during her stay at Grandview Marlene was in the middle of mini-riots, when isolated incidents of aggression among the girls sparked institution-wide brawls that saw chairs heaved, windows smashed, and some staff and residents injured. At least once, police were called in to help quell a disturbance.

One of Marlene's best friends at Churchill House was a bright and spunky but rebellious girl named Corry, who continually frustrated the authorities with her uncanny ability to escape from the most secure areas of the institution. She once took Marlene with her. The two fourteen-year-olds scaled the fence, stole a gun and a car in Guelph, and headed for Kingston, Corry's home base. Police found the pair stoned on "downers" sitting in a small park on Kingston's main street, and they were returned to the training school without being charged. It took Marlene close to a week to recover from the drug overdose.

According to Corry, Marlene wasn't one to start trouble but she was easily led into mischief. "If you wanted to do anything you could always talk Marlene into going first." Corry somehow overcame her own tortured existence at the training school, where she spent close to a year in a segregation cell. She once drank a bottle of bleach and spent an agonizing night writhing in pain on her cell floor. A compassionate guard named Marilyn Scrimgeour helped her by lying on the floor outside her cell all night, holding her hand through the space under the door.

Corry often wonders why she survived and Marlene didn't. She says, "Everybody liked her, I mean everybody. But Marlene didn't have that one piece of self-esteem that you can cling to. Nobody ever said to her you're a nice person, or maybe you could be a figure skater. Sometimes that kind of statement would be enough and at age twenty you would suddenly strap on a pair of skates and do something."

Despite her slight build, Marlene earned a reputation for toughness. Grandview officials responded to her misbehaviour by shutting her up in a locked room, where she would rock herself for hours on a bed bolted to the floor. Sometimes she would sit balancing on a wooden chair's back legs and crash monotonously against the wall, over and over. A decade later clinical psychologist Graham Turrall testified in adult court that "places like Churchill House precipitated slashings" and fostered an environment "certainly not conducive to any kind of growth." The Toronto psychologist once publicly denounced the maximum-security unit as "the most deplorable, depressing place" he had ever seen as a clinician. For Turrall, "It was the modern day version of the Charles Dickens workhouse."

For more than a decade, opposition members of the Ontario legislature had condemned the use of solitary confinement cells. In the late 1950s provincial CCF leader Donald MacDonald had exposed the caged existence of a girl placed in isolation for ninety-two days. The NDP MPP Stephen Lewis raised similar concerns in the legislature in March 1965. Girls locked in solitary-confinement cells at the training school lost all contact with the outside world, even visually, Lewis said. Cells consisted of three solid, concrete walls, a bare floor, and a barred and densely screened window. Two years later school officials said the seven detention cells had been converted into bedrooms and solitary confinement was reserved for rare and extreme circumstances. But residents of that time say Marlene and others spent days or weeks alone in locked rooms. Frustration, anger, and loneliness found expression in self-injury, from swallowing pins to cutting or biting their skin until the blood ran.

Corry, her own arms and legs covered in scar tissue from slashing, says blood-splattered walls at Grandview were commonplace. "There was a girl in there who literally used to eat her arms. They put casts on to try to get her to stop. She would pick up a heavy piece of furniture and drop it on her cast, and then she would start again to bite her flesh out."

For the most part, Corry says, the practice of self-mutilation – what the girls themselves called "carving" – was a private matter. "Nobody teaches you how to carve. For some reason, you just do it. But it wasn't something you did around other people." In fact, self-injury frequently resulted in girls losing points and, consequently, privileges such as movies or special outings. "You did it when you just couldn't get anything out. It never actually hurt. You just had too much pain in every way."

Grandview authorities frequently responded by stripping a girl of her possessions and, if that wasn't deterrent enough, moving her to a segregation cell. "You'd tear up your room and eventually they would take all the furniture out," Corry says.

"You'd bang on a cement wall and then they would take you to detention, and you couldn't do anything. I mean there's four brick walls there, what are you going to do?"

Once the girls were in segregation the measures used by security staff became even more severe. "If you got out of hand and started screaming or kicking doors they would come with the hose and hose you down," Patricia says. Sometimes girls were stripped of their clothing and left in their cell with nothing but a mattress. They had to sleep on the mattress no matter how wet the cell was and no matter how wet they were themselves.

Marlene's incarceration at the maximum-security unit co-incided with joint efforts by the corrections ministry and the University of Waterloo to develop treatment strategies for delinquent girls. By 1970 staff assigned to the Grandview complex included a psychiatrist, a psychologist, four psychometrists, three part-time university professors of psychology, three part-time medical officers, three full-time registered nurses, two part-time pastoral counsellors, and one part-time group therapist and counsellor. One of their long-term projects was to eliminate "carving."

When the University of Waterloo began its affiliation with Grandview, more than 80 per cent of the residents were identified as carvers. *Self-Mutilation*, the starkly titled text co-authored by Robert Robertson Ross and Hugh Bryan McKay (Ross served as chief psychologist for the Ontario corrections ministry for twelve years), offers this capsule view of the training school residents: "They were often grossly obese or emaciated, shabbily dressed and unkempt. What concerned us most was the fact that many of them, most of them in fact, were scarred." Investigators found that 117 of the 136 girls at the school had "carved" at least once. According to Ross and McKay, "The average girl had lacerated her skin eight times. The same figures describe almost any period in the 30 years or so of the institution's history. It was a perennial problem."

Some acts of self-mutilation took the form of a bizarre initiation rite. Residents pressured new arrivals to join in ceremonial carvings, sometimes sharing shards of a smashed light bulb with other girls seated in a circle. But, according to Ross and McKay, in most instances – about 70 per cent – girls were alone when they carved, either in segregation or in their rooms. The researchers found that staff attempts to curtail carving by keeping tight access over sharp devices such as razor blades or kitchen knives proved futile: "Although such instruments were used, the girls most frequently used broken bobby pins or needles smuggled out of sewing classes. Other objects could be used including plaster chipped off walls, pens or pencils, broken glass or china, wood splinters from furniture, strands of hair used as a saw, the metal ends of shoe laces, nails gouged out of shoes or furniture, or broken-off finger nails."

It was only after five years of frustration and failure that researchers made a radical discovery: Peer pressure was the key to changing the girls' behaviour. They developed a program known as "co-opting" – an unorthodox treatment strategy that subtly persuaded the school's ringleaders to act as therapists for other girls. The special staff trained a small number of residents in the principles of positive reinforcement and began to treat them as competent associates rather than clients. The researchers declared a moratorium on treatment programs run by the psychology staff and openly refused to support traditional methods endorsed by school authorities, such as punishing the girls for self-mutilation and offering concrete rewards for positive behaviour.

The peer-therapist approach was a resounding success, but the elimination of self-mutilation was only temporary. Predictably, the program was undermined and ultimately rejected by front-line staff and administrators. They could not accept that the girls ran the program with only minimal support from professional therapists, and they continued to treat the residents as pathological adolescents who had to be controlled. After a five-month hiatus, they revived old programs of psychotherapy and behaviour modification and introduced new and more elaborate treatment programs to replace peer therapy. The girls resumed carving.

While she was at Grandview Marlene adopted the perverse self-injury that would eventually become her own ritual response to frustration and powerlessness. At age thirteen she had entered an environment where self-mutilation was more than a way to manage overwhelming emotional pain. It was also a means of proving her allegiance to peers and of showing her defiance of authority, a way of gaining a measure of status in any penal institution. Patricia, who saw Marlene's arms wrapped in bandages more than once, says staff often singled her out among the other known slashers for body searches. In the dining room they would issue Marlene a plastic cup instead of a glass.

Marlene had become part of a corrections system that was also blatantly discriminatory. Before the repeal of Section 8 in 1975, Ontario studies conducted by researchers in both the public and private sectors found compelling evidence of the existence of one set of behavioural standards for boys and another for girls. Girls were far more likely than boys to be committed to training school for truancy, running away from home, sexual activity, and other status offences – even though adolescents themselves reported roughly equal rates of misbehaviour among both groups and higher rates of sexual activity among juvenile boys.

A study of juvenile court proceedings in Hamilton in the early 1970s confirmed that the rate of incarceration was much higher for girls than for boys. There was one girl brought to family court for every six boys, but one girl sent to training school for every three boys. A subsequent review by corrections ministry researchers of the records of 464 youths committed to Ontario training schools concluded that deviance by females, particularly sexual promiscuity, was less acceptable to society.

Training school administrator Les Horne, later the manager of the child and family advocacy office of the Ontario Ministry of Community and Social Services, describes Grandview as "a real good example of how wrong it was to use that kind of treatment for girls." Authorities failed to acknowledge the link between child abuse and behavioural disorders. Horne says training school residents were, for all practical purposes, youthful prisoners of the state. Although the staff resisted the idea of Grandview as a prison, Horne says the kids definitely saw it that way.

Thousands of girls passed through Grandview School before it officially closed on July 6, 1976. The site was converted to an adult remand facility and renamed the Waterloo Regional Detention Centre. By the time the school shut its doors, Marlene and many others had graduated to the adult corrections system.

Marlene appeared twice in provincial court in Richmond Hill in October 1974. Late in the month, just days before her seventeenth birthday, she received a conditional discharge on a charge of possession of stolen property under $200 and was put on probation for twelve months. For a time she bunked with her brother Curry and his girlfriend in Toronto, sometimes hitching rides up Yonge Street to Lake Wilcox to stay with friends and family. She belonged to the lost generation of street kids, meandering gangs of youth without education, without jobs, without hope.

3

When luck turns against me
it usually goes all the way

Just after midnight on March 6, 1975, Marlene stood, thumb
out, on Yonge Street on a dark stretch of the highway just north
of Richmond Hill. On a whim, she was heading north to see
her sister. Dressed in her customary blue jean jacket, her hair
dampened by a light snowfall, the seventeen-year-old girl
shivered from the onslaught of winter air that came with each
passing car. A man southbound in a purple Jeep passed her,
stopped, and turned around and came back to offer her a lift.
She was in luck, or so she thought.

The driver, a heavy-set, bearded man, drove only a short
distance with Marlene at his side before turning onto a side
road just north of the town of Oak Ridges. According to the
police records, Marlene told how he turned off the engine and
dimmed the headlights. Marlene asked him why he had
stopped, and that's when he turned mean. He ordered her to
remove her jacket. She refused. He grabbed her coat and while
they struggled he pulled a knife from his pocket and held it in
her face. "Don't make me angry," he said. She pleaded with

him to put the knife away. He demanded, "Take off your clothes." She refused. Then he threatened, "Get in the back seat and don't make me mad."

After raping Marlene on the isolated road, the man drove her back to the main highway, left her on the side of the road, and headed south again to Richmond Hill. Stranded on a deserted highway, Marlene flagged down the next car and asked to be driven to her girlfriend's place on Cedar Avenue in New-market. After she arrived there at 2:40 a.m. her friend Debbie Morrison contacted the York Regional Police on Marlene's behalf. According to Morrison's statement to the police, when Marlene arrived she asked for a cigarette and said, "I think I've been raped."

With the help of Marlene's description, a York Region constable caught the man on Yonge Street two days later. He told a different version of the events. He admitted picking up Marlene, but denied that he'd had sex with her. The two investigating officers wanted to drop the case. But Sergeant Bryan Cousineau, who knew Marlene, didn't. He says, "I had a feeling she was telling the truth the way she described it. I thought it was a good idea that we investigate this guy a little further." Cousineau's instincts proved right. Within a couple of days the man had changed his story. He now admitted having intercourse with Marlene in the back seat of his Jeep, but said it happened with her consent. He said that Marlene may have mistaken a piece of broomstick in his vehicle for a knife. Police later found a jackknife in his possession, similar to the one Marlene had described.

The man was charged with rape and, after a preliminary hearing, appeared in district court in Toronto in the spring of 1976 before a judge without a jury. The Crown attorney representing Marlene was Al Cooper, a tall, fair-haired Queen's University law school graduate who went on to practise criminal law in Hamilton. His faith in the case was bolstered not only by the evidence compiled during the police investigation but also by Cousineau's unshakeable conviction that Marlene wouldn't concoct such a story. Cooper believed the conscientious officer had presented him with an airtight case. "I've seen policemen on rape cases who are very macho types and they don't care. They'll slip it under the rug and not investigate it the same way they do other cases. But this wasn't the case. Cousineau did a good job on the case. He questioned the guy. He got a good statement from the guy. He treated Marlene with respect. It wasn't a sloppy investigation at all."

The defence lawyer, Ed Schofield, a former FBI agent who established a thriving criminal law practice in Toronto, was just as confident about his client's prospects for acquittal. A main feature of his defence strategy was that Marlene hadn't immediately reported the rape, even though the man in the Jeep had dropped her off directly across the street from the headquarters of the Oak Ridges detachment of the Ontario Provincial Police. Schofield and his client were so certain of their case they decided together not to bother putting the accused man on the stand to give his version of the events. "We opted for the joint view that her story just didn't hold water," Schofield says. He was unaware of the surprise Marlene had in store for his client in the event that the court failed her. Clearly prepared to seek her own bizarre form of retribution if the judge let her down, Marlene had carried a brown paper bag into the courtroom and placed it on the bench beside her. It contained the heads of slaughtered ducks, which Cooper believes she had salvaged from a restaurant in Chinatown, just around the corner from the court. "She told me she was going to throw them at the guy if the judge found him not guilty," Cooper recalls.

The district court judge declared the man guilty. But before the sentencing Schofield learned that Marlene had told the court officer assigned to prepare a pre-sentence report that she had been using speed (methamphetamines) the night of the incident. In the light of that revelation, the defence promptly applied to the judge to have the case reopened. This time the Toronto lawyer wasn't taking any chances. He called the accused to the stand and also brought in an expert witness – a pharmacologist who testified that the perceptions of a person under the influence of speed weren't to be trusted. Less than a month after the original verdict, the conviction was overturned and the man was acquitted.

Years later Cooper still feels outrage at the court's about-face. "I just couldn't believe that a person could be convicted, not having given testimony, and then all of a sudden they say I want another chance and they give evidence and the judge acquits. You can imagine how upset Marlene was. She believed very much in her case and I believed she was completely, 100 per cent, telling the truth."

Cooper put his concerns into writing in a passionate letter to the Ontario Attorney General's office, urging his superiors to authorize an appeal. The assistant deputy minister replied that the facts simply weren't strong enough. Cooper remains deeply troubled by the outcome of the case. He's convinced it marked a tragic turning point in Marlene's life. "Before that, her record was very minor. After that her record got bad, and I think she became completely disillusioned with life. I think this case had a devastating effect on her."

Curry Moore said the assault itself had a profound impact. "She told me she was absolutely terrified. She thought she was going to die." Workers at a halfway house in Hamilton who lived with Marlene eight years later say the debilitating effects lingered. One of them, Terri-Lee Seeley, executive director of the Hamilton Elizabeth Fry Society, says, "It was so traumatic for her that still, while she was in Hamilton, she was having memories, bad dreams of it and trying to cope with the rape." Marlene herself once said that the attack, along with the court's acquittal, drove her "nuts." Her experience of violence had now moved outside the home and into the world at large.

Craig Townson, a federal parole officer who befriended Marlene later on, says her attitude changed when her assailant went free. "I think at that point she said something like: To hell with you. I'm on my own. I'm going to protect my own individual rights. Nobody's going to hurt me any more. If you look at me the wrong way, I will construe that as a threat. I will take whatever action I need to take to protect myself. So if I have to be the aggressor to protect myself, I will."

But well before the acquittal, in the weeks and months that followed the roadside assault, Marlene's behaviour had become profane and fractious. She was arrested within three and a half weeks of the rape. First she was one of several people charged with breaking into a travel agency in the town of Newmarket. Two weeks later, along with other rowdy patrons, she was tossed out of a Newmarket restaurant. The next evening Marlene returned with two friends and hurled a soft drink bottle through the diner's window. York Regional Police charged her with causing a disturbance and malicious damage.

But that wasn't the end of it. After being released from custody, a spiteful Marlene crossed the parking lot at police headquarters, reached inside a parked cruiser, and grabbed a clipboard holding the reports of a Constable Gary Colangelo. She tore his notes into pieces and tossed the wadded paper into the Holland River next to the Newmarket Arena. That outburst got her re-arrested and charged with theft under $200. It also put her on the front page of *The Era*, the local weekly newspaper, beneath the waggish headline "Someone ripping mad."

Marlene pleaded guilty before Judge Clare Morrison and was remanded in custody for a week. On May 13, 1975, she was handed a suspended sentence plus probation for one year.

She got herself into more trouble when she accompanied a girlfriend to court in September. Marlene caused a ruckus in the courtroom, complaining loudly from the public benches about the way the judge was handling the case. She ignored the warnings of court officials to be silent and the judge ordered her removed. During a court recess, Bryan Cousineau noticed movement outside the judge's chambers. He discovered that someone had slipped a paper napkin under the door. It bore the scribbled message, "Hey, judge. Got an acre of space to rent?" – Marlene's impertinent way of accusing the magistrate of being empty-headed. The wisecrack drew a contempt of court charge that was later withdrawn.

Nearly seven months passed before Marlene had her day in court for the window-smashing episode. By the time she stood before Newmarket provincial court Judge C.W. Guest on December 8, she faced additional charges of mischief and theft for breaking into an apartment in the building where she lived. Convicted on all counts, she again received a suspended sentence. Her probation was extended and a few straightforward conditions were added. She was to reside at an address approved by the court and be off the streets between the hours of 11 p.m. and 5 a.m.

Marlene took little notice. Throughout the next six months she was in and out of trouble, courting arrest in a belligerent and boozy haze. She was also in and out of jail, spending weeks at a time in custody on various charges. Early on the morning of February 18, 1976, police found Marlene and another woman shouting and swearing in front of a crowd outside the Windsor House Hotel in Alliston. That performance garnered Marlene a disturbance charge and curfew violation. She staged an intoxicated curtain call eight days later at about 3 a.m., cursing and shouting at bystanders outside a doughnut shop in a Richmond Hill plaza. When police arrived she showered them with drunken epithets and was promptly arrested.

On June 22 police were called to a residence on Pine Drive in the small Innisfil Township community of Painswick, where they found Marlene seated in the back of a flatbed truck, swearing and shouting. A fracas ensued and the police charged Marlene with assaulting an officer. Just six hours later, after leading police on a foot chase, Marlene was arrested for the second time that day and held on a disturbance charge for intoxication.

In mid-August Marlene was brought before Judge J.W.P. Anjo at the Simcoe County courthouse in Alliston. She appeared on the court docket as offences 15 through 58. She pleaded guilty to seven Criminal Code violations: five counts of causing a disturbance, breach of probation, and assaulting a police officer. The assault charge – from the Innisfil Township incident – revealed the extent to which Marlene's relations with local police had degenerated.

When police had ordered her to get down from the flatbed, she refused and armed herself with a wrecking bar, a cutting torch, and a piece of chain she had picked up from the floor of the truck. Confronted by two officers who attempted to talk her into dropping the weapons, Marlene shouted, "The only fucking good cop is a dead fucking cop." As one of the policemen climbed onto the truck, she raised the wrecking bar over her head using both hands and yelled, "Don't come near me or I'll knock your fucking head off." A police constable got a glancing blow on the arm before Marlene was subdued and handcuffed.

Judge Anjo sentenced Marlene to twelve months in jail. But first he lectured the recalcitrant young woman: "I personally think that you're a very intelligent person. You can do what you want – you've already proved it. If you want to make a nuisance out of yourself, you're eminently successful at that. If you want to defy the police and vent your anger, your rage or your sense of rebellion, whatever, you can do that. You proved that to the court some time ago. I don't think that is going to be terribly important; what's terribly important is you are the key, and if you should be lucky enough to reach your life expectancy, which is about 50 years or more to look forward to, going in and out of jail for another 50 years would seem to me to be an awful waste of time and an awful waste of the government's money. You don't believe it, and I think you're kind of embarrassed if somebody tries to say something nice about you, but I really think you can make it. Until you decide to do that you're on your own. All you've got to do is make up your mind. It's your life, just yours. If you want to throw it up against the wall and smash it like a tomato that's your privilege. It's my privilege to pass the sentence though."

Marlene's curt response was, "You're all heart."

Marlene was incarcerated at age eighteen at the Vanier Centre for Women, the showpiece of the Ontario corrections system. When the Brampton facility opened in April 1969 the ministry had proudly declared the prison's treatment-oriented programs to be among the most innovative in the world. From the outset, Vanier adopted a "therapeutic community" model and broke with the military traditions still in vogue for adult corrections across North America. Open communication between staff and inmates was encouraged by the use of first names and nicknames, and prisoners were allowed to participate, in limited ways, in decisions that affected their daily routine.

Prisoners came to Vanier from all parts of Ontario, a mixed bag of repeat offenders and teenagers – like Marlene – doing their first stretch of serious time. The minimum age was seventeen, and all the women had sentences of between thirty days and two years. Most were young and had dropped out before completing high school, drifting in and out of unskilled jobs or surviving on the streets as hookers and petty thieves. Whether they spent their childhoods on the native reserves of northern Ontario or the cement playgrounds of urban centres, nearly all had known poverty and family strife.

There were few crimes of violence on the records of women held at Vanier. For the most part, the women had been convicted of property offences, break-and-enters, disturbance charges, and offences involving drugs, liquor, and prostitution. Corrections officials who studied the prison population in the early 1970s found that psychiatric problems and even past suicide attempts were not unusual.

When Marlene arrived at Vanier in the late summer of 1976, "She was extremely badly damaged from a psychological point of view," says Sylvia Nicholls, who spent nine years as director at the women's jail. "She had a horrendous family background, so when she came into Vanier she had very much an anti-authority approach to people. She had great, great difficulty relating to males."

Although Marlene was taciturn about her childhood, as she would be throughout her life, the young prisoner carried the badges of her distress on her arms. Nicholls soon discovered that Marlene was already badly scarred on her wrists and arms from attempting suicide – or sometimes not even from attempting suicide but just from punishing herself "by badly ripping open her arms."

During her first few months at the prison Marlene slashed herself on occasion and sometimes broke the rules. Once she took off from the institution, only to be caught walking along about ten minutes after staff reported her missing. According to a police report, Marlene's response on being picked up after her brief escape was in character: She stamped her foot and kicked the side of the police cruiser. But there were positive signs of change as well, and Nicholls believes that Marlene was "coping very well" under the concerted care at Vanier. Nicholls found there was still a lot of caring and compassion in Marlene at that time, that it still seemed possible to work with her.

Marlene was assigned to a unit known as Hochelaga, one of four medium-security cottages inside the fenced compound. Each unit was composed of three wings with eight single bedrooms, dining room, living room, kitchenette, laundry room, and staff offices. Weather permitting, Marlene worked outdoors on the groundskeeping detail, and over the winter months she worked as a janitor, operating industrial cleaning equipment.

And she rocked. Harriet Ironside, a grounds supervisor at the prison, would frequently see her seated in the corner of a cottage, rocking back and forth. When Ironside asked other staff about it they told her that Marlene rocked because it gave her some sort of peace. Marlene also had a dreadful habit of cracking her knuckles. Whe she became distressed during conversations with staff, she would inevitably begin cracking her knuckles and rocking back and forth.

Vanier had an individually tailored treatment program for each prisoner, and Marlene was soon meeting regularly with a psychiatrist. The institution expected staff to keep a watchful eye on their charges and to pass on their observations and concerns, which meant – in Marlene's case – regular reports about her insomnia and her extreme difficulty in dealing with frustration and anger.

According to Nicholls, there were other women at Vanier just as disturbed as Marlene. "The concern with Marlene was that she would turn on herself more than anyone else, and would injure herself very badly if she was depressed or upset." Without warning, Marlene would lose her fragile self-control and attack her own flesh with a razor blade or shard of glass. On occasion she cut herself so deeply that she exposed the muscle of her arm.

Marlene did open up to certain people she felt she could trust, but she was known for her radical mood swings. "You could see two sides of Marlene," Sylvia Nicholls says. "It was almost black and white. If she felt someone had let her down, she would go into a torrent of rage. But as long as she felt that she was able to trust an individual, then there was a quieter, more calm kind of personality in her. It was almost like two different identities or two different personalities."

Sympathy for fellow prisoners was part of that other side. Whenever she perceived some kind of injustice the young prisoner ignored the personal consequences of confronting prison authorities. According to Nicholls, no matter what the circumstances Marlene would stand up for the underdog. "If she felt someone was being treated unfairly she would go to bat for them," Nicholls says. "She didn't care what people felt about her, but she certainly did care about others. It's a side of her you don't hear much about."

Other women began to look to Marlene to voice their complaints, and one spring night in 1977 her imprudent compliance brought her close to disaster. On Monday, May 16, after the day's work was done, Marlene was talking and grumbling along with three other women confined to Invictus cottage, a maximum-security unit opened not long before on a trial basis. They were disgruntled about the introduction of new house rules – changes that had not yet been finally approved by the administration.

Marlene became increasingly agitated. She got up and paced around the room, joined by Isabella Fay Ogima, an eighteen-year-old native prisoner who once wrote in her own blood on the walls of her segregation cell that she hated all white people. The two teenagers vented their anger by banging doors and kicking furniture. But they didn't stop there. Just before midnight they set their mattresses on fire. Acrid smoke billowed under the bedroom doors and into a corridor, temporarily blocking access to the fire exit. A prison guard, Eileen Wingate, spotted the smoke and sounded the alarm that brought firefighters racing to the scene. Moments later Marlene and Isabella Ogima pushed the startled guard to the floor of the cottage. Both prisoners were armed with sharp-edged tin lids cut from fruit juice cans and folded in half.

They released Wingate, who was shaken but unharmed, after about twenty minutes. By then the fire brigade had turned hoses on the smouldering mattresses and grounds supervisor Harriet Ironside had rushed into the chaos. The two staffers herded the cottage residents outside, where Ogima doused Ironside with the contents of a fire extinguisher. Wingate, aided by the arrival of a male security guard, helped another prisoner overcome by smoke. They steered the woman away from the cottage, passing through a double set of electronically controlled doors that separated the command office from the inmates' living quarters. At almost the same instant, Marlene and Isabella Ogima, still brandishing their homemade weapons, rushed at Ironside, grabbed her, and pulled her inside the office. For the next five hours, the fifty-one-year-old guard, known as Heddy, was held hostage.

In a few rash moments Marlene had put herself in deep trouble. Nicholls, roused from sleep by a phone call, rushed to the prison to take command of the hastily assembled negotiating team. Later Nicholls said she viewed the incident as a "last-minute situation" and wasn't convinced the two girls had intended to take a hostage. It happened during a time when staff were being trained about hostage-takings, and Ironside, taught to be passive and a model prisoner in the event of a hostage-taking, didn't put up a fight. Years later she says she became convinced that some of the residents, including Marlene and Isabella Ogima, had come to know the procedure through an inadvertent breach of security. "They seemed to know exactly what we, the staff, would do if we were placed in that situation," Ironside says.

As the night dragged on, Nicholls talked on and off with Marlene over the internal phone system. The two prisoners had access to outside lines as well. At one point Marlene spoke briefly to Curry Moore in Toronto. He jumped into his car and headed for the prison but arrived after the drama had ended.

Images from the gruelling ordeal are fixed in Nicholls's mind – "as clear as if it was yesterday." At the outset the young hostage-takers were "flying high," drunk on power and the toilet-bowl fluid they had scavenged from the storage cupboards. Threats and vague demands punctuated their phone calls. At one point Ogima wrapped an electrical cord around the hostage's neck. Nicholls remembers Marlene's ominous warning: "Isabella wants to finish Heddy off." Ironside later said that she was "more afraid of Isabella Ogima than I ever was of Marlene."

Around 4 a.m. a crucial break came in the standoff. Marlene agreed to meet with Nicholls but insisted she come to the door of the cottage and personally escort her across the yard – out of reach of the contingent of armed guards surrounding the building. As Marlene stepped out the door, Ironside recalled, "my stomach sank." Nicholls, too, was deeply troubled as she turned her back on the cottage, an alarming threat ringing in her ears. Isabella shouted at Nicholls, "You might as well know, Nicholls, if Marlene isn't back in fifteen minutes, Heddy's had it."

The two women sat down with regional director John Main and went over the prisoners' grievances. Marlene read from notes she'd scribbled on scraps of paper. Nicholls remembers her complaints being "about program changes, nothing else." The meeting ended with vague assurances from the prison authorities but no specific demands or promises were made. On their return trip to the cottage, Nicholls steered Marlene across the vestibule where the hostage's distraught husband, Bill Ironside, sat with his head in his hands. On impulse, she stopped and introduced Marlene.

Bill Ironside had no idea that he was meeting one of the inmates who had taken his wife hostage. Nicholls said, "This is Marlene. She's going back into the unit to try to persuade Isabella to let your wife go." Ironside jumped up and grabbed her hand and said, "Oh, thank you, dear, thank you very much." According to Nicholls, "It was just like cold water had been thrown on Marlene's face." Marlene looked at Bill Ironside, who was "looking quite tearful," and said, "Well, I'll see what the fuck I can do."

With that, the two women retraced their steps across the open yard to the cottage. Before Nicholls had returned to the command post, Marlene was on the phone. Ten minutes later it was all over. Ironside was released unharmed, and her captors were manacled and whisked off to the Metro Toronto West Detention Centre. It was the last time Nicholls set eyes on Marlene.

Three days later, on Friday, May 20, 1977, Marlene and Isabella Ogima appeared before Judge John D. Ord in provincial court at Brampton to face seven charges. The abduction-related offences were distinctly more serious than any Marlene had faced before. Each of the accused pleaded guilty on all counts. Neither was represented by a lawyer. Crown attorney George Wouton proceeded reluctantly, having failed to persuade the teenagers to withhold their pleas, at least until they had secured legal counsel. Marlene was insistent: "No, I just want to get it over with."

The trial degenerated into farce, with the Crown's presentation of the facts of the charges frequently interrupted by giggles and shouts from the accused. When asked whether she wished to respond to the description of events, Marlene's answer was a respectful, "No, sir." But her demeanour changed within moments. When Judge Ord proposed to delay sentencing, pending psychiatric assessment and pre-sentence reports, Marlene countered: "I know it's a serious matter but that's why we're pleading guilty, just to get it over with and to get to where we're goin' and start our time all over again instead of puttin' up with petty shit that goes on in fuckin' Vanier Centre."

Once again, both women insisted they wanted to be sentenced. Marlene said, "We'll agree to five years." That sparked an exchange that stretched the bounds of courtroom decorum.

Judge: Well, that's okay but I can't operate like that, I've got to sentence you on certain principles I have.

Marlene: You've got the facts there. We've pleaded guilty, a pre-sentence report isn't going to help us in this case. A pre-sentence report is just like gettin' a piece of paper with shit on it.

Wouton: Why don't we hold it down and try to get a duty counsel in to speak to them because it's too serious just to giggle their way through?

Judge: Well, look . . .

Isabella: I'm asking you to sentence me now.

Judge: Look, kids, it's your life, and it's years of your life when you're young and while good things can happen to you. I'm not going to let you giggle this away or treat it as lightly as you are treating it. It's a serious matter and if you're not going to treat it seriously, I certainly am.

The prisoners finally agreed to retain a lawyer, who promptly asked that their guilty pleas be wiped from the record. The young women had unfortunately accepted the word of detectives that they would be going to the penitentiary, he said. They thought, "It didn't matter what would happen, they might as well get it over with." Judge Ord refused to withdraw the pleas but granted a request to delay sentencing until the following Wednesday, pending psychiatric assessment.

That order had not been completed when the proceedings resumed five days later. Marlene's lawyer informed the court that no psychiatrist was available because of the intervening Victoria Day holiday weekend, adding that his clients "wish everything to be over with as quickly as possible." In a series of brief exchanges with the bench, the two teenagers reiterated their demand to be sentenced and explicitly refused to co-operate with psychiatric assessment.

They turned down Judge Ord's invitation to address the bench. He sentenced each of them to six years in prison. By late May 1977 they were headed for the nation's only federal penitentiary for women.

4

I have the ability to
make something out of myself

Marlene Moore, at age nineteen, was now in federal custody, and "home" was a six-by-nine-foot cell at the Kingston Prison for Women. For female offenders, the limestone fortress known simply as P4W is the end of the line. In the late 1970s, women accounted for less than 10 per cent of the nearly 500,000 Criminal Code charges recorded annually by Canadian courts, and only a tiny fraction of female offenders ended up at the Kingston prison, serving sentences of two years to life. Fewer than a hundred women were housed at the Prison for Women when Marlene and Isabella Ogima joined the population.

The prison fronts on Sir John A. Macdonald Boulevard, one block from Kingston Penitentiary, the notorious maximum-security prison for men. A copper green dome atop the women's prison glints in the sunlight, its pretentious grandeur no longer spoiled by the sixteen-foot-high limestone wall that in Marlene's time encircled the grey building and outdoor exercise yard, an area the size of a small city block. Built in the early 1930s, the penitentiary's perpendicular block of ninety bar-fronted cells, each with a wash basin and open toilet, is a throwback to the maximum-security design favoured by prison authorities in the mid-nineteenth century. The women's prison was an architectural extension of Kingston Penitentiary, which opened in 1835 with two women convicts housed in "temporary" quarters that endured for ninety-nine years.

The Prison for Women was also a jurisdictional afterthought. From 1914 until 1960, when Isobel McNeill was appointed the first superintendent, the women's prison was an add-on to the responsibilities of the warden of Kingston Penitentiary. It was not until late 1965 that the prison secured administrative autonomy. It would be the early 1980s – following a widely publicized investigation by the Canadian Human Rights Commission – before federal bureaucrats began to take more than passing notice of the special needs of women, who represent less than 2 per cent of the nation's federal prisoners.

Capital construction did bring changes in the 1960s. The prison acquired fifty new dormitory-style rooms with wooden doors, a gymnasium, dining room, and an automatic locking device for the front door. About the time Marlene arrived blueprints were being drawn up for a multi-purpose activity centre, which finally opened in July 1982. One of the biggest capital projects was the $1.4 million spent in 1980 to replace the prison's crumbling exterior wall with an impenetrable barrier, eighteen feet high and containing some four hundred slabs of reinforced concrete, each weighing sixteen tons.

For nearly five years before Marlene's arrival Doug Chinnery had been director at the Prison for Women. For twenty-five years before that he had worked at Kingston Penitentiary. At the men's prison, one of the meanest and most dreary facilities in the federal system, Chinnery rose through the ranks, from guard to classification officer to deputy warden. At age forty-eight he moved across the street to head the Prison for Women. In those days it wasn't considered unseemly to assign the top post at the women's prison to a man or to refer to the institution's female guards by the undignified title of "matron." At one time, the guards were assigned the degrading task of scrubbing the toilets of the inmates in segregation.

As guards' working conditions slowly improved, so did the living conditions of prisoners. When the women's unit at a British Columbia prison was shut down in the early 1970s and several dozen drug offenders there were shipped to Kingston, the new warden relaxed protocol to accommodate the special privileges brought from the West by the newcomers. That meant abandoning the traditional dress code, which had restricted the women to standard-issue black stockings, dresses in three styles, and patent-leather shoes, and allowing them to wear their own clothes. Under Chinnery, double-blade disposable razors were also distributed to the women rather than loaned on request.

Despite gradual modifications in the routine, the imposing gothic edifice of P4W with its cavernous hallways and archaic plumbing and ventilation systems remains severe and oppressive. Countless coats of pastel paint applied to walls, cells, and cell bars have not softened the cold, hard reality of steel and cement.

Prisoners live on either the ranges or the wing. The wing is a long, narrow corridor of dormitory-style rooms with solid, wooden doors and small peep-through windows. Its use has always been reserved for two groups of inmates: those the administration has deemed deserving of relative privacy and quiet; and elderly women or those with handicaps who would find it difficult to adjust to the intimidating chaos of the ranges. The small compartments are creatively and individually decorated with plants, macramé hangings, posters, and family photos. Each prisoner gets a key to her own room.

The orginal double-tiered A and B ranges are quintessential jail: seventy-five open-barred, closet-like cells – each furnished with a metal bed, steel wardrobe, four-drawer dresser, wall unit, and open toilet. Privacy shams strung across the front of cells are required to be drawn eighteen inches apart for surveillance purposes. The prisoners can select paint for their cells from a range of approved shades. Personal touches – matching curtains and bedspread, a giant potted plant – also help to soften the impact of the rows of human cages.

When Marlene arrived at P4W the cells had no hot water. By day the clang and hum of electronically operated metal doors was constant. At night wind rattled through doors and windows. In the wing area women shoved socks and face cloths through the top crack in their doors in an attempt to alleviate the incessant creaking. They could sometimes hear bats swooping overhead. Even more alarming for the prisoners on the range were the inhuman sounds that travelled the antiquated vents: the screams of women housed in segregation.

There was little variation in the daily routine. Every morning at 8 a.m. a spin of the giant wheel at the end of each range disengaged the door-bar of each cell, releasing women for breakfast in the cafeteria, where they assembled at round tables, six to a sitting. In the winter the fare often included porridge or cream of wheat. On Sundays prisoners were served bacon. On most other days they got juice, eggs, toast, dry cereals, home fries, and percolated coffee. Marlene, known for her poor appetite, rarely ate breakfast, but she liked to mingle with the others over coffee.

After breakfast women lined up at the medication barrier, where nurses dispensed drugs, ointments, and vitamins. Women not confined to segregation or the infirmary spent their mornings at work or school. For a time Marlene was employed in the kitchen, washing pots or preparing food. Other prisoners staffed the laundry, the canteen, the yard crew, and the internal prison newsletter, or they worked as video technicians, cleaners, or clerks. Women also worked in the prison beauty salon, then the only occupational training at the prison.

At 11 a.m. the inmate-staffed cafeteria began serving lunch, the big meal of the day, which on Fridays was invariably fish and chips. Prisoners ate in two or three shifts, depending on the size of the current population. Time waiting was spent collecting laundry, opening mail, and socializing on the ranges. After lunch the medication barrier opened again. By 1 p.m. the women were back at work or school where they remained until dinner, which was served between 4 and 6 p.m.

In those days security was relatively relaxed. The pass system was rarely enforced. During the day women moved freely around most parts of the institution, visiting back and forth on the ranges, meeting with prison counsellors, or keeping appointments at the beauty parlour. Marlene, uninterested in make-up or the latest hair style, was one of the few prisoners who didn't take advantage of free cuts, perms, or color tints. But she would often drop into the hairdressing shop to chat with the manager, a woman she called Mrs. P. In her spare time Marlene mostly liked to sip coffee with friends in their cells, play cards – Spades and Canasta were the most popular games – or sit alone in her cell, wrapped in a blanket, listening to a Pink Floyd album and rocking back and forth in a distant, meditative trance.

In the evenings women were free to exercise in the yard or gym or attend support groups that included Alcoholics Anonymous, Ten Plus for those serving ten years or more, or the Native Sisterhood. They had to be back on the living unit by 10 p.m. and in their cells by 11 p.m., unless they were watching the late news. In deference to Canada's favourite national pastime, security also made an exception to the curfew during hockey playoffs in the spring. Locked in their cells for the night, the women could read or write letters before turning off their lights. Marlene could usually be heard rocking until well into the night.

The prisoners generally thought well of Warden Doug Chinnery. He was someone who listened to grievances and made concessions whenever possible. In Marlene's case, the soft-spoken administrator bent the rules on cell furnishings, allowing her to sleep on a mattress on the floor. Chinnery also intervened personally to arrange for visits from her brother Curry, by now incarcerated at Joyceville Institution, a federal medium-security prison about eighteen kilometres north of Kingston.

But the former head of the women's prison, who prides himself on being able to break through the tough exterior of the most hardened criminal, offers few benign recollections of Marlene. Her reputation had preceded her arrival at the prison, as details of the Vanier hostage-taking spread like wildfire through the guards' grapevine. Prison employees were aware that the teenagers had "put the fear of God into the staff of an institution," Chinnery says.

The warden found himself unable to establish any kind of personal rapport with Marlene, which rankles him still. "She was the most difficult inmate, male or female, that I ever met," he says. "Not the most dangerous – we had women who were more dangerous than Marlene Moore – but the most difficult. The reason she was difficult was this hatred she had that was free-floating. It wasn't aimed at anything." Mary Morissette, a career correctional officer and one-time union president who grew up in Portsmouth village, just two blocks from the prison, paints a similar portrait of Marlene. "She was well on her way to being one of the strongest, not by her strength itself but by her will and what she was capable of and what the other inmates knew she was capable of," the senior guard says. "Marlene's big thing was her bluster and pride. It was almost a macho thing." Morissette had her own theory about Marlene's behaviour. She says, "I believed she hated being female and she resented anything that was weak, so she had to be tougher and stronger and wilder. Because she wasn't a particularly strong person, she had to do it by being a little crazy."

In P4W Marlene seemed bent on living up to her reputation. The nineteen-year-old newcomer, says Chinnery, wasted little time in demonstrating that she belonged to a select group of prisoners – the one in ten whose behaviour "keeps a prison in turmoil."

But Chinnery was not insensitive to her sufferings. He saw her many times lying on her cell mat, flailing her head from side to side, and he knew her pain was real. "Let's face it, Marlene Moore brought out the motherly instincts in people," he says. Still, the young prisoner utterly exhausted his patience.

Marlene, who by then had learned to suspect the motives of authority figures, responded with contempt to his attempts to communicate. When Chinnery tried to talk to her she'd say, "What the fuck do you care?"

There were others among the prison staff, however, who Marlene felt she could trust. She frequently sat up talking with one of the guards late at night, when she thought other prisoners weren't listening. In those days, talking openly with guards was considered taboo, a breach of the unwritten inmate code. But Marlene wasn't a staff-hater like a lot of inmates were, Morissette says. "She would give that illusion a lot of times, but she was also one of the few who would bare as much to staff as she did." Marlene occasionally spoke about her relationships with members of her family or women in the institution.

Intense, devoted relationships have always characterized the women's prison. Separated from family and friends, the women turn to one another for physical affection and emotional support.

Television and film have promoted stereotypes of women prisoners as hardened, mannish personalities and convey the impression that prisons are overrun with knife-toting predator lesbians. The reality is different. Although homosexuality is officially forbidden in prisons, the administration tolerates, even passively condones, intimate sexual relations between women at the Prison for Women. While sexual liaisons between male prisoners are often coercive and violent, women offenders tend to form close, exclusive relationships that authorities perceive as having a stabilizing effect inside the institution. It shouldn't be surprising that many women prisoners choose other women as intimate partners. Most have been victims of male violence, whether physical or sexual or both.

Some women establish sexual relationships while in prison and resume a heterosexual lifestyle after their release. Many form passionate friendships that have nothing to do with sex. In the alienating and often volatile environment of prison, everyone needs at least one confidante. Marlene brought both fierce loyalty and tenderness to her close relationships. "The lovers she had were really beautiful women, really strong women – dynamic, gorgeous women," says Fran Sugar, a P4W prisoner at the time. Sugar says Marlene had an amazing ability to pursue relationships that lasted for months, sometimes years. "I don't know whether all these women had mother complexes or what but it was incredible – you could see parts of her personality emerging and the beauty of it. What she had to offer these women must have been really something because the flip side of her personality was so chaotic."

Few at the women's prison would openly call themselves feminists. But in prison many women discover just how much they have in common; how profoundly their womanhood accounts for the tragic patterns of their lives. They recognize that together they can fight the most oppressive conditions of incarceration. Whenever governments have pledged to close the women's prison in Kingston, prisoners have expressed the fear that their dispersal into smaller institutions across the country will silence their political voice.

Prisoner solidarity has its limits, just as it does in men's institutions. Prisoners revile women convicted of crimes against children, so those women are housed for their own safety in protective custody cells. Prisoner committees have strongly – and repeatedly – condemned administration attempts to integrate child-abusers into the general population. Although many prisoners acknowledge that child-abusers have often been victims of childhood violence themselves, understanding and sympathy don't come easily at the Prison for Women, where most of the prisoners have experienced childhood violence and where two-thirds have children of their own on the outside.

Marlene had been a federal prisoner for less than eight months when her close friend Isabella Fay Ogima died, at just nineteen years of age, of infectious hepatitis. Ogima had been moved from a cell in the segregation unit to the prison hospital a couple of weeks earlier and was then transferred to a Kingston hospital, where she died three days later on January 24, 1978.

Marlene, confined to the segregation unit when Ogima fell

ill, was called to testify at the coroner's inquest by Kingston lawyer Allan Manson, counsel for the dead woman's mother. She volunteered to wear a long-sleeved shirt, believing she would make a better impression if neither coroner nor jury saw the scars on her arms.

At the end of a two-day inquest, the five members of the coroner's jury ruled that Ogima had died of natural causes and recommended that medical services and record-keeping at the prison be upgraded.

Ten weeks later Marlene met with a psychiatrist. It's possible that prison officials were hoping that the first step had been taken in the development of a long-term therapeutic program for the troubled young inmate. Within weeks, however, the urgency of treating Marlene was dissipated by an Ontario Appeal Court ruling that reduced her sentence on the Vanier hostage-taking incident to three years. Her jail time was cut in half. In less time than Marlene – or Prison for Women staff – had dared hope, she would be released.

In the meantime, guards and prisoners steered a wide berth around Marlene and her closest friends, an exclusive club of young women known in joint parlance as "wackos" or "flippos" for their explosive anger and violent acts of self-mutilation. One of these women, Barb Dennis, had been shipped to the Kingston prison in 1979 from her native British Columbia after spending her teens in locked rooms at training schools and locked cells at provincial jails. A veteran prisoner in her early twenties, Dennis had a red-hot temper and quick fists, a red circle on her record to alert prison authorities to past escapes from custody, and red welts alongside faded scars that ran the length of her arms – mute testimony to a decade of self-mutilation. The blonde newcomer projected toughness and potential danger. Predictably, Marlene took the first opportunity to introduce herself.

The women became inseparable friends, then lovers, and remained staunch allies after the passion had left their relationship. Although their lives followed different directions on release from the Kingston penitentiary, the haunting description

Barb Dennis provides of her own horrific childhood, and the uncontrolled rage that drove her as a young prisoner, lend a sense of inevitability to the enduring bond she forged with Marlene. In some ways, each had found her mirror image: another spirit damaged by incest and beatings, another body scarred by self-hatred, another heart hardened by violence and fear, another life addicted to drugs and alcohol.

Barb Dennis and Marlene Moore were both manipulated into settling scores for other women. They would fight anyone for almost any reason. "When we got going, everybody just went the other way," Dennis says. "The old coppers will tell you that when we got going, they just backed off. We stuck together like glue, and a lot of people were afraid of us." Fighting and swearing earned Marlene disciplinary charges and punitive confinement.

Prisoners are moved from the general population to "dissociation" along three distinct routes. They are sentenced to segregation by internal courts as punishment for serious disciplinary offences. They are held in protective custody, usually at their own request, because their lives are in danger. Or they are segregated on the sole authority of the warden. The head of the institution, with sweeping powers under the controversial Section 2.30 of the Penitentiary Service Regulations, can isolate prisoners for the maintenance of "good order and discipline" in the prison.

At the Prison for Women, segregation and protective custody units were separated by a solid door. Each unit was a prison inside a prison. All three wardens who dealt with Marlene frequently resorted to Section 2.30 to bring her under the control of lock and key in "the digger," as the women refer to the eleven-cell segregation unit at the west end of the dissociation cell block. The daily routine in segregation was simple, the boredom excruciating. The women were locked in their cells except for a daily exercise period of thirty minutes during the mid-October to mid-April months, and an hour the rest of the year, weather permitting. Terse private conversations could be held via "kites" flown from cell to cell – notes scrunched into tiny balls of paper and passed from hand to hand. The monotony was broken by the hourly rounds, when guards handed out tobacco and lighted cigarettes. Prisoners were allowed only the bare necessities: pyjamas, blanket, pillow, mattress. Although cells and their occupants were searched regularly for contraband, the slashers found ways to cut themselves – and Marlene found more ways than anyone else.

Inmate committees will often rally behind a prisoner who is segregated without charges, but Marlene's unpopularity with some of the more influential prisoners made her more vulnerable to the warden's discretionary powers. In the summer of 1979, just a few months before Marlene was due for release, she was among a number of women moved to segregation on suspicion of involvement in a gang-stabbing at the prison. Dennis and the others, rounded up in the sweep, were released back to the general population without charges after a few days, but Marlene remained in segregation for more than two weeks without ever being charged because the inmate committee supported the warden's unilateral decision to keep her locked up twenty-three hours a day for the "good order" of the prison.

Without programs to distinguish work and leisure time, and without privileges to entice positive behaviours, segregation represents the most dispiriting aspects of incarceration. Being stuck in the hole meant misery. Inside this sealed, emotional pressure-cooker, the suffering is palpable. At one end of the section a cell has been converted to a guard station, where inmates believed to be suicidal or in danger of hurting themselves can be watched on four television monitors propped on a shelf. Cell bars are painted black to make it easier to see each woman's movements.

Less obvious, but no less real, was the general ennui that had spread throughout the Prison for Women by the end of the 1970s, spilling over into the ranks of prisoners, unionized staff, and management. The institution was stuck in a holding pattern. Prisoners and staff alike worried about their futures, following an announcement by federal Solicitor General

Jean-Jacques Blais that the women's prison would be closed "as soon as possible." In January 1979 the minister went public with his plans to phase out the women's prison, announcing a deadline of less than a year for negotiating an agreement with the provinces. Federal administrations had been urged at least a dozen times before to shut down the prison and relocate the women closer to their homes. Blais's commitment was unprecedented.

The first closure recommendation dates back to a 1938 Royal Commission, which concluded that "further continuance is unjustified," given the small number of female offenders. Over the next fifty years, pleas for decentralization were echoed by government-sponsored task forces, parliamentary committees, and advisory groups. Around the time Marlene was sent to Kingston, a special subcommittee of thirteen members of Parliament released a 75,000-word report containing sixty-five recommendations for changes in the operations and philosophy of federal corrections. Their unparalleled inquiry into the penitentiary system described the Prison for Women as "unfit for bears, much less women." The report vilified the institution as "obsolete in every respect – in design, in programs, and in the handling of the people sent there."

Another report issued in the spring of 1977, just weeks before Marlene moved into federal jurisdiction, offered the first comprehensive study of women prisoners in Canada since W.F. Nickle was appointed in 1921 to investigate the management of female offenders. Whereas his recommendations had led to construction of the Prison for Women, the National Advisory Committee on the Female Offender strongly urged that the facility be closed within three years. The seven-member committee proposed that one of two options be implemented by 1980: establish open small regional facilities under the federal jurisdiction; or hand over responsibility for all female offenders, regardless of length of sentence, to the provinces. Either way, committee members were adamant that Ottawa adopt a hands-on approach to the development and monitoring of standards of service. But talks between the two levels of government were sidetracked by a federal election.

On December 1, 1979, Marlene was released on mandatory supervision, having served the requisite two-thirds of her sentence and an extra couple of months for misbehaviour. She was back on the streets for only four weeks before she and a friend broke into an apartment over the New Year's holiday weekend in Toronto and stole twelve bottles of beer.

She was remanded in custody in Toronto and underwent brief psychiatric assessment on February 4, 1980. Three days later her temper erupted during a remand appearance. While being moved to a holding cell at the College Park provincial courtroom, Marlene punched a female escort in the cheek. Her mandatory supervision order was revoked soon afterwards, and she eventually received an additional 150 days for assault and 90 days for the stolen beer. She was sent briefly to St. Thomas Psychiatric Hospital for assessment and then back to the Prison for Women.

Daryl Dollan arrived at the federal prison in the spring of 1980 with an outlaw image and a life sentence, at age twenty-eight, for her part in a deadly crime spree with her boyfriend. She initially kept a safe distance from Marlene, acutely aware of the ribbons of welts that wound around the pale arms of this younger prisoner. "The first thing that hits you about Marlene is the scars," Dollan recalls. "She had scars everywhere, and she had a lot of tattoos." In time Dollan would become one of the most high-profile prisoners in Canada, earning an arts degree from Queen's University while in prison – and making both friends and enemies on the inside for her outspoken campaign for separate living quarters for those few prisoners whose violence or mental illness posed a threat.

For a time she and Marlene – nicknamed Shaggie by the inmates – lived on B range, one of the two double-tiered cell blocks in use since the prison opened in early 1934. They struck up a casual friendship. Marlene once became furious with Dollan for using sophisticated language that she felt "left her in the dust." After that, Dollan was careful to modify her speech so she wouldn't offend her friend. Although unschooled, Marlene had a quick wit and sharp instincts. "You could never pull one over on her. She was always quick to catch on to things," Dollan says. Still, Marlene was desperately insecure about her poor writing and speaking abilities. Dollan eventually moved to a room in the wing section, the living area of choice for most lifers because it offers more privileges, notably late-night TV on weekends and the relative quiet of an environment not unlike a spartan student dormitory. For a short stretch the next year, Marlene occupied a room in the south wing. The prison's chief security administrator arranged that temporary placement, in hopes that Marlene could be isolated from trouble brewing on the ranges.

A glimpse of Marlene's spontaneous generosity emerged one day when Dollan's father was visiting the prison on his birthday. Marlene – now working in the kitchen – baked him a cake, brought it to the visiting room, and sang Happy Birthday. "She was really embarrassed but she did it, and my Dad shook her hand," Dollan says. "I always thought my Dad was pretty naive, but he seemed to know which girls he could kiss and which ones he could shake their hands. If he had kissed Marlene, she probably would have decked him or something."

Sometimes Dollan acted as a sounding board during Marlene's confused ramblings about her relations with the few guileful prisoners who wanted to exploit her hair-trigger reaction to injustice. "She was questioning some of the motives that other people had for her and she wanted to sort it out," Dollan says. Dollan tried to be careful about not coming down on one side or the other of this discussion – "You've gotta be careful that way when you're in prison," she says. But she did say, "Marlene, you're smart enough to figure it out for yourself."

One of Marlene's closest friends, Brenda Hope, came to the prison from western Canada at the end of the summer of 1980. She was twenty-one. Hope and Marlene were assigned a work detail to build and assemble guards' lockers. After that they took on odd jobs in the prison's cleaning and supply services.

"If file cabinets needed to be moved, Shaggie and I would go and move them," Hope says. "We tore the rug out of the staff lounge and scrubbed the floor down to the terrazzo. Marlene loved working. She loved being really involved in something." They also teamed up on the softball diamond, where they formed the prison team's battery – Marlene on the mound and her buddy hunkered down behind the plate. The games played against teams from the Kingston area generated the few truly lighthearted recollections that Hope offers about her stretch at the Prison for Women.

One days Hope and Marlene gave themselves identical devil tattoos. "I looked through a mirror and drew it, and she traced it on my shoulder. We finished the tattoo and went out and played a baseball game and won," Hope says, laughing. On another occasion a bothersome bee disturbed Marlene's pitching. "She jumped off the mound and started going through all sorts of contortions," Hope says. "The umpire was yelling at her to pitch and she was laughing so hard she couldn't explain it was a bee. It was really comical and everybody was roaring with laughter before it was over. Marlene had a great laugh."

The young prisoners often passed the evening playing backgammon on a board balanced across chairs placed back-to-back, sipping mugs of coffee that Marlene would sweeten with two heaping scoops of sugar. They amused themselves with impulsive acts of rebellion, like the time they climbed the bars on A range to reach the cathedral-style windows at the end of the upper tier. "That's high up, and we stood in the window. We opened the window and just screamed at the top of our lungs, screaming at the world," Hope says. "It was just for something to do."

Their unruly behaviour was not always so harmless. When uncontrolled anger fuelled their energy, Marlene and Hope could be disruptive and intimidating. Both women spent extended periods in segregation for fighting or slashing or hurling obscenities at guards.

Hope now covers her scarred arms with a long-sleeved wardrobe when she leaves home, and she worries about how her infant daughter will view those symbols of her mother's troubled past when she is old enough to see the difference. Hope has travelled an immeasurable distance since her life at the Prison for Women. She is nevertheless fiercely loyal to the memory of her friend. She remembers Marlene as being well-liked, even admired by other prisoners. "Some people respected her because they feared her. But a lot – the majority of people – respected her because of what she stood for. She was solid. She was loyal to her friends to the very end. She was an honourable convict."

It was the special quality of their friendship that caught the attention of Canadian filmmakers Janis Cole and Holly Dale when they rolled their cameras onto the ranges of the Kingston prison for twenty-one days in 1980, producing an award-winning documentary entitled simply *P4W*. "As individuals, they both seemed like not particularly strong characters, but together, as one, they seemed like one strong character. They seemed like they had a very good friendship," Cole later said. She told the two young women that she was interested in including them in the film, especially Marlene because she had heard of her reputation. "I asked if it could really be as bad as people were saying. She started laughing. Shortly after that she started hanging around with us, and she asked if she could lift some cases of equipment and help out. I said sure and she was terrific."

Marlene initially balked at being filmed, saying she was too nervous, but toward the end of the shoot, after watching Cole and Dale at work, she agreed to participate. Her brief appearances offer a rare and poignant glimpse of the private hell that compelled her self-mutilation. About five minutes into the film, viewers meet Marlene, a slight, pale young woman, then twenty-three. She is seated, clad in a short-sleeved white T-shirt that exposes her tattoos and scarred arms, talking directly into the camera: "Like, I don't . . . sometimes I don't know how to deal with things the right way. Sometimes I won't be able to . . . like, Maggie, I won't be able to get to her in time. I hold so much inside. So I'll just go to my room and do it, right? It's not good but it happens." There's no mistaking the meaning of her words as the lens draws close to an angry-red slash mark on her forearm, then travels the length of her arm, revealing a roadway of raised scar tissue.

Maggie MacDonald, now released, was sentenced to life in prison in 1965 after fatally stabbing, for the second time, an abusive common-law husband. Marlene respected Maggie for the amount of time she had done and the fact that she was still a strong, proud woman. Maggie's life story was featured in the film *P4W*, and at one point Marlene offers a glimpse of Mac-Donald's matriarchal role inside the prison: "I go to Maggie a lot, sometimes when it's too late, sometimes when it's just in time. Most of the time I've been lucky that Maggie's been there. She's learned me a lot" – Marlene pauses, a quizzical expression on her face – "Taught me a lot? Yeah, right. And I think that, I don't know, I just know that I'm glad that she's there, you know."

The next time the camera swings back to Marlene, she elaborates on the build-up of pressure that culminates in slashing: "You know that through violence or whatever, it's not going to prove anything. You're just going to be in seg, right, for hitting a screw or for hitting one of the inmates, whatever. You have no choice. You either take it and take it and take it, and slash and get it out of your system somehow, or you just take it and take it and take the chance of somebody getting hurt, you know."

Years later Cole recalled that some prisoners had warned the filmmakers to stay away from Marlene, that she was very dangerous and it could be risky to be found in the same prison tunnel with her. But Cole never did see her as dangerous or scary. "I saw a person who had been quite marred and affected by the institutional experience and I thought that was impor-tant to include in the film."

When Cole and Dale returned to the prison to present the film to the prisoners, Marlene was locked in segregation and couldn't attend. But, Cole says, "One thing that was almost unanimous was how articulate Shaggie was because she didn't

usually express herself very well." Marlene later saw the film
with some friends at a private showing after her release from
prison and loved it. Cole recounts an amusing story about what
happened when she later took Marlene's mother to a Toronto
movie theatre to see *P4W*. By that time it had acquired a cult
following – like that of *The Rocky Horror Picture Show* – which
took the form of audience participation. "It was really wild,"
Coles says. "People were calling out everybody's name and
lines of dialogue. I hadn't expected that and I was wondering,
'What is she thinking?' But her mother really liked it too."

But in prison, Marlene's self-destructive impulse had become cause for mounting concern. She was at times manipulated by more sophisticated women. Her desperate insecurity
made her a pawn in the prison hierarchy, where status was
often the measure of crude power. But there was no clearly
identifiable pattern to the trouble she caused her keepers and
other inmates. Instead, there were random outbursts of aggression.

The most serious incident took place on the evening of
October 29, 1980, when Marlene assaulted another inmate,
stabbing the woman three times with a kitchen knife. In a
Kingston courtroom about three months later her lawyer did
not dispute the details of the incident, as provided by the
Crown attorney: Marlene entered the cell of Eva Baseraba, who
was visiting with two friends, and became provoked at Baseraba's use of a language she couldn't understand. A fight broke
out and Marlene cut the woman in the upper right shoulder,
arm, and just below her right breast. The breast wound was
described as "potentially serious" by a local physician. As it
turned out, Baseraba's injuries healed rapidly and she was
discharged from hospital after three days.

Marlene was represented in court by Allison MacPhail, a
self-possessed young lawyer who was then assistant director of
the Queen's University Correctional Law Project, a unique
legal clinic founded specifically to serve prisoners. MacPhail
put a senior guard on the stand and elicited testimony about a
series of incidents, including thefts and an inmate slashing,

which had increased the usual pre-Christmas tension in the prison. The witness noted obligingly that tension was particularly high on B range, where Marlene and Baseraba lived, the night of the assault.

But MacPhail didn't get the same help from her own client. At one point, Judge Paul H. Megginson commented that Marlene had been smiling smugly throughout the proceeding without apparent regard for the seriousness of the situation. "So what?" Marlene retorted.

MacPhail had negotiated a lesser charge in exchange for a guilty plea. In the end Judge Megginson accepted the Crown's recommendation that he impose the maximum six-month sentence allowed by law. In doing so, he noted that Marlene's record contained three previous assault convictions, as well as the fact that the Crown could have pushed for a more serious charge with a sentence ceiling of fourteen years behind bars. The judge ignored Marlene's tactless response when he extended her jail term. "Six months," she scoffed. "What a kiss. Hooray, all right."

Beneath the brazen veneer in the courtroom that day was an acutely sensitive and insecure young woman. It had become apparent to Allison MacPhail that Marlene longed for friendship beyond the prison walls. The Queen's lawyer began to stop by the penitentiary in the evenings. "We would talk about how she might deal with difficult situations and I encouraged her to think about the future, what she might do when she got out." Like other women who became entangled in Marlene's life, MacPhail finds it difficult to pinpoint what drew her to the disturbed young prisoner. "It's very hard to say why you like someone," she says. "But she was a very attractive person, very friendly, very warm, very sweet. There was just something about her." At the same time, she was becoming concerned about Marlene's behaviour. MacPhail and medical staff at the prison searched for help, finally locating Dr. Claudine Rodenburg, a Kingston psychiatric resident.

An initial meeting went well enough that Marlene began regular weekly visits, under guard escort, to the Barrie Street office of Rodenburg, a stately, grey-haired physician with a thick Dutch accent. The main objective of the therapy, Mac-Phail says, was to help Marlene learn to deal with frustration more constructively. Later on, during a 1984 trial, Kingston psychiatrist Dr. Philip Haden would speak positively about the doctor-prisoner relationship. Marlene had been very co-operative with Rodenburg and had improved considerably during the weekly treatment program, which lasted for a full year. Haden said Marlene was reported to be "enjoying success" within the prison as well.

But the outside visits presented Marlene with an opportunity she couldn't resist. On February 27, 1981, while she was on medical temporary absence for her session with the psychiatrist, Marlene slipped away from her guard escort and headed downtown. Authorities picked her up a few hours later, but the stunt cost her an additional five months.

Marlene's impetuous escape occurred just as a new warden was settling into the job. From the outset there was plenty of friction in relations between Marlene and George Caron, who had graduated to the warden's chair from the office of deputy warden in January 1981. While her dealings with retiring warden Chinnery had led more or less to a stand-off, her relations with the new warden were closer to outright war. A former parole officer, Caron was an unyielding administrator who lacked Chinnery's diplomatic instincts. Maggie Mac-Donald, the long-time head of the inmate committee, temporarily resigned her post in disgust at the appointment. In her 1987 autobiography, *The Violent Years of Maggie MacDonald*, she has bitter words for the new prison chief: "Just before he was made warden, he wanted the gym scrubbed, waxed and polished for the big presentation. So one of the staff asked two girls if they'd do it. They got up at five in the morning and scrubbed it from corner to corner, making it sparkle. And they didn't even get a thank-you from that ungrateful man."

According to MacDonald, slashers especially hated the new warden. "He had them in seg more than out, and I was still on the inmate committee, forever running back and forth to seg, talking to the girls and taking razor blades off them, and then back to the warden, trying to get answers on why they were in the hole and when they'd be coming out. But the new warden would never give any answers."

Caron says that despite all his trouble with Marlene, he never had any personal animosity toward her. Yet when the National Parole Board went to court in 1982 in a bid to block Marlene's release from prison, one of the reasons the board chairman cited was a violent verbal threat Marlene had directed at the warden.

In summer 1981, Felicity Hawthorn, the lawyer who would act for the Canadian Association of Elizabeth Fry Societies at the coroner's inquest into Marlene's death, first met Marlene. Hawthorn had signed up as a volunteer with Kingston's Elizabeth Fry Society within days of enrolling at Queen's University law school. She saw Marlene often during visits to the prison. One day stands out in her mind. A politically active student who had become exasperated by the conservative politics and "low level of social consciousness" among many of her fellow classmates, Hawthorn decided to stir matters up a bit. Bent on bringing co-workers at Queen's Legal Aid, a student-run community service, face-to-face with some of those designated as Canada's worst female criminals, Hawthorn organized a softball game at the prison. Her plan was to mix all the players up so each team would have both students and prisoners. "I thought it would be more fun," Hawthorn says. Marlene, pitcher for the prison team, vetoed the idea. She wanted her team left intact, poised to prove itself against the outsiders. She also unilaterally rejected Hawthorn's suggestion that the group play slow pitch rather than the more competitive softball. "It was an awful day," Hawthorn says. "Marlene was determined she was the softball pitcher and she couldn't pitch for beans. She didn't pitch a single strike the whole game. She just kept walking us round and round and round."

Hawthorn had many contacts with Marlene over the next seven years and grew fond of her. "I really liked her. Everybody liked her. She was just a really likeable person, despite everything," she says.

That same summer Marlene was somehow able to obtain medical authorization for a hysterectomy. She was twenty-three. The circumstances surrounding the operation are unclear, and confidentiality between patient and physician make it unlikely that the full story will ever be known. People close to Marlene say that she linked recurring bouts of depression to her menstrual cycle.

It's not so surprising that she was able to convince a doctor to perform the operation. Research has shown that the invasive surgical procedure, which involves full or partial removal of the uterus, is often performed without medical justification. Women health critics have long held the view that some doctors see hysterectomies as a way of treating women's mental health. If a woman's anger and irritability can be attributed to premenstrual syndrome, the medical solution becomes removal of her uterus. The truth may in fact be that a women who is premenstrual experiences a heightened sensitivity to the conditions of her life. Her anger is not a biological reflex but rather a healthy response to the injustices attached to being female.

The reports of the Kingston psychiatrist Philip Haden make two official references to the operation. In his first assessment of Marlene in 1982 Haden stated, "A hysterectomy has been performed at her own request partly on account of premenstrual tension which, allegedly, exacerbated her violent tendencies." In a follow-up report about two years later Haden quoted Marlene as saying, in reference to her hysterectomy, "I'm glad it's gone." According to his subsequent courtroom testimony, Marlene was "more communicative and less tense" following the surgery.

June Callwood, the Toronto author and columnist who befriended Marlene, interprets Marlene's hysterectomy as the young woman's rejection of her own womanhood: "Her sense of all the violence was that being hurt, being vulnerable, had something to do with being a woman." Curry Moore says Marlene simply couldn't bear the humiliation of having to beg guards for sanitary napkins. "She was spending a lot of time in solitary confinement. They would leave her bleeding without giving her sanitary napkins, and she just hated it."

Until the early 1980s an official policy at the Prison for Women prohibited all personal effects, including tampons, in segregation cells. For years the prison allowed a woman housed in segregation only one tampon at a time, supposedly to ensure that no inmate could vent her displeasure by flooding the toilet in her cell. The inmate committee took up the issue with prison management and finally got the rule rescinded.

Around the same time as Marlene's hysterectomy, P4W had its first brush with feminism. Maude Barlow, who would soon become Prime Minister Pierre Trudeau's senior consultant on women's issues, was allowed into the prison to conduct a series of life-skills workshops. Barlow belonged to the group Women for Justice, which had lodged a formal complaint about the women's prison with the Human Rights Commission in the summer of 1980. The group had alleged "systemic discrimination," pointing to the lack of programs and opportunities for inmates. After a seventeen-month investigation, the commission agreed with nine of eleven charges cited by Women for Justice and appointed a conciliator. But because of unresolved disagreements between Correctional Service officials and the complainants, no settlement was ever signed.

During that human-rights investigation Marlene volunteered for one of Barlow's workshops, a pilot project designed to help participants develop self-confidence and draw strength and support from one another. They were to begin by identifying common themes in their lives. Like Marlene, most of the women at the Kingston prison had experienced assaults, both physical and sexual, which had taken a terrible toll on their self-esteem. Repairing the damage would take sensitivity and patience, and Barlow quickly discovered that the stumbling blocks on that painful journey of self-healing would come from the most unlikely sources.

Although Marlene was enthusiastic, she sat apart from the group on a window ledge. For the first whole day she was "in the sun like a little cat," Barlow says. After lunch on the second day, as the women filed back into the room, Marlene went to the flip chart and wrote the words self-respect and self-love. Soon afterwards the prison chaplain walked into the room, picked up a pen, stroked out the handwriting, and rewrote the word respect, which Marlene had misspelled. Marlene, who was by that time sitting with the group, retreated to the window ledge.

Though her personal confidence was fragile, Marlene intuitively grasped the co-operative aspects of feminism, Barlow says. "For some of the women, they'd had a whole history of hating women, hating themselves, not supporting each other. Marlene understood right away the feminist context which I was addressing." When the women in the seminar expelled a native prisoner convicted of killing a baby – a crime that engenders repugnance in a prison setting – Barlow found an ally in Marlene. Barlow had a showdown with the inmates, telling them that if they didn't let the native prisoner back in, she would leave. She says Marlene was "right on side" with her. "She immediately knew what I was talking about." After some discussion, the native woman was allowed to return.

Barlow eventually became friends with Marlene, corresponding regularly and sometimes visiting her at the prison. Barlow says, "There was something so genuine, so open, so unaffected about her and her pain and her story, and her desire to understand. She had a real political instinct about who was there to take advantage and who was there for the women."

5

My fears sometimes force me to *get into trouble*

During her first stretch at the Kingston prison in the late 1970s, Marlene added scores of slash marks to her arms and legs. Her unpredictable rage and self-mutilation kept guards and other prisoners on edge. She would struggle wildly with staff for possession of the piece of glass she carried like some kind of perverse security blanket. Her appearances before the internal disciplinary court inevitably ended in a heart-pounding scuffle.

"As soon as she was sentenced she would start pulling out this piece of glass, and the custodial officer would get cut before they could subdue her," former warden Doug Chinnery says. Chinnery would ask staff, "Why didn't you search her before she came in?" Staff would say, "What's the difference? Someone would get cut then instead of later." Chinnery says Marlene "always carried a piece of glass, always."

Marlene had toyed with slashing as early as age twelve, but at Grandview she had turned on her body in earnest. By the time she reached her nineteenth birthday her arms were crisscrossed by ribbons of scar tissue. She cut herself with the savvy of a surgeon, once yielding a fifty-six stitch wound without severing an artery. At the Prison for Women her chronic self-mutilation became legendary, her scars ultimately becoming a metaphor for her pain. By the time of her death at age thirty-one she had slashed as many as a thousand times, disfiguring nearly every reachable part of her body. "I have never seen a set of arms as badly scarred, either through slashing or tattooing, as Ms. Moore's," a psychologist once testified. A Toronto lawyer who represented Marlene said, "she wore her scars like a badge of courage."

Razor blades, fragments of glass, the broken edge of a plastic knife – they were her defences against internal demons. In prison she usually concealed a "sharp" inside her cheek, but a Kingston guard remembers once having to summon a nurse to Marlene's segregation cell late at night to dislodge a fragment of glass from her vagina. Marlene felt naked and vulnerable if she didn't have a piece of glass stashed somewhere.

Guards who tried to talk Marlene out of slashing were left frustrated and bewildered by the intensity of her need to injure herself. "You'd talk and talk and talk for two hours and you'd walk away and, not always, but half the time she'd still slash," says Mary Morissette.

Marlene didn't speak easily about the feelings that drove her to wound herself. In one conversation with a prison nurse she explained that self-mutilation relieved her feelings of victimization. "When I'm hurt or I feel someone is going to hurt me . . . I have some control over the pain and control of what I do, rather than letting someone else have control of me," she told the nurse.

While the frequency of Marlene's slashing was extraordinary, her anguished behaviour is not uncommon. Self-mutilation has been documented in all nations, among people of every social rank and age, from infants to the elderly. Self-mutilation has existed "for at least as long as man has left a record of his activities," says psychiatrist Armando Favazza of the University of Missouri. Archetypal myths of creation are replete with ritualistic self-mutilation and the symbolic power of blood-letting. Self-flagellation and other forms of self-injury have accompanied the quest for spiritual purity and atonement for centuries. "The Bible contains a description of how the priests of Baal gashed themselves with knives and lances in a rainmaking ceremony. Self-cutting as homage to God or to cure others has been described among the Chinese, Semites, Tartars, and the Flagellants in America," writes U.S. psychiatrist Marc D. Feldman.

There is a direct relationship, as well, between involuntary confinement and the frequency of self-mutilation. In U.S. prisons, psychiatric wards, and mental institutions, 750 of every 100,000 inmates mutilate themselves. That's two million U.S. citizens who cut or burn or otherwise wound themselves. In Canada researchers in social welfare, psychiatry, medicine, and corrections reported in 1987 that the average rate of non-fatal, self-inflicted injuries in the federal prison system during the previous five years was "more than twice the estimated rate of 1,400 to 2,000 per 100,000 found in the general population."

Statistical evidence shows that such self-injury occurs at least three times as often in females, and research links the discrepancy to the ways men and women express anger and aggression: Men who have been abused are more apt to lash out violently against others; women turn their anger inward against themselves.

The lives of children and adults who self-injure are fraught with anguish and anger so disturbing that we choose, for the most part, not to see or hear. Society turns away from scarred bodies and souls with revulsion, incredulity, and guilt, maintaining silence about the Marlene Moores in our midst. Favazza, author of *Bodies Under Siege: Self-mutilation in Culture and Psychiatry*, writes: "Despite their numbers, self-mutilators have never received much attention from physicians. In the bustle of the emergency room, where the medical establishment first encounters these patients, physicians find them unsettling in the extreme; the standard approach is to close their wounds quickly, dress their burns, and ignore their psyches."

In 1974 an epidemic of slashings at the men's maximum-security Millhaven Institution, just west of Kingston, led to the first concerted internal investigation by federal prison authorities. A twenty-page report confirmed the direct link between self-mutilation and the frustration of imprisonment. During the one-year study period there were seventy-two self-inflicted injuries, most of which involved self-cutting, including twenty-two cases designated by medical staff as severe wounds.

Years later self-mutilation remains a chronic problem. In 1986 fifty-two of ninety-eight self-mutilations at federal prisons in the Ontario region occurred at the maximum-security prison. In 1987 Millhaven Institution accounted for half of the seventy self-inflicted injuries reported.

The records of the Correctional Service of Canada show that a disproportionate number of self-mutilations in federal penitentiaries occur at the Prison for Women. In 1988 the women's prison accounted for thirty of the fifty-nine reported self-mutilations in the Ontario region, although women prisoners represent less than half of 1 per cent of the jurisdiction's inmate population.

Many theories have been advanced to explain this high rate of self-mutilation among prisoners. Certainly, it is becoming increasingly recognized that many inmates have extensive histories of childhood abuse. But studies also indicate that most inmates don't have a history of wounding themselves before incarceration, which has led some psychologists and criminologists to conclude that the prison environment itself contributes to self-mutilation. "The inmate must find new strategies to restore his sense of freedom and power," U.S. psychiatrist Mario E. Martinez writes. "He must learn to manipulate an environment that has limited his options. Noting that no degree of confinement can restrict what the inmate does with his body, he can restore some of his desired options by manipulating the environment through self-mutilation."

Kim Marie Thorburn, a U.S. doctor who works in prisons, characterizes self-mutilation among inmates as "a desperate coping mechanism designed to counter the stress of violent, isolated penal environments."

The response of Canadian penal authorities to self-mutilation in prisons has often been simply to deny the problem. The 1974 report on Millhaven recommended additional research in several broad areas. But the matter was closed – over the protests of the chief of psychological services – by a terse memorandum from the prison system's director of living units: "Further to our discussion on this proposed study," wrote Jean Garneau on April 7, 1975, "I was informed that the problem has ceased to exist and consequently the project has been abandoned."

The belief that self-mutilation is a suicidal gesture – a view that has long dominated the thinking of social scientists, prison authorities, and mental health workers – is now being seriously challenged. At the forefront of the research in Canada is Ottawa therapist Jan Heney, who advances startling new insights into why women injure themselves. Heney is the architect of a controversial treatment approach that has helped women overcome their self-destructive urges. The key to her work is the belief that the common bond among women who slash or otherwise self-injure is their history of incest. The sexual abuse nearly always originates with a "significant other" – a father, brother, or uncle with close family ties. Heney estimates that about 70 per cent of the incest survivors she works with engage in some form of self-injury. Her analysis is provocative: Women hurt themselves to help themselves. Rejecting the orthodox view that acts of self-mutilation are compulsive and pathological, she sees them as a controlled, well-intentioned response to "feelings of powerlessness" in situations that mirror, consciously or unconsciously, the anxiety evoked by childhood sexual abuse.

According to Heney, official statistics underrepresent the incidence of self-injurious behaviour and misrepresent the phenomenon by locating self-abusers almost exclusively in psychiatric hospitals and prison. "For the women whom I deal with who are living at home, typically the slashing or burning is quite a private act. In a hospital or a prison, it becomes much less private because the person doesn't have the ability to go away and do it in secret. They're typically watched all the time, so the slashing or burning would seem to be more prevalent, but there's just more people who can monitor or see the behaviour."

Heney contends that it is vital to therapeutic intervention to first dispel the notion that self-injury is synonymous with attempted suicide. Although the two behaviours can exist in the same individual, they are distinguished by "clinical, dynamic, and experiential differences." In Heney's experience, clients can themselves quite clearly differentiate feelings that accompany acts of self-mutilation and suicidal urges.

Julie Darke, a psychologist at the Prison for Women who worked with Marlene, agrees. "Although there was often danger associated with Marlene's slashing, in that she could inadvertently go too deep and do more damage than she intended, like most other women who frequently slash, the intention was rarely suicidal."

Modern research springs from U.S. psychiatrist Karl Menninger's classic 1938 work on suicide, *Man Against Himself*. Since then the research has been voluminous but insights about why people wound themselves are wildly divergent, speculative, and contradictory. In addition to the predominant views of self-mutilation as a suicidal gesture, researchers have advanced many other theories to illuminate motive. Self-injury has been described, for example, as a ritualistic means of initiation into a group. It has been dismissed by penal authorities as a calculated form of protest against mistreatment or as manipulative, emotional blackmail. Investigators have concluded that self-injury is a means of transcending overwhelming emotional suffering through physical pain – and conversely, a way to counteract emotional numbness.

Dr. Richard Korn, an eminent penologist and former assistant warden at New Jersey State Penitentiary, says prisoners who are forced to undergo long stretches in solitary confinement often slash or burn themselves. "If you keep people [in solitary] long enough, they will engage in self-torture, simply to focus the pain. . . . Physical pain, which is definite, which they can control, is much more bearable than the torture they can neither understand nor control."

According to Julie Darke, women who slash are also often motivated by self-loathing. Their seemingly bizarre behaviour is a troubling yet rational response to childhood sexual abuse. "Their bodies are the most obvious expression of femaleness, which is seen as the problem, and they quite rightly feel that if they weren't female this wouldn't be happening to them," Darke says. "A logical consequence of that kind of abuse is for adult survivors to continue to abuse their bodies when they feel a sense of failure or helplessness, or frustration, or anxiety." Slashing can also be a way of expressing pain "to the outside world when silence about the abuse has been enforced and often continues to be enforced." Graham Turrall, the Toronto psychologist who would treat Marlene during her last stretch of freedom, describes the motives for slashing in psychoanalytic terms – as a drive to maintain the sense of an autonomous self. "The ego is splitting so badly they don't know where the body begins and where it ends; and if they feel pain, and they do [when slashing], they have some sense that their ego is still intact." Darke says some women injure themselves to alter consciousness; that they cut so they'll feel something different. "It's a way to end the feeling of deadness, rather than to move closer to it." Slashers themselves often compare their actions to silent screams.

Sheila Gilhooly, a woman who survived three years of mind-numbing drugs, shock treatment, and the oppression of a psychiatric system that viewed her lesbianism as a sickness to be cured, documented her experience in an art exhibit, a book, and a videotape. Titled *Still Sane*, and produced in collaboration with Vancouver artist Persimmon Blackbridge, the work includes twenty-seven life-sized clay figures created from plaster moulds of Gilhooly's body. In *Still Sane*, Gilhooly describes her own and others' feelings about her self-mutilation. "I remember the rush of blood as I slashed as hard as I could, sort of not looking and then looking, seeing the skin all white and puffy-like, splitting and then blood welled up and I sat there and let it run in the bath. I've felt mostly ashamed of my scars till just recently. Covered them up and lied about them. Even after I realized there was nothing wrong with me. I felt like it had all happened to someone else. I kept my distance. And other people encouraged that. Of the people I did tell, nobody ever asked me questions or seemed to want to know more about it or anything."

Asking questions of women who self-injure was exactly what Jan Heney did in 1982 when she first began working with rape and incest survivors. An undergraduate student in the psychology department at Carleton University, Heney had volunteered to work on the crisis lines at the Ottawa Rape Crisis Centre. She had almost no previous knowledge of the alien world of self-injury.

The Crisis Centre would turn out to be the ideal place for Heney to carry out the research that led to her controversial treatment model. Through the centre's twenty-four-hour phone line she had direct access to women in crisis and asked the ones with a history of self-mutilation to telephone the centre as soon as they felt an urge to injure. These callers were rerouted to Heney, so she was able to talk to women in the moments just before a possible self-injury such as slashing, or sometimes even while the client slashed or immediately afterwards.

It was a unique methodology that gave her valuable insights into the women's feelings and needs. Callers consistently related extreme anxiety about some aspect of their lives or reported a feeling of "deadness" or "numbness" that subsided only after they had slashed or somehow self-injured. Heney soon discovered that there was nothing to be gained by merely trying to talk women out of hurting themselves. She says, "There was obviously an incredible need and simply saying 'don't do it' wasn't enough."

Heney found little correlation between self-injury and being raped as an adult. In her experience a woman only begins slashing if the rape triggers suppressed memories of having been sexually abused as a child. Unable to accept the notion that the parent or another family member is the villain, a child assumes all responsibility for the abuse, blaming herself and setting up a treacherous pattern of self-loathing and punishment. "She is being assaulted by someone she has ambivalent feelings for," Heney says. Although the child hates what the abuser is doing, he may also be the person who takes her for walks in the park or comforts her when she's scared.

Darke has seen this pattern many times. "Victims of child sexual violence, particularly victims of incest, internalize the messages communicated to them by their abusers, that they're of little worth, of little value, and that they're to be used. Most child victims blame themselves in some way for the abuse, feel that they are bad and the abuse is often experienced as deserved punishment for who they are or their acts." In a child's mind there is a lot to be gained by taking responsibility for the abuse, including the illusion of control and predictability. As Heney says, "If she believes that she brought the abuse on, then by consequence she believes that somehow she can stop it." Some become "perfect children," convinced that a better report card or a tidier bedroom will win them a respite from abuse. Their actions prove futile.

The abuse goes on and the cumulative effect is devastating, Heney says. "As they get older they believe that they're really bad, that they're really evil, and that the abuse happens because of something that's wrong with them and they also believe that bad things are going to happen to them. When they're put in situations that bring back feelings that they experienced as a child there's often an incredible amount of tension and anxiety, and they believe, again, that something bad should happen to them."

Heney believes that a similar recurring psychological process is being played out when a woman slashes. When events in her life trigger the feelings of powerlessness that she experienced as an abused child, she becomes convinced that something bad has to happen to her. "Waiting for the bad thing to happen" is the source of the intense anxiety a woman feels in the moments just before injuring herself. Her defence is to take control by slashing or burning. "A woman may not want to cut," Heney says, "but at least she knows that she can deal with the cutting or the burning, and that that's the bad thing and the anxiety is released from that." ✓

Heney says a woman may act symbolically when choosing which part of her body to injure, her actions serving as a metaphor for the type of abuse she has experienced. Some of Heney's clients who slash emphasize the importance of blood; the relief comes as they watch the blood – "the badness" – flowing out of them. Others practice genital self-mutilation as a way to punish themselves for responding in a physiologically normal way during the sexual abuse. Headbanging is often seen in women who speak of the need to control bad thoughts "that just won't stop."

Advancing a theory that, at first glance, seems to defy logic, Heney characterizes self-injury as an adaptive and resourceful way of dealing with anxiety "in the same way that if you have a headache you take an aspirin." When women slash or burn, they are "trying to look after themselves," she says. These women are saying, "I can't deal with this anxiety. It's far too difficult and I have a way that will get rid of this anxiety." For Heney this is "a health-seeking behaviour, a way of trying to look after yourself." It's that perception of self-injury as a "coping strategy," as a way of gaining a sense of control over the extent and timing of the inevitable pain, that undescores Heney's bold new treatment method. Her approach recognizes the futility, even harm, of insisting that a woman immediately abandon all forms of self-mutilation. Her early attempts to negotiate with women not to hurt themselves failed miserably. Self-injurers felt too defenceless and vulnerable trying to cope day by day without a substitute for their usual practice of slashing or burning when anxiety mounts. The first step in therapy, Heney says, is to help a woman find "safer ways to get the pain" until she is ready to adopt non-injurious methods of coping with emotional distress.

After establishing a pattern for the kinds of situations that induce a woman to injure herself, Heney explores less dangerous ways of achieving the same kind of powerful and quick release. In the early stages of counselling this may even include some form of "safe cutting" or "safe burning." Heney has instructed clients about safety features such as using new blades to reduce the possibility of infection; waiting thirty seconds between slashes if they desire blood as opposed to pain; cleaning the area with disinfectant before and after wounding. She has advised women who scorch their skin with cigarette butts to instead burn a candle and drip hot wax on their arms. Beeswax should be avoided, however, because it burns at too high a temperature. Other clients have been encouraged to exercise to the point of pain by running, lifting weights, or practising yoga. The goal in the early stages, Heney says, is to achieve "equivalent pain" in a safer way and to alleviate anxiety.

Her methods have outraged some medical professionals, who accuse her of advocating inappropriate, damaging modes of dealing with emotional pain. But Heney argues that those working in therapeutic relationships with women who self-injure understand you can't strip them of their coping strategies until they learn about alternatives. Together, therapists and clients must explore the intense feelings that compel self-injury, and move toward the women reclaiming personal control and power in their lives. Heney's treatment strategy has produced impressive results. Virtually all her clients, including some with a long history of engaging in dramatic forms of abuse, permanently stop wounding themselves within a period of three months.

In January 1989, Jan Heney would be called to the Prison for Women to discuss plans to introduce her methods to the institution. But this potential change would come all too late for Marlene.

In P4W Marlene was banned from working in the kitchen, where she would have easy access to knives and glass. But that didn't stop her self-mutilation. "When she got to the pen, it was either a daily or weekly occurrence," her friend Patricia says. Marlene once slashed her arms so deeply that "Blood was hitting the ceiling, and there was blood everywhere."

Mary Morissette remembers escorting Marlene, in the middle of the night, to the prison nurse to get her stitched up after she had slashed. The nurse asked the guard to assist him by holding the wound closed. He looked at Marlene and asked her if she was all right. Marlene said "I'm fine but I think Morissette's going to pass out." "It was true. I can't stand blood," Morissette says.

There were times when Marlene would make earnest attempts to curtail her slashing. "It was almost like Lent," Patricia says. "She would give up slashing for a month, and that was a goal and a big achievement and she was so happy that she could actually go a month without slashing. And when she promised herself that she wouldn't, she would not – no matter what was going down."

When her brush with freedom in early 1980 turned into disaster, Marlene reacted with predictable self-violence, cutting herself with horrifying frequency. In early April, around the time she was convicted of the break-in, Marlene slashed herself so badly that dozens of stitches were needed to close the wounds. Prison and medical officials moved to have her certified under the province's Mental Health Act, which meant she could be committed to the St. Thomas Psychiatric Hospital for a minimum thirty-day assessment. Dr. Paul Gatfield, then the director of the facility in southwestern Ontario, would later remark on the severity of Marlene's physical and mental deterioration when she was brought to the hospital on April 9. Although he had seen lots of self-mutilators, Marlene had the most scarred arms he had ever come across. "At the time Marlene had fifty-two stitches, "and she was removing the stitches prematurely herself and threatening to do so again," Gatfield said.

Now a forensic psychiatrist at University Hospital in London, Gatfield assumed personal responsibility for Marlene's care at St. Thomas. But by his own admission, he paid little heed to the violence she turned on herself. During a subsequent court proceeding in 1984, Marlene's lawyer, Rebecca Shamai, grilled Gatfield on his lack of response to Marlene's severe self-mutilation. Gatfield said: "I don't think there is any question that she's slashed a lot. Why didn't I direct more attention to it? My experience is that that's a blind alley. You never find out anything except that people have got a lot of unexpressed anger."

Shamai: Did it concern you, as a medical practitioner, that she should be causing such damage to herself?

Gatfield: Sure.

Shamai: And in terms of describing psychiatric disorders, it would seem, in my perception, to be of some significance but it was not something that you explored?

Gatfield: That is correct.

Shamai pressed the issue. Given that Marlene had been admitted to St. Thomas hospital as a direct consequence of savaging her own body, why had he not gone into greater depth in his assessment of her self-mutilation? At that point, Gatfield revealed that Marlene would have virtually nothing to do with him from the outset. She was a hostile patient, whose behaviour he described as belligerent in the extreme. For Gatfield, treatment wasn't even an option.

Marlene's P4W friend Barb Dennis had been transferred involuntarily from the segregation unit at the Prison for Women to St. Thomas before Marlene was committed. Dennis says her heart just fell when she first spotted Marlene. When she saw her walk in she thought, "She don't have a chance. She's going to flip and they're going to hurt her." Dennis felt that although she knew Marlene and how to handle her, the St. Thomas people didn't. "The first thing they showed her was violence, and that's what she was so damn used to," Dennis says. "And the next thing I knew they had her on the floor and they were cuffing her." To Dennis's way of thinking, things didn't get appreciably better after that.

At St. Thomas Gatfield would put male rapists in therapy sessions with women who had been raped. "The program there was unreal," Dennis says. "I was sexually abused as a child and I walked in there where the patients ran the group, men and women, and all the men were in there for rape or killing a kid. And they wanted me to talk about my childhood. No, no – I'd rather go and die somewhere." When Dennis told Marlene about the sessions, Marlene said, "Well, fuck this, I ain't hanging around here. I'm going back."

Marlene and Barb Dennis soon ended up back at the Kingston prison, each apparently beyond the reach of the medical professionals at the psychiatric hospital. Only their close friendship afforded some relief from despair, enabling each to break her silence and share the darkest of secrets. They confided their own histories of incest and physical abuse and pledged each other to secrecy. And they wept, in the haunting remembrance of childhood terror. Marlene gently insisted that her friend explain the cruelty behind her scars.

"I started crying," Dennis says, "then I held her and I told her, and she was the first one I told that I was sexually abused a lot when I was a kid." Marlene, in turn, revealed her own tormented childhood. The women groped for words to explain the connections between anguish and guilt, anger and self-mutilation. Marlene said, "Is that why you slash, Barb, because of what happened?" Dennis said, "Yeah, I didn't know how to deal with it." Marlene told Dennis, "That's what I'm going through." And the two prisoners drew closer together. "We were so damn close," Dennis says.

Around that time another young prisoner went from Kingston to St. Thomas with the questionable benefit of Marlene's warnings about what to expect on her arrival. Brenda Hope had marked her twenty-first birthday not long before. Nearly eight years later she described the hospital environment with both fear and agitation, speaking of nightmarish memories of physical restraints and mind-numbing drugs. Like Marlene, she says, she raged against the doctors and pulled out the stitches meant to repair her self-mutilation. When Hope returned to the Kingston prison to finish her sentence she spent the next year alternating between the ranges and segregation. Much later, seated in the living room of an Amherstview townhouse with her fourteen-month-old daughter, Hope bluntly describes the months she spent at St. Thomas as providing the worst memories of her troubled youth. "I spent a lot of time tied to a mattress," she says. "They almost overdosed me on drugs." She once fell off her chair in a drugged stupor in the midst of an interview with a parole officer. Hope assumes that he kicked up a fuss and ordered changes in her medication because, after that, her memories of the hospital come into sharper focus. Mostly, though, she recalls how desperately she longed for the day she could leave the hospital and return to the relative sanity of prison.

Gatfield, who headed the forensic unit at St. Thomas Psychiatric Hospital from 1976 to 1984, says that most patients from the Prison for Women stayed only the requisite thirty days as stipulated by Ontario law. The hospital's "secure ward," which was established under his direction in the late 1970s, was designed to accommodate prisoners and other patients, both men and women, designated as security risks. From the outset the ward normally housed between one and three women from the Kingston prison. "They were the women who were the really difficult management problems in the prison – women who were slashing," Gatfield says. Self-mutilation was their common link. Abused as young children, they experienced another type of abuse at the hospital. They would be locked in physical restraints to prevent them from slashing themselves. The most difficult patients would be tied to a mattress with a sheet so they couldn't move. Some of the women spent nearly all of their time in hospital in restraints. "I don't think we were very successful with very many," Gatfield says. "I can't give a blanket answer as to what would determine when they went back [to prison]. But certainly, how long they persisted in going against the grain would be one of the reasons."

Gatfield remembers Marlene as typical of the patients from the Prison for Women. "She was maybe a little more aggressive and out of control at times, but not appreciably different from a lot of the others."

About a week after Marlene was admitted to St. Thomas

her mother and her sister Maureen came to visit. They went away shaken by her rundown appearance and her accusation that she'd been manacled to a bed and left to urinate on herself. "Her wrists and ankles were bruised and red," Maureen says. Marlene told them she'd be chained up again after the visit.

Marlene was discharged from St. Thomas at the earliest opportunity. In response to the demands of her lawyer and her mother, she was returned to the Prison for Women in early May. But at P4W there was no treatment for Marlene. She was simply back where she started. The only tangible consequence of her admission to the psychiatric hospital was to have her behaviour officially labelled. Gatfield's diagnosis concluded that Marlene had an antisocial personality disorder.

Back at P4W, Marlene was again among old friends and about to make new ones. After her four weeks inside the St. Thomas hospital the fresh smell of spring was welcome. Windy days brought a hint of the spray off the cold waters of Lake Ontario as the women walked and jogged, often in pairs, around the well-worn path that marked the perimeter of the exercise yard at the Prison for Women.

On any given day more than half the one hundred or so prisoners in P4W are unmarried young women between the ages of twenty and thirty-four, serving between two and five years. In age, at twenty-two, and in length of sentence, Marlene was representative of the majority of women at the Kingston prison. But her appearance and temperament set her apart. It was no secret that the odds of Marlene getting into a fight jumped astronomically whenever the general mood in the prison turned ugly, as it did in the fall of the following year, 1981, when a load of pills was smuggled onto the ranges.

It was a time of high tensions, says Daryl Dollan, who had become acting head of the inmate committee. Three slashings occurred in rapid succession after prison officials searched for the contraband drugs. Marlene was one of these and, as Dollan says, "Predictably, she slashed the worst." Soon afterwards Dollan and another veteran committee member went public with their concerns about the chronic problem of self-mutilation and the lack of treatment options.

At the time, the only psychiatric facility that would accept women from the Kingston prison was the St. Thomas hospital. The Correctional Service of Canada operated its own eighty-five-bed psychiatric facility, but the Regional Treatment Centre, located across the street at Kingston Penitentiary only a few yards from the front doors of the women's prison, accepted only male prisoners.

For the most part prison authorities responded punitively to women who slashed. They officially viewed self-mutilation as manipulative behaviour. After a woman was stitched or bandaged she was charged with "disrupting the good order of the institution" and moved to an inhospitable cell in the segregation unit, sometimes stripped naked as insurance against a repeat offence.

On one occasion, after being stitched up, Marlene had second thoughts about being returned to segregation, so she went to Dollan's cell with a grim request. She had been told that if she removed the stitches she would be put "on charge." So she had removed the stitches – but then had second thoughts. She asked Dollan to stitch her up. "I used a regular sewing needle and some dental floss and I stitched her back up," Dollan says. She sat there with a facecloth in her mouth, biting on the facecloth, and never said a word."

The segregation unit was – and is – a dirty, dreary, oppressive place. One particularly chaotic summer night in segregation sticks in Brenda Hope's mind, a snapshot of the hysteria that would break out after endless days of unrelieved boredom. "It was so hot it was just sickening in there," she says. "People were laying there with nothing on. We were singing – Janis Joplin and stuff like that. You'd get going and everybody was just cooking. It was our only way of passing time that was really enjoyable. So we were all lying on our bunks and singing our hearts out. The girls in protective custody cells didn't like our singing. They didn't want us to be causing noise, so one of the guards came in and slammed all our windows and told us to shut up."

The mood turned ugly. Marlene set her mattress on fire, stuffed her bedding down the toilet, and flooded her cell. Two prisoners in cells on the top tier slashed themselves. In the cell next to Hope's, a woman hanged herself. "You could see into the next cell, and I was lying on my bunk and all of a sudden I see this person hanging in the cell. I started calling the guards. Marlene was screaming. Everybody was screaming. It was wild. It was just a wild, wild time and a lot of people got punished. The people who slashed got punished. Everybody who hurt themselves got punished for hurting themselves. We always joked about how you couldn't slash because you were destroying government property."

In 1981 two women legally challenged the punitive discipline. One of them, Constance Diane Davidson, had slashed her arm with a razor blade and was sentenced to ten days in segregation. Marlene Hunt, a senior guard supervisor with fifteen years' experience, articulated the prevailing view of the corrections staff. Slashings, Hunt told the Federal Court, had a "ripple effect" on the prison population: "One slashing invariably encourages other inmates to slash." Moreover, Hunt said, "Slashings invariably create serious administrative problems, since emergency medical personnel need to be called and prison routine is disrupted. In my experience, inmates are aware that slashings affect and disrupt the discipline and order of the institution."

Constance Davidson presented a different perspective. She said that she had acted out of "total frustration and despair" after being denied a temporary absence pass to spend Christmas with her family. She said she had encountered problems in getting the psychiatric treatment she felt she needed, and this difficulty had also led to her self-mutilation. Slashing her forearms served "to focus or release" her "feelings of despair" and was in no way intended to disrupt the good order of the prison, she testified. The Federal Court of Canada later quashed Davidson's conviction, and the practice of charging women for hurting themselves ended.

A few years later, during an interview with a journalist, P4W warden George Caron offered a calculated assessment of the perennial problem of slashing. "A lot of them were not attempting suicide. They were looking for attention." For Caron, a main problem was the cost. "When they're slashing their arms, and we have to bring in a doctor or a nurse and take them out in an ambulance, sometimes it would lead to hundreds of dollars" being spent, he said.

6

To me the future looks
hard, awfull, scarry

Marlene's second stretch at the Prison for Women ended with her release on mandatory supervision on October 25, 1981, some eight months before the official completion of her sentence. She left the prison with her youngest sister, Retta, and they drove to Toronto, where Marlene was to report the next afternoon to the parole office in Etobicoke.

The filmmakers Janis Cole and Holly Dale greeted their friend with open arms. By the end of an afternoon celebrating Marlene's freedom, she had accepted their invitation to share their downtown apartment. For the past year they had exchanged letters, and the partners in Spectrum One Films had spent time with Marlene at a few social events at the Kingston prison. They knew that she would have difficulty adjusting to life outside and had discussed asking her to live with them. Cole now admits that she felt some apprehension at first. "I was the one who was not into the idea of taking Shaggie on. I said to Holly, 'I don't know if this is a very good idea. We're awfully busy. I don't know if we can handle it.' And Holly sort of made the plan and, of course, when Marlene came it was me who went into it wholeheartedly, who sort of jumped in."

A main concern at first was Marlene's poor health and resistance to nourishing foods. Cole and Dale encouraged her to take vitamins regularly and, as a way to tempt her appetite and fatten her up, began adding a bottle of beer to pasta dishes and just about everything they cooked. Soon Marlene was concocting her own recipes and preparing meals for her roommates.

She also began lavishing her scarred arms with Vitamin E cream in an attempt to erase the evidence of years of pain. Only once did she slash during that period, an incident that Cole describes as "very minor" and something Marlene found difficult to talk about. Cole says Marlene talked about slashing just a few times, "but sometimes when Marlene talked you could just tell the depth of her privacy, and family and slashing were two of the tough areas."

Marlene enrolled in a basic upgrading program at George Brown College, attending school on weekdays and spending most evenings at home with her friends. They took turns going to and from school with her and coached her on how to get around by bus and subway – travel that Marlene viewed with fear and suspicion. It was not only the prospect of getting lost that jangled her nerves; she was alarmed by the unavoidably close contact with men and routinely carried a small paring knife in her back pocket. Cole and Dale talked to her about other ways of handling a crisis, and eventually Marlene began leaving her knife at home.

Marlene's friends felt optimistic about her prospects for adjusting to life in the community, given her willingness to give up old habits and take better care of herself. Marlene was starting to eat, was taking vitamins, and had stopped carrying a knife. She was becoming more talkative, opening up a bit and, they felt, trying to deal with things more logically. "She was doing well with her life skills and she started having friends in our group who she went out to see individually," Cole says.

"We had half a dozen friends who took a real interest in Marlene."

Six weeks passed without any signs of serious trouble, but in November Cole had to break up a scuffle between Marlene and another former inmate of the Kingston prison. When the visitor and Marlene got into a wrestling match, she reacted in the only way she knew: she ran into the bathroom, smashed a mirror, and threatened to slash. In the end Marlene put down the broken glass, sent her friend on her way in a cab, and sat down at the kitchen table, where she and Cole talked for hours. At some point during that evening Marlene cut herself slightly on the arm in a superficial imitation of the slashing that had been her outlet for at least a decade. Later, when she was asked about the events of that evening, Cole said, "Even at that time the logic that she was handling the situation with was understandable, and we were able to communicate. And at that time I wasn't scared and nothing came to mind about my being scared of Marlene."

In early December Cole and Dale went away on business for about a week, leaving Marlene alone in the apartment. She had turned down the chance to spend the time with another friend of the filmmakers, wanting to demonstrate her growing independence. Instead she moved into the apartment of Donna Turner, another friend from the Prison for Women. Not long after, on December 14, the two women got into a fight and Marlene stabbed Turner in the shoulder with a steak knife. When the police arrived Marlene identified herself as her younger sister Edith. For that she was later convicted of obstructing justice. For the stabbing, she was arrested and jailed in Toronto and charged with a weapons offence. "It was heartbreaking when we got the news because Marlene was part of our family," Cole says. "We didn't want her to go back to prison. We wanted her to come back and live with us."

Marlene spent the next few months at Metro Toronto West Detention Centre, a remand centre in Rexdale. One of the guards at the provincial jail, a soft-hearted woman named Tammy, says she was terrified to learn that Marlene Moore, the same woman who had taken staff hostage at Vanier, would be on her shift. But her preconceptions about Marlene quickly changed after working a number of shifts with her. She says, "I spent many evenings just talking to Marlene about anything. I usually would call her out to mop the floors or something. She always obliged and loved keeping busy."

Marlene eventually grew to trust the correctional officer enough to share a humiliating secret. One morning she slipped the guard a note: "Tammy, please don't tell anybody but I wet my bed again last night. I need clean clothes and sheets. Keep this between you and me because I like you. It would kill me if everyone knew. Thanks, Shaggie." After that, whenever she came on shift, Tammy would discreetly smuggle clean linen to Marlene.

Marlene, Tammy found, was acutely sensitive to other people's feelings. One day Marlene found Tammy quietly weeping in her office about an incident involving a fellow worker. Marlene asked Tammy if she was okay and Tammy said, "Yes, but I don't know how much more I can handle." Marlene asked to sit down, and then she put her hand on Tammy's shoulder. She said, "Tammy, you can handle anything if you want to. Don't let the other screws cause you to come down on yourself. I don't. I always fight back and you can too." They talked for a few more minutes, until Marlene got up and said "Keep smiling" and went back to her work.

Another day, while working together in the jail laundry, Tammy saw Marlene at her playful best. "She and the other girls grabbed me and threw me in a laundry cart," Tammy says. "Then they threw sheets over my head and started tickling me. Marlene was so proud of herself. She thought it was hilarious and smiled and laughed and laughed."

Marlene was reunited at the remand centre with Harriet Ironside, the guard she and Isabella Ogima had taken hostage at Vanier. Ironside had been transferred to Metro West in 1978 and was working in the women's wing. Just before Marlene was admitted to the provincial jail, she had a chance to ask another staff member how Ironside felt about the possibility of seeing her again. Ironside told the staff member to tell Marlene that she didn't bear her any malice whatsoever, and that she was sorry Marlene hadn't been able to stay out of jail longer. When Marlene got to Metro West she was placed on Ironside's unit and the two got along well. After a while Marlene found the courage to tell Ironside how sorry she was about the hostage-taking.

The National Parole Board eventually revoked Marlene's mandatory supervision and ordered her returned to the Prison for Women. On March 25, 1982, she was shuffled back to Toronto for trial on the stabbing charge. Judge P. B. Pickett, of the provincial court, accepted a joint recommendation by the Crown attorney and defence lawyer David Cole for a one-year sentence, to be added to her remaining prison time. For Judge Pickett, Marlene's return to the courtroom was more a comment on the corrections system than on Marlene herself. "I guess it is a terrible indictment on our prison system," he said.

After Marlene returned to Kingston, prison officials investigated the possibility of having her committed to hospital for psychiatric treatment. In mid-October they sent her back to Toronto, to the Queen Street Mental Health Centre, for assessment. But after four days medical staff there concluded that Marlene was not certifiable. The hospital also indicated that it was not prepared to accept her as a voluntary patient after her release from prison. At the time Marlene was anticipating her release on mandatory supervision within two months. She told her case management officer that she would like to go to a halfway house operated by the Elizabeth Fry Society.

In late October negotiations began with society workers from Hamilton. Terri-Lee Seeley, who joined the agency in 1980 as a social worker and later became executive director, had spoken with Marlene a number of times during her regular monthly visits to the Kingston prison. Seeley felt confident that Marlene was determined to stay out of trouble, more so than ever before, as she made plans for her release in December. Marlene's primary concern was to work out arrangements so she'd be able to continue a relationship with a friend due for release to the Hamilton area around the end of March. "She had to make it on the street for the sake of this relationship – that was her agenda," Seeley says. "And I think that's what kept her going, because she knew she couldn't have this relationship unless she stayed strong on the street."

On November 5 Seeley and Justine Howarth, the executive director of the Hamilton society, interviewed Marlene. Over the next several days Howarth reviewed Marlene's files and discussed the situation with prison staff, parole officials, Hamilton-area police, and agency workers at the halfway house. On November 15 the Elizabeth Fry presented an acceptance proposal with several conditions: An extra staff member would be assigned to night duty to ensure that "special attention" was available around the clock; arrangements would be made for psychiatric counselling and vocational training; and Marlene would have to abstain from using alcohol and all non-prescribed drugs. The conditions also stipulated that any display of aggression or self-destructive behaviour inside the house would be cause for the society to recommend that Marlene's mandatory supervision be revoked. The terms were both strict and supportive, and designed to help Marlene learn how to cope with anger and frustration without hurting herself or anyone else.

Before the invitation was extended, halfway-house workers talked at length about Marlene's history and her already legendary reputation for violence. Seeley says the decision to accept Marlene was unanimous. The Hamilton house felt adamant that it couldn't turn its back on a woman like Marlene, who had already been so victimized by the system.

The first obstacle came just a week after the Elizabeth Fry Society had presented its acceptance conditions to prison authorities. The Hamilton area parole office rejected the proposal. The recommendation came from Craig Townson, a man who would one day invite Marlene into his home as a guest. Despite the knowledge that Marlene would most likely go to Hamilton unsupervised in only four months anyway and that Hamilton Regional Police didn't object to her release to Hamilton, the parole board's area manager turned thumbs down to the proposal, saying Marlene Moore represented far too great a risk to the community. The National Parole Board went further. It set out to stop Marlene from going anywhere.

In the early 1980s, Canadians were inundated with media reports about brutal crimes committed by men fresh out of prison. In the fall of 1980 a man released on mandatory supervision murdered a twenty-one-year-old Ajax woman. Shortly after his release in 1981, another man attacked a fifteen-year-old Vancouver girl who was jogging near her home, choking her to death. The same year a man raped and murdered a two-year-old girl in Kingston only eleven days after he was let out of Kingston Penitentiary. Another man – Clifford Olson – was arrested in 1981 after killing eleven children. He too had recently been released from prison. In the wake of these tragic events, no one felt the sting of public outrage more acutely than William R. Outerbridge, chairman of the National Parole Board.

As board chairman, Outerbridge symbolized the failure of the parole system and frequently found himself a personal target for public hostility. His appearance in the early 1980s before one angry organization for victims' rights in Vancouver left him devastated. "There is a real sense of helplessness that you get after spending three hours with 150 to 200 people, all of whom have had their families decimated in one violent way or another," he commented.

The tall, grey-bearded bureaucrat was faced with a complicated dilemma that few members of the public clearly understood. Most of the devastating crimes that had captured media attention were committed by people over whom the parole board had no control. Nonetheless, Outerbridge couldn't shake the nagging feeling that there might be something more the board could do.

He asked his legal advisers whether the laws governing release on mandatory supervision could be construed in a way that would give the parole board the power to delay the release

106

of "those few very scary inmates" who would otherwise routinely be set free before the end of their terms. (Before 1986, inmates who earned time off for good behaviour were automatically released after serving two-thirds of their sentences.)

Outerbridge's advisers told him that the most direct way to legally test the board's powers was by re-arresting an inmate at the gate of the penitentiary at the moment of release: the process that came to be known as "gating."

Outerbridge first tested this advice in 1982 on a sex offender in British Columbia. The parole board's strategy backfired, however, when the man allowed himself to be gated without launching a legal challenge. Stymied and frustrated by the turn of events, Outerbridge sought the advice of one of Canada's best known criminal litigators.

David Cole runs his Toronto law practice out of a refurbished three-storey red-brick building on St. Nicholas Street. The flamboyant lawyer has acted for some of Canada's most notorious criminals, including police murderer Rene Vaillancourt, and in some of Canada's most sensational cases, such as that of nurse Susan Nelles. One of the country's few specialists in prison law, he has made significant contributions to the development of new rights and safeguards for inmates.

In fall 1982 Cole received an unusual phone call from Outerbridge. According to Cole, the parole board chairman said, "Look, we need this challenged. We need the courts to tell us whether we're doing the right thing. Can you challenge it?" Cole told Outerbridge that he couldn't do anything without a client, and Outerbridge was only too happy to oblige. He supplied Cole with the names of a handful of prisoners in Ontario whom the board was planning to gate. One of them was Marlene Moore.

That private, behind-the-scenes conversation set the legal machinery in motion. Cole was convinced that Marlene's was a winnable case. He knew her, because he had represented her on the 1981 weapons charge, after she had stabbed Donna Turner. She was young, just twenty-five, and she was a woman.

"Gender was definitely a factor," Cole says. "I felt frankly that a judge would be somewhat happier releasing Marlene than holding his nose and releasing some dreadful sex offender." Marlene's record had none of the shock value attached to the cases of some of the other gating candidates – one of them was rumoured to sit in his prison cell leafing through magazines with scissors, snipping out the genital areas of children. Cole was also keenly aware that media interest in gating would be intense and that the case would reach the Supreme Court of Canada.

Regardless of what the parole board did, and regardless of what the courts might decide, Marlene had to be released at the end of her sentence on March 24, 1983, only four months away. The entire purpose of the exercise was the precedent, not the person.

The parole board wasted no time building its case against Marlene. Only two weeks before Christmas 1982, Philip Haden, the Kingston psychiatrist, received an urgent phone call from prison officials. He was asked to determine whether Marlene's release into the community posed a danger to herself or others. That same day Marlene was brought to Haden's office in handcuffs, dragged along by a phalanx of three guards. Haden was aghast at the scene. His interview, conducted in the presence of a custodial officer, proceeded along delicate lines. Marlene adamantly refused to speak about her early family life. Her answers were "punctuated by frequent obscenities" and slurs on select prison staff. But Haden would report that she also demonstrated her ability to be reasonable and responsive. "She responded appropriately quite often to my direct comments on the falsity of her logic and she was smiling and relaxed when we parted," he wrote.

Before she left his office, Marlene asked the doctor what his recommendation would be. His answer was frank. He told her that he did not think she was in a fit state to be released on mandatory supervision because she might be dangerous. Her relief was "barely concealed," Haden wrote. "Her blustering talk was her way of trying to hide her feelings of tension and extreme insecurity."

As a result of that one-hour interview and his review of her prison files, Haden diagnosed Marlene as an antisocial personality of extreme degree: someone "more disturbed and disturbing than many mentally ill people" but still not certifiable under the Mental Health Act. But the doctor demonstrated a concern that went beyond the simple question of Marlene's suitability for early release. He recommended that before her sentence expired she be allowed a series of escorted passes to a halfway house "to help mitigate her apprehension" at the prospect of leaving prison. He also strongly urged an end to the use of disciplinary segregation: "I confirm the opinions of others that in the interest of her mental health involuntary segregation is highly undesirable and ultimately will exacerbate existing problems."

Haden's report gave the parole board the ammunition needed to block Marlene's release. The report nonetheless ended on a hopeful note. "Despite her lurid history and current rebellious demeanor," Haden wrote, "there are several rather favorable features in her make-up and the outlook for the future is not necessarily hopeless."

A four-page court affidavit, signed by Outerbridge, spells out the reasons for the parole board's decision to gate Marlene. It cites violent offences on her criminal record along with twenty-four institutional convictions on charges that included stabbing another inmate, assaulting guards, and setting fire to prison property. The document also alluded to "numerous threats of violence to institutional staff, other inmates and the warden of the women's penitentiary." An enraged outburst directed against Warden George Caron became a focus of subsequent legal proceedings. "On September 27, 1982," the affidavit states, "she slashed her arms and threw a cup of blood and urine in Warden Caron's face. She has apparently said 'When I get out I am waiting in the parking lot for Caron, and I'm cutting him to ribbons.'"

It was Allan Manson, an intense, bearded law professor at Queen's University, who first discussed Marlene's legal options with her. Manson, who teamed up with David Cole to represent Marlene, watched her growing indignation. "Having to fight over release seemed to be a bit of a relief. It postponed the prospect of release, and she was very much energized. She became quietly angry that it was going to be denied to her and was very enthusiastic about fighting."

Official notification came in a letter from the National Parole Board dated only six days before her scheduled release date: "The board believes that you would continue to pose a danger to the public if you were released despite every effort to find a release plan which would offer the highest degree of supervision and control you require."

On December 13 – less than twenty-four hours before her official mandatory supervision date – Marlene slashed her wrists and was moved to the prison hospital. The next day dawned cold and blustery, and Marlene didn't bother with the ritual walk through the prison gates. She simply accepted the bureaucratic paperwork informing her that she had been gated and returned to her cell.

Marlene's case went before the Supreme Court of Ontario the following week. On December 21 Cole argued that nowhere did the existing laws give the parole board the power to interfere with an inmate's release on mandatory supervision.

Manson, an expert in constitutional and prison law, was waiting in the wings with supplementary arguments based on the new Charter of Rights and Freedoms. It was a highly technical proceeding, with much of the time spent briefing the judge on the complicated rules of parole and mandatory supervision.

On January 26, 1983, Mr. Justice John Eberle ruled that gating was illegal. He ordered Marlene's immediate release. If Parliament had intended to give the board the discretion to prevent a prisoner's release on mandatory supervision, it would have said so clearly, he said in his seventeen-page judgement. But Mr. Justice Eberle didn't circumvent the dilemma presented by the case. "Moore's desperate unhappiness, as revealed by her record of offences, readily evokes sympathy, but for many members of society, her record will be regarded as terrifying rather than depressing," he wrote. "Society has a legitimate interest in protection from Moore's persistent anti-social behavior. But how is this to be accomplished?"

The National Parole Board released Marlene within an hour of the ruling. On January 27, Marlene travelled under police escort to the Elizabeth Fry halfway house in Hamilton. John Nugent, the regional executive officer of the parole board, told reporters hungry for details about Canada's new celebrity criminal that her travel schedule had been given to every police department along her route and that the Hamilton police had been fully briefed about her case. "Marlene Moore will be back," Nugent prophesied. "Marlene is the type who threatens anyone who looks at her."

The board had no intention of giving Mr. Justice Eberle the final word on gating. In February the case moved to the Ontario Court of Appeal. Mr. Justice Charles Dubin upheld the lower court decision, saying an inmate's mandatory supervision can be revoked only on the basis of his or her conduct after release.

But the legal waters were muddied by a same-day ruling in the Federal Court of Canada, in which Judge Paul Rouleau upheld the board's gating powers in the case of another prisoner in Edmonton. In less than three months Marlene's case vaulted into the Supreme Court of Canada for the final decision. Again, Allan Manson and David Cole appeared on her behalf. Cole argued in the Supreme Court that the law simply doesn't allow officials to prognosticate. Manson's supplementary arguments made legal history, marking the first Charter-based defence to be heard by the Supreme Court. After only fifteen minutes of deliberation, Chief Justice Bora Laskin delivered the unanimous judgement: Gating was illegal and must stop.

Marlene was one of eleven inmates gated as part of the parole board's legal experiment. She was the only woman. When he retired in the spring of 1986, Outerbridge would dismiss any suggestion that he had been motivated by politics or a desire to publicly demonstrate the powerlessness of the parole board.

His actions were inspired, he said, by a sense of personal duty. "I didn't want somebody down the line saying you had the authority and didn't use it, and now look at the number of people whose killing or maiming could have been prevented if only you had acted."

Once she got to the Elizabeth Fry halfway house, Marlene appeared to thrive on the structured routines and family atmosphere. The large, white-painted brick building is located in a quiet residential neighbourhood only a few blocks from downtown Hamilton. Founded in 1974 as a hostel for sixteen- to eighteen-year-olds, it was converted two years later to a halfway house for adult women offenders. Residents share in household chores, taking turns cooking meals in the large sunny kitchen. The women can spend their free time at sewing machines in the basement or conversing quietly in the living room. A plump orange and white cat named Fry has the run of the place.

Funded by the United Way and the three levels of government, the house has room for twelve residents. Whether they've come from a provincial or the federal jail system, the women all need time and individual support to make the difficult transition from the highly structured conditions of prison to life in the community. Staff are relaxed and casual but meticulously record the comings and goings of residents and control all medication and money for travel and other extra-ordinary expenses. Although women can live in the house for a year, the average length of stay is three or four months. Women are expected to search for housing and employment or secure an income through some type of government assistance program.

Elizabeth Fry workers resolved from the outset to receive Marlene as they would any other resident. They introduced her to the other women and told her about the house routine and what would be her duties. They kept their fingers crossed that she would fit in. The approach seemed to work. Marlene seemed to get along and the other women quickly warmed to her self-effacing humour, her openness, and raw honesty. She developed an exceptionally close rapport with a couple of staff members and grew instantly attached to the household cat. She was eager to contribute to daily chores. She stayed away from drugs or alcohol and never missed a curfew.

The terms of her supervision order allowed her to go out unescorted during the day, but she seldom did. Shy and fearful of her new independence, she stuck close to home, never venturing out alone for more than a brief period. In need of constant attention and approval, she followed staff members around like a shadow. "She was very much a house mouse," Terri-Lee Seeley says. "Staff sometimes described her as a little girl because they'd turn around and almost trip over her."

Most of the residents are required to take part in a highly structured, five-day-a-week program of life skills and vocational training. With Marlene the staff's first concern was her physical and emotional well-being. Rather than involve her in group programs, the staff worked with her one on one. A main concern was her general health. She was thin and rundown. When she needed to be taken to outside physicians for medical and psychiatric care, Marlene, who would consider only women doctors, had trouble choosing someone she could trust and feel comfortable with. Staff treated her almost like a child, constantly urging her to eat regular meals and take better care of herself. Slowly, she began to gain weight.

In the supportive environment of the halfway house, Marlene gradually opened up to some staff about her feelings, taking a few small steps toward resolving some of the horrors in her background. But her unrelenting emotional pain was raw, and she frequently became frustrated and despondent. Marlene was also haunted by memories of her time at the Prison for Women. One time she told Seeley that if she ever returned to the federal institution she was sure she would die. "She wasn't getting assistance there, and there was a sense of helplessness and hopelessness" about the Kingston prison, Seeley says.

Marlene expressed an interest at the halfway house in working as a mortician. Toward the end of her stay she met with funeral directors and arranged a tour of the McMaster

University medical centre. She also took out a card at the Hamilton Public Library. When a Toronto psychiatrist asked her some months later about her career choice, Marlene replied, "Well, dead people can't talk to you and you don't have to talk back to them." Another time she said that preparing bodies for burial was a way of "helping people who can't help themselves."

One of the conditions of acceptance that the Hamilton house negotiated with Marlene was an agreement not to slash. Staff made a contract with her that she would not hurt herself. If she did she would be evicted. "It was a very strict rule," Seeley says. Marlene somehow managed, with the help of patient and supportive staff members, to honour that pact until the end of her mandatory supervision. But on March 24, the day her supervision order expired, she took a blade to her arms and abruptly announced she was leaving the halfway house.

Despite the agreement on slashing, Seeley says that Marlene's action was not used to expel her. In this case, Seeley told Marlene, the extraordinary circumstances involved justified making an exception to the rule.

Marlene was leaving to make way for a woman who had visited the Hamilton house on passes in early 1983 but whose request to go there after her release had been turned down by the parole board. Marlene assumed it was her fault. She had developed a close relationship with this woman at the Prison for Women and had looked forward for months to a reunion.

The Elizabeth Fry organization was still appealing the parole board's ruling on Marlene's friend when Marlene's mandatory supervision period expired. But Marlene refused to go along with a staff plan that she stay on at the house on a voluntary basis. "Marlene wouldn't listen to staff urging her to wait until the appeal was heard," Seeley said. Two days after the slashing, wearing fresh bandages on her wrists, she said her goodbyes and – with her younger sister Retta – headed north to trouble.

She met it head-on on March 31, 1983. It was a cold, clear night, with the temperature holding at about minus five degrees Celsius. Constable Brandon Weir of the Ontario Provincial Police detachment in Midland was alone on patrol in Tay Township in the County of Simcoe. Just after midnight the young policeman spotted a tan Chevrolet pick-up truck weaving conspicuously as it travelled west on Duck Bay Road. The officer could make out a male driver and two female passengers.

Constable Weir pulled the truck over. As the driver, a man named Frederick William Dickenson, opened his door to step outside, one of seven puppies corralled on the floor of the vehicle scrambled to freedom. For several minutes the officer stood and watched a comical scene unfold as the two sisters, Marlene and Retta, and their male companion fell over themselves trying to capture the wayward pup. But the levity soon dissipated. When Weir asked Dickenson, who was plainly intoxicated, to accompany him to the police cruiser, Marlene pulled a serrated knife from her back pocket, pointed it at the officer and said, "He's not going anywhere." Then she threatened, "Stay away or I'll cut ya." In courtroom testimony, Brandon Weir later described Marlene as bouncing around on her feet in an extremely agitated state. She continued to wave the knife at him. Retta tried to calm her sister but Marlene repeatedly broke loose from her grasp. To try to pacify Marlene, Weir told her he was simply taking Dickenson to the cruiser to check on his licence. Once inside the car, the worried constable radioed for assistance. Marlene now banged on the cruiser window and waved around four hypodermic needles pulled from the breast pocket of her jean jacket. Weir then remembered a special police bulletin that had been relayed to all stations in the area, advising officers to watch for a young woman matching Marlene's description.

"The situation was relatively tense and rather than provoke a further confrontation with her I was just going to sit there and wait for some assistance," Weir later testified. But when he saw Marlene and Retta fall into a scuffling match at the rear of the cruiser, he became concerned that someone would get hurt and got out of the cruiser. To his relief, he saw the knife on the ground. As he approached the two women, Marlene lunged at him and took several swings with her fist. Weir grabbed her to handcuff her, but Retta draped her body over his arms to prevent the officer from securing the steel bracelets.

Marlene broke away and ran off down the road, but she went only a few yards before turning back. The constable, who had put in another radio call for help, coaxed her into the back seat of the cruiser next to Dickenson and electronically locked the rear doors. At 12:55 a.m., about twenty minutes after Weir first stopped the truck, another cruiser appeared on the scene with red roof-lights flashing and two officers inside. At this point, Weir testified, Marlene leaned over and seemed to attack Dickenson. "When I went over to the cruiser, his left ear was bloody and it appeared that she either bit him or scratched him on the ear," Weir said.

Marlene climbed into the front seat of the police car and got out the front door. Weir and the other two officers caught her, handcuffed her, and told her she was under arrest. The charge was possession of a weapon dangerous to the public, an offence punishable by a ten-year maximum sentence. Later Weir distinctly remembered his discomfort as he closed the steel handcuffs over the fresh white bandages on Marlene's wrists. She was taken to the Midland detachment and locked in a holding cell, where she remained extremely hyperactive for several hours. Throwing herself fiercely from side to side on her cot, she hurled obscenities at jail staff, occasionally breaking into rowdy saloon songs.

Weir had retrieved Marlene's weapon – a kitchen knife with a six-inch blade – which he later referred to in court as a "butcher knife." In the pocket of her jacket Weir also found a folding Swiss army knife. He later testified that at the time of his confrontation with Marlene he detected no smell of alcohol and assumed that she was under the influence of drugs. Shortly after Weir went off duty at 8 a.m., Marlene was transferred to the regional jail in Barrie.

Early that morning, David Cole was awakened by a telephone call from a Kingston *Whig-Standard* reporter who had learned of Marlene's re-arrest and wanted his comment. It was the first the Toronto lawyer had heard of the incident and he had no grasp of its seriousness. His glib response was printed in the next edition of the paper. "Well, at least she made it through mandatory supervision," he said.

Soon after Marlene's arrest, Elizabeth Fry workers Terri-Lee Seeley and Justine Howarth drove to Barrie on a Saturday morning and met with Marlene for about two hours, urging her to consider returning to the Hamilton house if they could persuade a justice of the peace to release her into their custody. The two social workers were convinced that they could get Marlene a conditional release from the Barrie jail but that, once transferred to Toronto, her chances of getting bail would be slim. They told her they were willing to take her back that day and gave her the news that her friend had finally been released from P4W after winning her appeal to go to the Hamilton house. Marlene refused the offer, saying she was being well treated in Barrie. Her complacency disturbed Seeley, who says, "She was very calm and coherent, almost too calm." On the way back to Toronto, Seeley told Howarth that Marlene had given in. "She's given the power back to the system."

David Cole initially tried to turn Marlene's case over to an old roommate of his who was practising law in Barrie. Marlene didn't hit it off with the man. In the meantime Cole learned just what his client was up against. The Crown attorney in Barrie, a tough-minded lawyer named John McIsaac, let it be known that he would seek permission from the Attorney General of Ontario to attempt to have Marlene declared a dangerous offender. If McIsaac succeeded, Marlene could be sent back to the Prison for Women indefinitely.

7

The men over me
are stupid

Under a controversial section of Canada's Criminal Code, a person can be labelled a dangerous offender and sentenced indefinitely if he or she is convicted of a "serious personal injury offence" and if there is strong evidence that the person is a threat to others. It's the only law under which someone can be detained as a preventive measure for something they might do in the future rather than for crimes committed. It is the most draconian measure the government has at its disposal for dealing with violent criminals. Although entitled to parole board review initially after three years, and every two years after that, designated dangerous offenders never really know their fate.

Before 1977 the government had two means of incarcerating indefinitely those believed to be a public threat: habitual-criminal legislation and dangerous-sex-offender provisions. In 1977 both laws were replaced by the dangerous-offender provisions. Since then ninety-two men – and one woman – have been designated dangerous offenders. The legislation continues

118

to be used mainly against violent sex offenders. Some provinces – indeed some Crown attorneys – have made much more use of the law than others. Ontario accounts for nearly half the instances of its use. Quebec has not designated a single dangerous offender.

In early April 1983, David Cole travelled to a Penetanguishene courtroom where Marlene made her first appearance in connection with charges arising out of her showdown with Constable Brandon Weir. On April 7 Marlene was denied bail, and Cole worried about leaving her in the Barrie jail. The facilities for female offenders were poor and he believed that there was a strong likelihood, because of Marlene's tendency to act out her frustrations, that she might explode again in custody. He wanted Crown Attorney John McIsaac to authorize Marlene's transfer to Metro West. Cole again tried to get Marlene released on bail. Despite a sworn affidavit by Marlene's loyal friend, Janis Cole, offering to provide a residence at her Toronto apartment as soon as she returned from a filming job in Vancouver in June, a Toronto judge flatly refused to entertain the idea of bail.

"She has a horrendous record," said Mr. Justice Thomas P. Callon of the Ontario Supreme Court at the June 27 bail hearing. "She is obviously a human being out of control. There is a high degree, I would almost say probability, that if she were released she would commit another criminal offence. I have never heard any application that had less merit than this one. The record speaks for itself."

On August 25 Marlene was committed for trial in Penetanguishene provincial court. She elected trial by judge and jury. The day's events were anything but routine. During an adjournment a friend rushed up to Marlene, kissed her, and, while officials and spectators looked on, dropped a handful of pills into her mouth and onto the floor. A stunned Marlene, who suffered an overdose as a result of the episode, watched as her friend was promptly arrested on a drug charge. Soon afterwards, Marlene was transferred to the more secure Metro Toronto West Detention Centre.

David Cole, for his part, was beginning to ask himself whether he should continue acting for Marlene now that she was facing another major legal battle. Cole had been representing her for a couple of years, first on the December 1981 weapons charge and then through the gating challenge. Marlene resisted the idea of a new lawyer. But Cole told her he would be of more use to her as a witness at her dangerous-offender hearing than as her lawyer – which wasn't entirely true, he now says. "I realized I wanted out. I had been representing her a fair amount of time and I really didn't think that I could do as good a job for her. There was a selfish element in me that said, 'I've done enough on this case. It's time to move on.' "

Marlene was a difficult client, Cole says. She frequently called his office from jail and threatened to slash herself. "At that point I was trying to distance myself a little bit because frankly I was a little tired of Marlene and her constant problems. That sounds callous, but I'd had enough."

Cole also believed that it would be a strategic advantage for Marlene to be represented by a woman. The person he had in mind was Rebecca Shamai, a criminal lawyer in Toronto well versed in issues related to women and their dealings with the criminal justice system. Cole reasoned that while the male bias in the system often works against women, there are times when it can be exploited to the advantage of a female client. He believed Marlene would have an edge with a woman as her lawyer.

"My rationale was that a judge was going to balk at declaring a woman a dangerous offender and particularly would do so if the counsel standing up was a woman," Cole says. "Let's face it, counsel speaks for the client. In a sense, counsel is the client. Rebecca is very dignified, very poised, and I thought she would do a good job for Marlene."

On September 2 Marlene pleaded guilty before Chief Justice Gregory T. Evans of the Ontario Supreme Court to carrying a dangerous weapon and assaulting a police officer. The next day Mr. Justice Evans ordered her remanded for psychiatric assessment. At the same time, Cole was removed as the solicitor of record and replaced by Shamai. Sixteen days later Constable Weir transported Marlene from the Toronto detention centre to St. Thomas Psychiatric Hospital near London. His passenger was quiet and pleasant during the two and a half hours it took to make the trip, sometimes making small talk about the weather or points of interest along the way.

Marlene spent about four weeks in September and October at St. Thomas. As part of her pre-trial assessment, she was observed daily by staff on the ward and underwent several psychiatric interviews with Dr. Paul Gatfield, the same man who had found her unreachable three years earlier. In mid-October a judge ordered her sent back to the Toronto detention centre. Before the month was over Marlene met yet again with Dr. Philip Haden, who a year earlier had found her too dangerous to be released. He travelled to the Metro West centre to do an assessment of Marlene, this time at the request of her lawyers, Rebecca Shamai and Allan Manson. Haden noted in his report that Marlene, only days away from her twenty-sixth birthday, had a serious slash wound on her leg. It was a fresh cut. Her anxiety was well founded. Once again, the state was mustering its political and legal might, this time in a Goliath effort to lock her up indefinitely.

Barrie Crown Attorney John McIsaac wore the giant's shoes. Though many Crown attorneys balk at the complicated, time-consuming preparation and onerous red tape involved in launching a dangerous-offender application, McIsaac was not one of them. His record for using this particular section of the Code outstrips that of most Crown attorneys across the country. By the time Marlene's case came along, he had initiated four such actions, only one of them unsuccessfully.

In the early 1980s Ontario Attorney General Roy McMurtry was chastising the province's Crown attorneys for not making more appropriate use of the dangerous-offender legislation. The province's chief lawmaker was taking his cue from the Ontario Court of Appeal. On several occasions the high court had berated Crown prosecutors for seeking life sentences

instead of taking the dangerous-offender route, which prosecutors were avoiding simply to get around the periodic review
built into the legislation.

In Marlene's case McIsaac knew that the only way to win a
lengthy prison sentence was to have her jailed indefinitely as a
dangerous offender. By itself, her knife-wielding episode was
relatively minor. It would in no way warrant a heavy prison
term. McIsaac also didn't have the usual option of striking a
deal with the defence. He couldn't drop the dangerous-
offender action in exchange for a ten- or twenty-year sentence.
"He couldn't do that because it would have been a ludicrous
proposition," Cole recalls. "He knew what I would have done.
I would have accepted the ten years and then told Marlene to
go ahead and appeal. You've got the monkey of the dangerous
offender off your back and the appeal court will reduce the
sentence to one which is appropriate."

In mid-November 1983 McIsaac got the go-ahead he needed
from the province. Marlene's lawyers countered with a constitutional challenge to the dangerous-offender legislation. Many
others had contested the onerous law but Rebecca Shamai and
Allan Manson were among the first to test it under the new
Charter of Rights and Freedoms. On December 14 they tried
to convince Mr. Justice Eugene Ewaschuk of the Supreme
Court of Ontario that the section was unfair and contrary to
rules of due process and fundamental justice. While Marlene
waited anxiously for the outcome in her cell at Metro West, her
lawyers argued that no one could accurately predict who would
be dangerous in the future and that an indefinite term of
imprisonment was cruel and unusual punishment.

Mr. Justice Ewaschuk disagreed. Almost a month later, on
January 10, 1984, he ruled that the law reflected standards of
justice that most Canadians would find tolerable and fair. "It
is difficult to comprehend how the dangerous offender provisions of the Criminal Code would shock the general conscience
so as to be intolerable in fundamental fairness given all the
requirements and safeguards written into the process," the
judge said. "Not only is the dangerous offender eligible for

parole long before a life offender, but he or she has greater rights of appeal." The Crown was now free to advance the case of Marlene as a dangerous offender and would take the case to court on January 30.

The day following Mr. Justice Ewaschuk's ruling, Marlene was officially notified of the Crown's intent in a letter delivered to Metro Toronto West by Constable Weir. When she had first learned of McIsaac's plans from David Cole the previous spring, Marlene had responded almost indifferently, too overwhelmed by the chaotic events of her life to absorb the shocking implications. But what had been an intangible threat for so long had now become a reality: She was to become the first and only woman in Canada that the Crown has moved to declare a dangerous offender. She was twenty-six, and she was terrified. The prospect of spending her life in prison was horrifying enough. But the idea that she was on the brink of being singled out as the most dangerous woman in Canada was devastating to her.

Marlene braced herself for an extended stay at the overcrowded provincial jail. A remand centre used mainly for men and women awaiting trial or sentencing, Metro West wasn't the proper place for her. But when Vanier refused to accept her back, and she resisted any attempt to send her to St. Thomas, there was no alternative. At that time the top floor of the four-storey brown brick complex on Disco Road in Rexdale, a few miles from Pearson International Airport, was reserved for female inmates. She lived there in one of the jail's maximum-security cells – one of about a hundred women whose movements were heavily controlled and whose visits with friends and family were conducted through glass barriers.

Marlene, aware that she had edged dangerously close to a legal precipice, was determined to make the most of her stay at the Toronto jail. She got a job in the laundry, one of the institution's prized work details. She enrolled in an English course and joined the jail's chapter of Alcoholics Anonymous. An important influence now was Craig Townson, the federal parole officer who a year earlier had recommended against her release on mandatory supervision from the Prison for Women. When the Ontario Supreme Court had ruled that gating was illegal and ordered her release, Townson had acted briefly as her parole supervisor.

A tall, lanky man of conservative dress, whose conversation is laced with philosophical and literary references, Townson remains somewhat mystified by the friendship that evolved during Marlene's imprisonment at Metro West. "It's odd that I would have developed this type of relationship at all. I think it's the only occasion, because I take a fairly tough-minded view of the job I'm in. I'm not a social worker."

Their unlikely bond was forged a couple of months after Marlene arrived at Metro West. On a whim he wrote her a perfunctory note saying, "Dear Marlene. What's Happening? Sincerely, Craig Townson." She responded in kind with "Dear Craig. Not much. Sincerely, Marlene Moore." They were soon writing real letters to each other regularly. One day on his way through Toronto, Townson dropped by for a visit. He saw something in Marlene that he couldn't turn his back on. "The more I saw her and the more I wrote, the more I thought there's this little tiny kernel of a worthwhile person, and in principle there's no good reason why a decent person couldn't emerge."

Townson attempted to open up new vistas for Marlene by sharing his love of music and literature. Her brought her a copy of *The Catcher in the Rye* and she ploughed through it. He got permission from the institution to bring in a Walkman with two sets of headphones and set about making tapes, playing everything from jazz to Laurie Anderson to Kate and Anna McGarrigle to the last movement of Beethoven's Ninth Symphony. There was a period, Townson says, when Marlene was receptive to almost anything. "It was like dealing with an eight- or nine-year-old kid. She was starting all over again to try and fill in the things she'd missed as a kid. She was embarrassed about her lack of knowledge, her lack of education. But when she was prepared to make gains, she would put all that aside and show this kind of curiosity."

The two struck a deal, Townson says. He would start visiting her on a regular basis if she worked hard to improve her performance in the institution. "I really don't know how much effect that had, but it seemed for a while that she was able to hold things together."

Marlene once told Philip Haden that she was puzzled by Townson's interest in her and didn't understand why he stood by her. Even after her eventual release from Metro West, Marlene kept up her friendship with the parole manager. She visited him and his wife at their home just outside of Guelph on a couple of occasions. It was the first time Townson had ever had someone he'd dealt with as a client in his home. They listened to music, had a pizza, and watched a video. He remembers how his wife, initially apprehensive, took to Marlene. "She couldn't quite reconcile the image of Canada's most dangerous woman with the person who was actually a model guest. She was very agreeable and congenial and did her best to fit in. She was a bit shy at first, but the second and third times were more relaxed. We played Scrabble and on both occasions Marlene showed a native intelligence. She was actually quite good at it. My wife won. She always does. I came third."

At Metro West Marlene alternated between hopeful moments and horrible bouts of despair and frustration. One day Terri-Lee Seeley found her in a rage at the concerted efforts being made to imprison her indefinitely. "She said there wasn't anything that could help her now, and I really see that as a turning point for her."

During her stay in the remand centre Marlene met up again with her old training school friend, Patricia. On more than one occasion Patricia saw Marlene lose her self-control and lash out at others or herself. One evening while Marlene, Patricia, and two other prisoners sat playing cards, Marlene was provoked by something that one of the women said. She leapt from her seat and began flailing and kicking at the woman. Patricia broke up the fight and followed a trembling Marlene into a prison bathroom. She was struck by the fragility of her friend's ego.

"Marlene sat on the bench by the toilet and she looked at me, and I often saw that look," Patricia says. "She couldn't believe that people cared about her or what happened to her. I think she recognized the neediness in her and she knew it was great, and it was too much for her to handle – so how could somebody else possibly handle it? I sat down beside her and I put my arms around her and when she let her walls down she was just this frightened, frightened little girl, and she just broke down crying." Patricia says Marlene was embarrassed by her tears – as if it was something that would give other people an advantage. But the two prisoners sat there for about half an hour, with Patricia's arms around Marlene. Then Marlene apparently began to feel awkward. Patricia says, "She jumped up and acted like, let's get back to being a piece of concrete."

For the most part staff and other prisoners saw Marlene as one of the 'heavies' in the jail. She appeared fearless, wasn't afraid to say what she thought to anyone, and sometimes played on her notoriety. One day a guard named Sean Muldoon, who had been assigned to work on the female side of the institution, gave her a simple order that raised her ire. "Don't you know who I am?" she asked. But she sometimes also used her influence to assist security staff. When an item that Muldoon feared could be made into a weapon went missing one day, Marlene promised to track it down, and she did.

At one point Marlene barricaded herself in her cell with her mattress pushed up against the bars and began to slash. "When she wanted to slash she took all her clothes off," Patricia says. "She would take it out on any part of her body. It wasn't just her arms." Security staff cleared other prisoners from the range. According to Patricia, "She started slashing that morning and they took all of us off the unit and put us into another unit on the other side because they knew when she started she did not stop."

Marlene's cell mates, aware of the impending hearing to determine whether she should be classified a dangerous offender, often went out of their way to conceal behaviour that could get her into trouble in the institution. Patricia remembers Marlene once being so high on drugs obtained illegally inside that she could barely stand upright. "Everyone was trying to hide her and not make it obvious because if the screws found out, for sure she'd be going to the hole. That wouldn't look good when she was coming up for trial."

It was the jail's shift supervisor, Diane MacKinnon, a determined and compassionate woman, who offered the day-to-day support and encouragement that helped sustain Marlene through that difficult period. According to David Cole, MacKinnon decided she was going to do all she could to make sure Marlene didn't kill herself or commit more offences, and she thought maybe they could even "turn Marlene around." Cole says, "Diane MacKinnon worked like a dog with Marlene. Basically she took her on as a special project. I know the two of them behind closed doors had some pretty good battles and I believe that punches were thrown. Diane is a very fine human being and really, really tried hard with Marlene."

The historic hearing opened on January 30, 1984. The event attracted the Toronto media and the outcome would determine just how big a story it would be. A crew from CBC-TV's national news stood by waiting to give coast-to-coast coverage of the verdict, but only if Marlene were to become the first woman in Canada designated a dangerous offender.

McIsaac tried to persuade Mr. Justice Eugene Ewaschuk that Marlene's criminal history contained a pattern of repetitive violence and that she was a "time-bomb" who would inevitably explode. In terms of predicting future violence, he would later say, "She was at the highest level of the scale that I've dealt with." Throughout the four-day hearing, McIsaac painted a portrait of Marlene as a woman "totally out of control." That she could stay out of trouble while in prison was irrelevant, he said. It was her behaviour on the street, where she had easy access to alcohol and drugs, that was at issue. Her latest offence, he stressed, occurred only six days after her departure from the Hamilton halfway house, proof that she was "allergic to freedom."

The Crown built its case on the details of Marlene's criminal record and the testimony of only two key witnesses: psychiatrist Paul Gatfield and Constable Brandon Weir.

As Marlene's counsel, Rebecca Shamai was the last line of defence against the threat of endless imprisonment for her client. It was a daunting responsibility that required her to take calculated risks and sometimes pursue delicate lines of questioning from which there could be no turning back. Much of the evidence was equivocal in terms of whether it was favourable to Marlene.

A steady and confident woman, Shamai threw herself into the case, devising a multi-layered strategy to undercut the Crown's arguments. Her biggest hurdle was persuading the judge that Marlene could survive outside of prison, where she had spent most of her adult life. Only three of the eleven witnesses she called had known Marlene in the community. The Toronto lawyer had to strike a precarious balance in eliciting testimony that would show how Marlene coped outside of prison but that might also bring out potentially damaging information. It was no simple task to convey the extent of Marlene's progress while living in the community; what seemed like minor feats for others were momentous achievements for Marlene. Shamai also had the sometimes agonizing job of persuading her client that certain information Marlene found personally difficult to confront or simply too private would help her cause if revealed. The relationship between lawyer and client was frequently strained. Marlene often became antagonistic if she didn't get her way. While Shamai respected and sympathized with Marlene's desire to steer the course of the proceedings, the lawyer also knew she was working with a badly damaged young woman whose judgement was impaired.

In court Shamai argued that Marlene suffered from serious psychological problems that had never been properly addressed. The fact that she carried a knife shouldn't be grounds to label her dangerous, when she was much more apt to use it against herself than anyone else. Shamai also hammered home

A police photo of Marlene, aged thirteen, taken around the time she was committed to Grandview Training School.

Deputy Superintendent Sylvia Nicholls on the phone to Marlene during the hostage-taking at Vanier.

Harriet Ironside and her husband at Vanier moments after Marlene and Isabella Fay Ogima released her.

Kingston's Prison for Women (P4W). (Neil Ward, *The Whig-Standard*)

Marlene (left) and Daryl
Dollan in Daryl's cell in the
prison wing, 1980. (Courtesy of
Daryl Dollan)

On the B range at the Prison
for Women. (Neil Ward,
The Whig-Standard)

Marlene during a 1981 softball
game at P4W. (Courtesy of
Daryl Dollan)

Filmmakers Holly Dale and
Janis Cole, who befriended
Marlene during the making of
their film *P4W* in 1980.

Marlene, her sister Retta, and a friend at a family day, 1982, in the
Prison for Women. (Courtesy of Daryl Dollan)

Rebecca Shamai, Marlene's lawyer during the Dangerous Offender application hearing in 1984. (Ian MacAlpine, *The Whig-Standard)*

Dianne Martin, Marlene's lawyer during the appeals of Judge Ewaschuk's decision on the Dangerous Offender application. (Ian MacAlpine, *The Whig-Standard)*

John McIsaac, the Barrie Crown attorney who initiated the Dangerous Offender application against Marlene.

Craig Townson, who befriended Marlene during her stretch at the Metro West Detention Centre, 1983-85.

Marlene in 1988, shortly before
she was returned to the Prison for
Women for the last time.

A portrait of Marlene taken in 1987,
while she was living on her own in
Toronto. (David Littman)

June Callwood, Marlene's staunch
supporter and advocate.

Part of the crowd at the candlelight vigil held for Marlene soon after her
death in November 1988. (Rob Cowperthwaite, *The Whig-Standard*)

Marlene's family at the inquest into her death held in Kingston in June
1989. Her brother Tom, sister Arlene, and mother, Edith.
(Rob Cowperthwaite, *The Whig-Standard*)

Bonnie Diamond of the Canadian Association of Elizabeth Fry Societies at the inquest. (Michael Lea, *The Whig-Standard)*

Lawyers Allan Manson and Felicity Hawthorn acted for the Association of Elizabeth Fry Societies during the inquest. (Michael Lea, *The Whig-Standard)*

Brenda Blondell, a witness at Marlene's inquest, being escorted from the court house. (Neil Ward, *The Whig-Standard)*

Mary Cassidy, warden of the Prison for Women, leaving the court house after testifying at the inquest. (Michael Lea, *The Whig-Standard)*

Graffiti sprayed on the Kingston court house wall during the inquest.
(Michael Lea, *The Whig-Standard)*

Marlene Moore,
1957-1988.
(David Littman)

the point that Marlene didn't come close to displaying the type of threatening behaviour that would qualify a man as a dangerous offender.

The hearing opened in the dead of winter in Courtroom 21 on the sixth floor of the University Avenue court building. Each morning Marlene was transported under guard escort from Metro West detention centre to the modern court edifice in downtown Toronto. She waited for the start of the proceedings in a holding cell in the court basement. Later, perched in the prisoner's dock facing the judge, she would turn her head to glance over the crowded courtroom. She chewed incessantly on her fingernails through close to twenty hours of testimony. The pressure would eventually take its toll, and toward the end Marlene arrived at court wearing fresh bandages on her wrists.

The first witness took the stand just before noon on the opening day. Constable Brandon Weir, twenty-nine-years old, had been a police officer for about eight and a half years. For close to forty minutes the uniformed officer, frequently leafing through his notes, recreated the events of March 31, 1983. He said that he had feared for his own safety. "It was the manner she was holding the knife at me and the comments she made to me," he told the court. "I considered her to be very dangerous."

Shamai's cross-examination established that Marlene was standing at least five feet away from the constable when she produced the knife and that she had never made a move toward him. "She was just standing there yelling at me," Weir said, "and she was waving the knife more or less in a circular or semi-circular motion in front of me." Weir also conceded that Marlene had voluntarily abandoned the knife.

Next on the stand was Paul Gatfield of St. Thomas Hospital. In his last meeting with Marlene, he said, he had noticed a marked change. The threat of the dangerous-offender designation had "made her look more into what was actually happening to her, that she's wrecking herself and her life and hurting people in the bargain."

Still, Marlene refused to undergo a physical examination or psychological testing, as she had on her first trip to St. Thomas in 1980. She did complain about symptoms that "were typical of some kind of serious kidney disease," Gatfield said. But the hospital did not initiate treatment because Marlene was transferred back to the Toronto detention centre "before a complete investigation could be undertaken." Marlene was referred to a specialist who made rounds at the hospital once a week, but she refused to let him examine her. Gatfield speculated that her reluctance was rooted in her general distrust of men.

The psychiatrist diagnosed Marlene as suffering from an explosive personality disorder. Unlike schizophrenia or other such "affective disorders," which are treatable and which become less severe as time passes even without treatment, Marlene's disorder normally continues well into middle age, he said. This finding was a slight variation on the initial label he attached to Marlene in 1980. His new diagnosis, which he described as "sort of the same class but with a different emphasis," made him more optimistic that she would respond to what he called an "authoritarian therapeutic community approach" to treatment.

Gatfield said Marlene had demonstrated that she had no control over her aggressive impulses, and that she was very sensitive – at times overly suspicious – and profoundly insecure. He added that her tenuous self-control was exacerbated by her severe drug habit. He said Marlene used drugs almost daily whenever her funds allowed.

Gatfield conceded, however, that Marlene adhered to a moral code. She was loyal to her friends, didn't lie, and didn't make up excuses for her wrongs or attempt to manipulate others, he said. She was unusual even among those who fit the description of personality disorder because of her acute sensitivity to the attitudes of people around her and the ease with which her feelings were hurt. He also attested to her honesty. "I got the impression that when she told me things, they were true, and if she wasn't going to tell me about something, then she would say, 'I'm not going to tell you.' But she wouldn't make things up."

The doctor's most damaging testimony came in response to

a question about whether Marlene's violent outbursts could escalate. Citing some ten incidents of violence in her life, Gatfield said it was due more to good luck than good management that Marlene had not caused serious injury. "I wouldn't be surprised to hear that someone has been killed or permanently injured, although I certainly can't predict that's going to happen."

By late afternoon on the first day of the hearing the Crown had concluded its case. Shamai's first move was to put forward a preliminary motion challenging the very legitimacy of the proceedings. She argued that Marlene's crime didn't even fall into the category of a serious personal injury as defined by the dangerous-offender provisions. The motion was lost, but Shamai's point wasn't entirely lost on the judge. Despite the media hype that surrounded her case, Marlene's actions on the night of March 31 could hardly be seen as a life-threatening standoff between a dangerous criminal and a cop on a deserted road.

Dr. Philip Haden, who took the stand on the second day of the hearing, had taught psychiatry for many years at Queen's University and is frequently called upon by the parole board to assess inmates. His assessment report was one of the exhibits in the hearing. Mr. Justice Ewaschuk noted that even though Haden was now being summoned on behalf of the defence, he had formerly been aligned with the parole board on Marlene's case. "I question why there was not an independent psychiatrist used on behalf of the respondent," he later remarked.

Haden also described noticeable changes in Marlene since his first assessment two years earlier. He said that in their recent meeting, after initially telling him "I don't like shrinks," Marlene spoke freely with him for about two hours. "She was completely changed. She was very communicative and pleasant in her demeanour, courteous in her language." She even allowed the doctor to probe for details of her childhood, an area that she had previously declared strictly off limits. Marlene told him about parental beatings, sibling incest, and how she "hated menstruation."

In reporting his assessment, Haden continued: "She said

that she had been told that she should have been a boy. I enquired of any feeling she might have about her hairstyle and she said, 'I'm bitchy if it grows – I feel like a girl.' Regarding her breasts: 'I hate them – they made me put a bra on in here.' "

This time Haden diagnosed Marlene as borderline personality disorder, saying he had been "perhaps a little loose" when he had labelled her a severe personality disorder earlier on. Mr. Justice Ewaschuk asked whether the bad side of Marlene's personality would be deterred by a prison term. "A prison term seems to make matters much worse," Haden responded. "She's been in prison for seven and a half years and it doesn't seem to have helped her much." He added that while people with personality disorders don't commonly change quickly, they do tend to improve in a caring, structured environment. Asked whether the Kingston women's prison could provide such a setting, Haden answered unequivocally. "The Prison for Women is a place which would tend to provoke inmates of this type of personality," he said.

In his report Haden noted that Marlene's "destructive behavior has been treated punitively in the past which only aggravates her symptoms. Although she is potentially dangerous, she is also potentially harmless if properly managed. Treatment in her case is difficult but not impossible."

The doctor sternly condemned the prison's practice of locking inmates in a segregation cell for slashing themselves. A punitive response to Marlene's self-destructive behaviour only makes matters worse, he said. "It's no good punishing behavior of this nature because it has the effect of reinforcing it. There's no good locking somebody in a little cage because they are behaving in socially unacceptable ways. They come out and behave worse."

Despite Marlene's history of violence, Haden said, "When her confidence is gained, she expressed considerable interest in justice and in the welfare of disadvantaged people." Her aggression had been her way of exercising control.

Haden said that Marlene was afraid of life outside an institution. "If in the future she can be confined for a prolonged period in a structured, firm but emotionally warm environment, such as a special halfway house, the future is not necessarily hopeless." He described her as "much more an emotional casualty than a person with criminal intent desiring to harm others for their own gain. She is indeed more sad than bad."

When the proceedings resumed later that afternoon, at Marlene's request Shamai received permission from the bench for the prisoner to leave the courtroom during the testimony of the Elizabeth Fry workers, Justine Howarth and Terri-Lee Seeley. Shamai has refused to speak about what was behind Marlene's unusual request. Seeley recalls Marlene's vehement outburst when she went to the witness stand. "She stood up in court and screamed, 'I don't want your help.' It was almost as though she didn't want to hear how well she had done at the halfway house." On the stand Howarth speculated that Marlene's feelings were still tender over the issue of her leave-taking from the Hamilton house, when she slashed after learning of the parole board's decision to deny her P4W friend a placement there.

Howarth's testimony addressed the circumstances under which Marlene was delivered to the house. Normally, the prison provides three days' notice of a woman's release date. Elizabeth Fry staff were informed only three hours ahead that Marlene would be arriving at 6 p.m. that day. Howarth explained how difficult it was to design programs and plans on the street without reasonable notice. She said the Elizabeth Fry had urged the parole board to release Marlene at least four months before her sentence expired – providing sufficient time to build some structure into Marlene's new life. Marlene had made progress while at the house, but her eight-week stay wasn't enough time to prepare her for life in the community, Howarth testified.

Marlene was highly regarded by both staff and residents and had learned how to discuss sensitive issues in a calm way, Howarth said. Given her history of self-mutilation, it was seen as quite an accomplishment that Marlene had handled her feelings without slashing for two months. She vented her anger and frustration in other ways, like walking, Howarth said. Under questioning by Shamai, Howarth said that four of the six women from the Prison for Women whom the agency was working with around that time had a history of slashing.

One of three prison guards called to the stand by the defence the next day was Harriet Ironside, then working at Metro West. In her thick Scottish brogue, the matronly officer – glancing occasionally at Marlene in the prisoner's box – related the details of the 1977 Vanier hostage-taking. As her testimony unfolded, it became increasingly apparent that the woman who had been victimized by Marlene was now one of her strongest supporters.

Ironside: I haven't been afraid since with Marlene. I have been afraid for her.

Shamai: What do you mean by that?

Ironside: Well, I think Marlene is very loyal to her friends and she hasn't known very many friends except prison friends.

Shamai: Why does that make you afraid?

Ironside: Because somehow or other I think Marlene always comes off with the heavy end of the stick. You know, when there is any trouble going, Marlene seems to get herself right in the middle and I don't know if she actually realized how much harm some of her friends cause her to get into.

Over the years, the two women's paths had crossed several times. Ironside was working at Metro West when Marlene served time there in late 1981 and early 1982, and she had almost daily contact with her while Marlene was at the jail awaiting the dangerous-offender hearing. Ironside had come to know Marlene well. "I know she's very bothered by her conscience," she testified. "I have spoken to her often. She won't like me saying this, but she's many times cried. I know she doesn't like people to see her cry."

When Shamai asked Harriet Ironside whether she could envision any situation where Marlene "just wouldn't get into trouble" inside or out of jail, Ironside responded: "What Marlene needs is somebody to love her and give her the support that she really needs. I don't think there is anybody who's ever given her the love that she would like to give back. I could see her out in an open-air community, out in open spaces in a country setting with someone who cared and understood, maybe somebody a little bit older, mature, who wasn't afraid to accept a girl of Marlene's calibre."

Alice Whitson, another important witness from the ranks of the prison staff, was a correctional officer who supervised the laundry at Metro West. The inmates there called her "Hawk-eye," a pet name reflecting her keen powers of observation over those in her charge. She testified that she had noticed changes since Marlene's return to the detention centre in March 1983. Marlene, she said, no longer answered to the beck and call of other inmates looking to her to fight their battles. "This last time she wasn't interested at all. She just says keep me out of it. She's been doing that for quite a long time now," Whitson said. "I would say that in the last two years, Marlene is growing up and she's taken more responsibility on herself."

Whitson could recall only one violent incident involving Marlene. Several years earlier, eight male officers were deployed to break up what Whitson described as a relatively harmless tiff between Marlene and another inmate. Marlene took a swing at one of them.

"Has there ever been an occasion, when you thought she was being dangerous?" Shamai asked the witness. "No," Whitson said. "We are shut in the laundry, locked in the laundry all day. I have nine other girls. If I thought she was dangerous she would be up in the unit. There are some inmates that I have had down in the laundry that have been sent back because I wouldn't turn my back on them. Marlene is a pussycat compared to some of them."

Janis Cole was the last witness of the day. She and film partner Holly Dale had continued to write to Marlene and visit her at Metro West after her arrest in December 1981. The two women also visited Marlene while she was living at the Elizabeth Fry halfway house in Hamilton.

Shamai's examination of Cole focused on how Marlene coped

with the day-to-day pressure of life in the community. The witness didn't try to underestimate the help Marlene would need to make the transition from prison to the street.

"With the isolation she's had, she needs really more care than most people because she needs years of socially growing. She needs the chance to interplay with a lot of different people in situations to get used to making up her mind and working out logic in situations, to get used to weighing one option against another."

Cole said that Marlene had made steady progress while living with her and Dale. Asked how long she thought it would take for Marlene to become self-sufficient, Cole answered: "I think that if she could get into an environment that was healthy for her growth, without stagnating her growth any more, that she could grow by leaps and bounds and probably become self-sufficient within a short period of time, maybe a half a year or so." What Marlene needed most, Cole said, was a friend – "someone to understand the kind of questioning periods that she goes through when she doesn't know how to cope."

In his cross-examination McIsaac stressed that Marlene had been re-arrested after a stabbing, which occurred while Cole and Dale were out of town on film business and landed Marlene back in jail. "It would appear," he said, "that she seems to need a warm, loving, understanding environment twenty-four hours a day."

Of the many witnesses at the hearing, Maude Barlow clearly impressed the judge with her credentials and expertise. The prime minister's senior adviser on women's issues flew in from Washington on the final day of the hearing to testify. She spoke of her personal friendship with Marlene, and of her understanding of the connections between women as victims and women as criminals.

Barlow also raised the question of why someone like Marlene would be seen as a legitimate candidate for a dangerous-offender application, and she didn't hide her indignation. "The thing I wanted to say so much," she later commented, "was, dammit, there are these guys out there who have raped and sexually abused countless little girls or little boys, and yet they were testing their dangerous-offender legislation on a woman who had never seriously hurt anyone. The slashing was always against herself. . . . It was the oddest thing that they would pick her." Barlow was an invaluable witness, Shamai says. "She obviously had a tremendous amount of authority to lend to the proceedings."

Shortly after noon on February 2 the judge adjourned the hearing. Marlene waited eight days for his verdict. On judgement day, David Cole went downstairs to Marlene's holding cell to wish her luck. She had a special request. She told him that she wanted to apologize to Constable Weir and asked Cole to bring the officer to her. When Weir came they spoke through a glass barrier and Marlene told him that regardless of the outcome of the hearing, she wanted him to know that, on the night of her arrest, she was "all messed up on pills" and she was sorry. The police officer accepted the apology, wished her luck and said he hoped that she would be able to straighten out her life.

At 2:25 p.m. on February 10, a court constable led Marlene into the courtroom. After distributing copies of his written judgement to the Crown and the defence, Mr. Justice Ewaschuk began to read his twenty-four-page decision. He began with a brief summary.

"Her unhappy and indeed pitiful plight started as one of 13 children. Evidently her father beat her because of her nocturnal enuresis [bed-wetting] which unfortunately was a regular occurrence until she was about 16 years old. Furthermore, it seems her brothers sexually abused her and when she reached 16, she was raped.

"It also seems that Miss Moore has had difficulties coping with her feminine state. She has rid herself of part of that state by having had a hysterectomy. In that regards, evidence has been heard of fights with girl lovers and her general distrust of most men.

"As far as schooling is concerned, Miss Moore has Grade 6 education. She has no countervailing trade, but seems to possess some considerable skill in woodworking and auto mechanics. She has additionally expressed great interest in becoming a mortician."

But, the judge continued, "perhaps the most striking feature of Miss Moore's background is her criminal record resulting in her almost total exclusion from the outside world during the last eight years. It has been estimated that in that period Miss Moore has been out of custody, at most, some four months."

Mr. Justice Ewaschuk said that while Marlene's actions had in fact met the legal test for a personal-injury offence, her offence was at the "lower range of misconduct" required for a dangerous-offender application. The crime of carrying a weapon dangerous to the public was punishable by a maximum of ten years' imprisonment and didn't necessitate actual harm to a victim for a conviction. "Without minimizing Miss Moore's conduct," the judge said, "I would again note that she did not advance against her potential victim, who never had his gun withdrawn." As far as the judge was concerned, Marlene had contained her violent impulses on the night of March 31. "She was about five feet from the officer and it is important to note that although highly agitated, she took no step toward the officer."

The judge said he accepted the Crown's argument that Marlene was a threat to others. But he also faced conflicting evidence. The psychiatrists had told him there was little likelihood of a "cure" for Marlene in the near future. On the other hand, social workers and prison guards claimed that her reputation for dangerousness was unfounded; that all she needed was to trade the prison environment for a warm and loving setting. "I had the feeling that for some of [the witnesses], the criminal justice system, and not Miss Moore, was on trial."

In the end the judge said Marlene qualified legally as a dangerous offender. Nevertheless, he declined to make that designation. He cited discretionary authority, which he said had been granted by Parliament. He wanted to spare Marlene a label that some predicted would only cause her to act out her violent reputation. The judge was unconvinced that indefinite incarceration was warranted. While an "element of luck" may have been involved, he said, none of the violent incidents in her past had resulted in serious harm.

But he issued a strong warning: "Miss Moore is on notice that should she exhibit any form of violence toward another person in the not-too-distant future, she will likely be the subject of a successful dangerous-offender application."

After a ten-minute recess the judge returned to the bench to sentence Marlene. Clearly persuaded by testimony about her potential for rehabilitation, he refused to send her back to the Prison for Women. He gave her two years less a day – just short of a federal term – to be followed by probation for three years with conditions including mental health counselling. He recommended that she be "immediately transferred" to the St. Thomas psychiatric hospital if she consented. "She requires psychiatric treatment and the hospital setting would be less harsh and more conducive to rehabilitation than a prison setting," he said. Marlene's lawyer, aware of her client's aversion to St. Thomas, asked the judge to amend his order and remove the reference to a particular hospital.

Marlene, who had already spent eleven months in custody awaiting the hearing, demonstrated none of her usual cheek. Before the court officially adjourned and she was returned to Metro West, she stood to thank the judge for sparing her the prospect of a lifetime in prison. "When I've been on the street, I've tried to make it," she told him. "It's hard because I've been in so long. I need a lot of support."

It wasn't over yet. Seven days later, on March 2, the Attorney General's office filed a notice with the Ontario Court of Appeal. Three days later, a letter stating the government's intention was hand-delivered to Marlene at the detention centre. The letter informed her of her right to appear at the hearing and to seek legal counsel and callously instructed her to "fill out the enclosed form informing me of your intentions." Marlene was crushed. In a fit of anger and frustration, she turned on her lawyer. Shamai won't discuss what was said. "I don't want to speak badly of Marlene," she says. But it was clear that Marlene took the appeal to mean that Shamai had lost the case.

Marlene's letters to Janis Cole during the period of the dangerous-offender trial and subsequent appeals were filled with apprehension about the future. "As time went on, the anxiety grew," Cole says. "Every time she had a success that turned into a failure because it was appealed the anxiety grew, and my concern grew with it because there was nothing I could do. It became a bigger battle than a support system for Marlene. . . . It was bigger than all the people around her. It was sort of like machinery that surged forward."

8

I don't like people who
make judgements on others that aren't true

At the Metro Toronto West Detention Centre Marlene heard through the inmate grapevine about a lawyer named Dianne Martin. Martin worked in a three-storey, red-brick Victorian house converted to law offices on Toronto's Gerrard Street East, in the same block as an abortion clinic where pickets are a common sight. A consultant to the CBC-TV drama "Street Legal," Martin is part of the first wave of female law graduates who gravitated toward the specialties of criminal and correctional law. Later she got a master of laws degree from the London School of Economics and went on to teach at Osgoode Hall, becoming academic director of its poverty law program.

A passionate crusader on justice issues, Martin served as one of a team of lawyers for Leonard Pelletier. The American Indian leader fled to Canada after being accused of killing two FBI agents during a protest on a South Dakota reservation and was later extradited to the United States. She is one of those hard-working lawyers who puts in fifty to eighty hours a week and constantly struggles against a system that comes down hard on the poor and disadvantaged. "I sometimes cried in my early years," she once said. "Sometimes more with frustration and anger than sadness."

In mid-1984 Martin agreed to take on Marlene's case. She knew from the experiences of other lawyers that her new client could be demanding and at times unreasonable. "Marlene wanted to be responsible for herself," Martin says. "She wanted to make decisions and instruct her lawyer and, at the same time, it was almost impossible for her to do that. She was not only an interesting and delightful and very strong woman, she was also very damaged."

During the next three years Martin would see her client through two appeals and an ensuing snarl of legal and emotional crises. Martin tried hard to maintain a professional distance, but that wasn't always easy with Marlene. "There are many clients you get to know well and get to care about, but I kept saying to Marlene, 'I'm not your buddy, I'm your lawyer.'" Yet, she says, "It was impossible not to care about her and impossible not to go that extra mile. I try to view all my clients as something more than a file. Marlene was one, for sure, who could really get to you."

On January 9, 1985, the Ontario Court of Appeal dealt with Mr. Justice Eugene Ewaschuk's disputed conclusion. The Crown argued that the judge had erred when he held that the law allowed him the discretion not to declare Marlene a dangerous offender. The appeal court agreed. It ruled that once the judge had found that Marlene met the Criminal Code definition of a dangerous offender, he had no choice but to make that finding. The appeal court ordered the matter returned to Mr. Justice Ewaschuk and set aside his sentence of two years less a day.

Marlene, still at Metro West and with the spectre of an open-ended prison sentence again staring her in the face, now sank into depression. "It's going to kill me if I blow it," she said. "I'll string up."

By then her case was attracting more public attention, most of it packaged under the sensational banner of "Canada's most dangerous woman." Her brother Curry was unlawfully at large at the time but, riled by media reports, surprised a *Toronto Sun* reporter by dropping into the newspaper office and making a plea for public sympathy for his sister. He said the appeal court order was tantamount to burying his sister alive. "If they now declare her a dangerous offender, there will be no turning back, no chance at rehabilitation. It's a death sentence. She will kill herself, and I know she will."

On March 1 the case returned to Mr. Justice Ewaschuk. The issue ostensibly turned on the principle of whether Marlene should have been declared a dangerous offender. The real battle, though, would again be whether she should be imprisoned indefinitely. Once more Crown Attorney McIsaac tried hard to convince the court that Marlene was a dangerous public threat. But Mr. Justice Ewaschuk held firm. Marlene's violence had been "fairly minimal," he maintained. Neither Brandon Weir nor Harriet Ironside had suffered any bodily harm, and Marlene's two prison assaults amounted to little more than "a couple of spats." Apart from her own slashing, her record contained nothing, the judge said, "which has been in any way life-threatening." He rejected outright the Crown's contention that Weir had witnessed Marlene in a fit of homicidal frenzy. "She didn't lunge at him, didn't go towards him; so she wasn't that out of control."

Mr. Justice Ewaschuk informed the Crown that, had he dealt strictly with Marlene's dangerous-weapons offence, without considering her criminal record and the psychiatric reports, he would most likely have sentenced her to a mere two to three months in jail. The Crown had argued that Marlene's performance in jail wasn't a true test of her ability to cope on the street. The judge disagreed: "It's not as if she has been in a germ-free situation where she hasn't had the chance to become engaged in violence triggered by alcohol or drugs." He and others knew that inmates have routine access to drugs in jail. Harriet Ironside had testified during the original hearing that sometimes prisoners even returned from a court appearance high on drugs.

Despite the court's evident sympathy for Marlene, Dianne Martin took nothing for granted. To drive home the extent of the headway that Marlene was making at Metro West, she solicited letters of commendation from supporters inside and outside of jail. The overall impression created by the strategy – that Marlene had suddenly metamorphosed into the sweet, wholesome woman next door – wasn't true. But the point was made: Marlene was far from incorrigible.

In a letter to the court, Metro West guard Lynne Hooker said that Marlene had made remarkable progress in learning to deal with feelings of anger and frustration. "Her struggle to stop slashing herself has been difficult, but she is doing her best to deal with disappointment in a positive way and has been succeeding."

Another woman named Iris, a reformed alcoholic who worked as a volunteer in Toronto and Brampton jails, wrote of her experiences with Marlene in the twenty-three months since Marlene had joined Alcoholics Anonymous. "Marlene's attitude has become more positive, fear has left her eyes, and she has worked hard at trying to cope with her life in a positive, constructive way. If she is able to continue with her AA program, she will develop even more self-respect. She is a kind, loving person with a real love of life and happiness." Iris ended her letter: "I would trust her with my life."

Craig Townson, the parole supervisor who had befriended Marlene, prepared a detailed release document including plans for educational upgrading, alcohol counselling, finances, and even how she might spend her leisure time. In a separate letter he pledged his friendship and support and attempted to describe the qualities that had attracted him to Marlene. "One factor," he wrote, "is that Marlene is not totally preoccupied with her own problems which, by any normal criteria, are extremely serious." He said Marlene had always "made a point of inquiring" after his welfare and interests. "This seemingly innocuous rule of courtesy is generally conspicuously absent in dealings with the majority of conditionally released inmates."

Martin also submitted a copy of Marlene's certificate from the Ontario Ministry of Education, showing that she had completed Grade 9 English at Metro West with a respectable grade of 69 per cent. Her accomplishment was especially impressive, the lawyer noted, given that she was in a noisy, overcrowded jail that offered scant opportunity for quiet study or concentration. "She has taken advantage of what little is available and made extraordinary progress," Martin said.

Another entreaty to the court came from Marlene herself in a painstakingly composed, three-page letter. Given her self-consciousness about her literary skills, the document was testimony to her growing confidence and her desire to assume responsibility for her own welfare. "I have made a lot of mistakes," she wrote. "I have caused family, my friends and myself a great deal of unhappiness. I guess I was at a point in my life where I couldn't see past my anger and pain, to feel for any one else's. I've grown up a lot sense [sic] at the Metro West Detention Centre."

Marlene also wrote that she was in the process of having her tattoos removed – words or phrases like "Love Hurts," "Hate," and "Speed." While working in the laundry at the detention centre, she had received a ghastly injury when a corrosive acid accidently spilled on her arm. During treatment for the lye burn at Etobicoke General Hospital, she had asked if the numerous jailhouse engravings in her skin could be erased. "The image I had at Kingston Penitentiary should have been left there. I am a woman and I am grown. I have a lot more I want to learn."

Before imposing sentence, Mr. Justice Ewaschuk asked Marlene if she had anything to say. With her mother Edith looking on from the public benches, Marlene expressed her relief that the proceedings seemed finally to be coming to an end. "It has been a long drawn-out case. I do have some of my family in the court, my mother and brother, a couple of other members, and I just want to get it over with. Thank you."

The judge was brief in making his ruling. Correcting the technical flaw that gave rise to the appeal, he made the legal finding that Marlene was a dangerous offender. But again he denied the Crown's bid for an indefinite sentence. He described Marlene's weapons offence as "about a two, maybe at best a three" on a scale of one to ten for dangerous offences.

Marlene had already spent two years in custody since the offence that had launched the dangerous-offender application. Mr. Justice Ewaschuk was determined to find a way to cut through the complex rules of sentencing to make sure her confinement wouldn't extend beyond mid-July 1985, which was when she was scheduled to be released under his previous sentence of two years less a day.

Taking into account that Marlene had committed no acts of violence since her admission to Metro West, as well as the new evidence indicating "substantial rehabilitation and motivation to change," Mr. Justice Ewaschuk sentenced her to six months in jail and three months' probation. "It is my firm opinion," he said, "that an indeterminate detention is unwarranted and that this dangerous-offender application has been misconceived on the part of the Crown."

Before the end of the month, Marlene was notified that the Crown would appeal again. Casey Hill, the government lawyer who assumed responsibility for this second appeal, was worried that Marlene would be on the street again before he could get the case back into court. So he wrote to the Court of Appeal urging an expeditious hearing. After all, he wrote, "the Crown appeal is premised upon the fact that she is too dangerous to be in the community." Marlene, on the other hand, was hoping the appeal would be held up long enough to allow her to be released from prison in the summer so she would have a chance to prove she could live responsibly as a free woman. "If I mess up then, I'll have no one to blame but myself," she said.

This time – the fourth time the Crown had made its case against Marlene – Casey Hill faulted Mr. Justice Ewaschuk for giving too much emphasis to Marlene's immediate offence as opposed to her overall record; for weighing matters that should be left to a parole board; for minimizing "uncontradicted psychiatric evidence" about her dangerousness; and, ironically, for depreciating the evidence of Dr. Haden by implying that he was a less than independent witness. Although the psychiatrist had appeared as a defence witness, the Crown felt he had aided its case.

The crux of Dianne Martin's defence was, once again, to drive home the conviction that Marlene wasn't an intractable criminal but a sensitive, resilient young woman who, though deeply troubled as a result of past traumas, would respond in a kind, caring treatment environment.

Martin had commissioned Graham Turrall, the clinical psychologist with a special interest in predicting dangerous behaviour, to conduct a thorough assessment of Marlene. Over a two-day period in June 1985, Turrall administered a battery of tests to measure Marlene on everything from intelligence and academic aptitude to self-image and mental stability.

On June 20 Turrall was cross-examined by Crown Attorney Hill, with his written report filed as a court exhibit. Turrall said he had found Marlene reluctant in interviews to talk about her slashing and rocking. He testified: "The rocking is similar to what emotionally disturbed kids do when they go to sleep. Most of the adolescent treatment centres in the city would be filled with kids who would rock themselves to sleep."

Although Marlene did poorly on intelligence tests, Turrall maintained that her low scores were due more to lack of self-esteem than anything else. He described her as an "intuitive, sensitive, productive individual who has learned to distrust her own judgment. But when pushed to the limit she was able to come up with relatively good answers." The psychologist predicted that she would be capable of handling a community college program.

In the classic Rorschach test Marlene was asked to respond to a series of ten abstract pictures. To the first image she responded, "A butterfly that's been shot." After a brief pause she added, "It looks like a scientist has picked it apart." Another card, specifically meant to tap capacity for empathy and human interaction, elicited the response: "That could be two people with one leg. Maybe they just shot each other with blood in between." Her answers were "bizarre" and implied an emotional disturbance, Turrall noted. But more significant was the fact that she had rejected six or seven of the cards. Her sparse and very tentative responses led the psychologist to conclude that she was "extremely insecure and feels incredibly inadequate."

A sentence-completion test designed to measure self-image produced more disturbing results. For example:

To me the future looks . . . hard, awfull, scarry

I know it is silly but I am afraid . . . [of] fucking almost everything

I feel that a friend . . . is a backstabber 9/10 times

At work, I get along best with . . . the machines

Some day . . . I will die by my own hand

My sex life . . . I hate it

Marlene responded to five open-ended sentences about her relationship to her father, who was no longer living, by striking lines through all of the questions. It was an overreaction that signified deep trauma, Turrall said. "Most people just say deceased and continue moving on." But overall, he said, "her responses, with the exception of ones relating to her father, are all complete, and none seem to me as a clinician to be psychotic in any way."

To test her learning abilities and capacity for abstract thought, Turrall asked Marlene to write a paragraph about something in her past. Her reply was unequivocal. "I don't approve of writing down my past for no one." As a compromise she sent Turrall a sample of her writing on a topic of her choosing. According to the psychologist, it revealed not only an impressive faculty for abstract thought but also a deep resentment about her past dealings with psychiatrists. She wrote: "Shit. If people would stop to think and explain things, so I could understand them, then I could become a perceptive person, but no. Everything is confidential and if I don't have a right to know anyways, although I have never heard of it. It definitely makes sense. I understand it and how can I correct it? Is there a way I can do it myself? Sure not where I am now, but I can watch out for it. Shrinks piss me off. I went to St. Thomas for 30 days, right? So they got a stupid report off this waterhead. I rapped to him approximately two hours, out of 30 days, and the scatterhead was on the stand for three and a half hours. And I understand fuck-all, nothing of what he said. If you come down and explain it and now I become aware that it is a problem."

Turrall noted that in all her years in jails of one sort or another she had received only six and a half hours of psychological assessments and no "sustained professional treatment." (He was unaware at the time of Marlene's year-long weekly sessions with Claudine Rodenburg at the Prison for Women.) Turrall concluded: "Ms. Moore's potential for treatment remains a potential only. She has never been treated. In the nine years in the adult correctional system, and at least five years within the juvenile justice system, Ms. Moore had not been sufficiently assessed to determine whether an intensive, in-patient treatment program could be of any value in re-integrating her into the community." His own test results, he said, showed that "her motivation to improve her current functioning is substantial." He said she would require about five years of carefully planned treatment and that, with her consent, he had forwarded her records to the director of pre-admissions of a widely extolled program in Hartford, Connecticut. There was no such treatment program available in Ontario, he said.

Looking back four years later Turrall explained that he had recommended the Connecticut program for Marlene because it specialized in severe character and personality disorders and had a good substance-abuse program. "It was expensive, private, but at that point it didn't matter. I was recommending the ideal situation for a person who hadn't responded and wasn't responding to any of the services provided her."

The Connecticut program didn't operate on a behaviour modification approach in which, he said, "if you earned five peanuts, you got to move two steps. It was psychodynamically based, very sensitive, very skilled people working in tandem in a totally therapeutic environment. Eventually they would have moved her out into an apartment, and then in my idealistic fantasy we could have brought her back to Canada where she could have established roots again. They have a very good success rate. We lose a lot in Ontario. We lose the tough ones."

In the hearing, Crown Attorney Hill confronted Turrall's generally optimistic assessment, suggesting that Marlene had manipulated the psychologist during his sessions with her. Was her sudden openness to treatment simply "a technique by which she might put herself in a better position for the upcoming appeal?" Turrall rejected the suggestion: "I don't think Marlene Moore is sophisticated enough psychologically to manipulate people with good educations."

On June 28, 1985, the Court of Appeal dismissed the Crown's appeal and upheld Mr. Justice Ewaschuk's order for a six-month sentence. Marlene's legal ordeal had finally come to an end.

But the question remained: What had compelled the government to invoke the most severe measure at its disposal against this troubled young woman? Interviewed one day on the steps of a Toronto court, John McIsaac said, "It wasn't a matter of being out to get Marlene." He said her criminal background and psychiatric profile made her an ideal candidate for a dangerous-offender application. Later McIsaac would add that Marlene's case had presented the government with a fertile testing ground "for some very interesting legal issues that had never been litigated."

Her supporters say the experience devastated Marlene. "The labelling was desperately bad for her," Dianne Martin says. "It had an incredible effect, and it's something to be really angry about." She makes a sweeping gesture toward the row of legal files behind her desk. "Pick half of these files, and I'll show you far more dangerous men, and no one would dream of bringing a dangerous-offender action against these guys."

Rebecca Shamai had also worked hard during her defence to establish that Marlene was being judged by different standards than male dangerous offenders. "We had to establish that her conduct was not so bad as any man's conduct would have been.

In fact, the police response to her was probably as much because she was a woman and because it was unusual for her, as a woman, to be doing these things. It seemed to charge the situation more than if a man had been doing those things. So you come up with the question, What makes a woman so incredibly dangerous? And the answer has to be, It's not the same conduct that makes a man so incredibly dangerous."

David Cole and Allison MacPhail, Marlene's lawyer and friend from P4W days, maintain that there were times when Marlene was treated leniently by the courts and, as a result, did not draw the lengthy sentences typical of most dangerous offenders. But still, MacPhail says, "She was not the kind of repetitive violent offender that normally the dangerous-offender provisions are used for. Marlene was perceived as being more dangerous than other women, and therefore that's why they would use it. She certainly wasn't more dangerous, or the record wasn't nearly as bad, as many of the men."

Martin insists that Marlene's biggest liability was her refusal to accept quietly whatever the system doled out. "Men are afraid of women, and they are afraid of women who fight back. The system isn't used to women who mouth off. It's abnormal, unnatural, threatening, dangerous, scary."

Once Marlene had been branded a dangerous offender, the lawyers who acted on her behalf felt a tremendous burden. "You had to work incredibly hard just to get simple justice for her," Martin says. "You really had to work hard against incredible odds to do a decent job."

There was always the threat that the government could at any time revive its indeterminate-sentence application. "There was that overwhelming kind of paranoia that became associated with defending Marlene," Martin says. "Because if you lost – look at the risk she faced."

9

My friends don't know I am afraid of *living outside jails*

On July 4, 1985, Marlene was released from Metro West and headed north to stay with family near Midland. The three-year probation order imposed by Mr. Justice Ewaschuk instructed her to "be of good behavior" and to make "reasonable efforts" to find employment. It also required Marlene to "undergo mental health counselling" and to report regularly to the Midland probation office. Within a few weeks she was referred to a job-training program operated by the local Canada Employment Centre, and her probation officer took initial steps toward finding psychiatric support.

Before the end of August there was friction between Marlene and some members of her family, and she abruptly returned to Toronto with no clear idea of where to go or how she would survive. Probation services turned to the Elizabeth Fry Society, arranging a temporary placement at the society's halfway house – a placement that would stretch into more than six months' residency at 215 Wellesley Street East in the downtown core.

Since 1955, staff and volunteers at the Toronto agency have provided support services for women in conflict with the law, working with both provincial and federal offenders. Since 1972 the Wellesley Street location has housed both administrative offices and a fourteen-bed residence, where a staff of twenty women provide individual counselling and support groups designed to ease the transition from prison to life in the community. Some residents come to the house as a voluntary condition of their parole or mandatory supervision orders; others, like Marlene, move in from the streets. In the early 1980s the Toronto agency redesigned its halfway-house operations and upgraded staff training to provide a more structured, therapeutic environment. There are house rules that must be obeyed and prohibitions on weapons and the use of alcohol and other nonprescription drugs. Otherwise, daily routines and programs are adapted to suit individual needs.

The Elizabeth Fry society made an attempt, Dianne Martin says, "to replicate a caring community" for Marlene. She spent many hours in conversation with social worker Billee Laskin, and she had regular sessions – sometimes as often as three times a week – with psychologist Graham Turrall. The Ontario corrections ministry supplemented its basic probation services, contracting with Elizabeth Fry to provide around-the-clock crisis intervention for Marlene during her stay at the halfway house. The ministry arranged for two women, one of them a former slasher, to be available on pagers.

At first Marlene fit in beautifully. She was happy to be back in the community and responded well to the highly structured routine that occupied her days. Though Marlene chafed at the strict rules, sometimes grumbling aloud at what she saw as the overly attentive concern of house staff, she worked at learning to control her pent-up anger and to direct her frustration in ways other than slashing. For a while it seemed that she was making strides and finding a rhythm to her life on the street. "She didn't slash, that was a plus," Turrall says. "She didn't drink and she didn't use drugs and that was a plus and she went back to Elizabeth Fry every night. We were gaining, step by step."

Like others who became professionally involved with her, Turrall grew fond of Marlene. At first she hid her scarred arms from him. But as she grew to trust him she began to wear T-shirts. And she began to open up. "I liked her anger," Turrall says. "It was upfront. I liked her style and how she had learned to deal with herself and the rest of the world."

Before the end of 1985 Turrall came up with an innovative plan to help Marlene: she would get involved in a canoe-making business. He had somehow found a woman who built canoes and was willing to work with Marlene. The Elizabeth Fry Society agreed to cover the cost of building materials for the first two canoes. But Marlene, who was initially keen, soon lost her enthusiasm and the project never got off the ground.

During this period a few close friends, new and old, looked out for Marlene. For a while Marlene used Dianne Martin's office as a drop-in place where she could engage in friendly ribbing or even be put to work for a couple of hours over the photocopy machine. Martin was optimistic about Marlene's future. "With the resources and continuity and support, I always thought Marlene was going to make it. I liked her." Martin says that in some ways Marlene seemed to be healthier and less of a victim in her attitudes than other clients of hers. "She responded very well to straightforward, uncomplicated caring. I was often really straightforward with Marlene and would yell at her. But you didn't need to coddle Marlene. In fact, that would irritate her. She could handle you being really angry with her if it was fair for you to be that angry, so there were a lot of areas where you could see there was real hope."

Writer June Callwood was another friend. Callwood had first met Marlene in late 1984 when a *Globe and Mail* editor suggested she arrange to interview the young woman held at Metro West – the prisoner the state wanted classified as a dangerous offender. Her journalistic interest in Marlene soon developed into something much larger. They met by chance – their first conversation outside prison – when Callwood dropped by the

All Saint's Church for homeless people one evening and Marlene was there visiting friends. The two women soon fell into a pattern of almost daily contact.

"It felt good being with her," Callwood says. "She was tense and edgy but she was keeping her curfew, and she was very merry at the same time." By late summer 1985 Callwood had begun "drifting together" with the spirited young woman. Marlene's scarred limbs and wry humour had left an indelible impression when the writer first met Marlene in the jail's visiting room a few months earlier. "I just liked her," Callwood says. "I thought she was terrific. She was funny and she was smart. She had a lot of insight, she had humour, she seemed a really appealing person. The story she gave me of her life was a classic story of societal neglect, a family of violence."

Marlene's mastery of day-to-day life on the street, however, was still limited. After years spent inside the surreal confines of prison, the vastness of the city caused her torment. As slight a misstep as staying on the subway past her stop could leave her ashen-faced and trembling. Brenda Hope says Toronto was just not the place for her. "It was too big and too cold and too empty." Hope ran into Marlene again on a brisk winter day in early 1986. It was the last time she saw Marlene. "I really felt bad, and I really felt guilty because I couldn't do anything. All I really wanted to do was pull her out of her past, and I couldn't." Hope and Marlene went off for a coffee and Hope was surprised by how skinny her old friend had become. "When I hugged her it was like I hugged a bag of bones. She was so frail." Still, at least Marlene was out of prison and among people who cared about her and had reason to celebrate. That Christmas she bought the tree for the halfway house.

Eventually tensions between Marlene and the Elizabeth Fry staff began to escalate. No longer content to abide by house rules, Marlene had fallen back into using drugs and alcohol and was resisting attempts by the staff to supervise her. More than once during this period Dianne Martin was called upon to mitigate crises for Marlene. Martin says the staff were "worn out and burned out" by Marlene's intense need for support and supervision. Twice the house workers concluded they simply couldn't cope and threatened to evict Marlene. Martin was concerned that, without a permanent residence, Marlene would be sent back to jail. "It was really rather horrible because, in a way, it was because she was so exhaustive of resources – rather than that she was doing something so seriously bad they should turn her back."

A serious threat to Marlene's freedom occurred in January 1986 – six months after her release from Metro West – when she appeared in court on charges of assault with a weapon. She was alleged to have cut a man with a broken beer bottle in a fit of temper during a drunken brawl at the Brass Rail Tavern on Yonge Street.

Martin says Marlene – and a sister who was with her at the time of the incident and appeared as a court witness on her behalf – presented a vastly different version of the event. They insisted that one of the men involved in the fracas had been "coming on to" a woman with Marlene and that Marlene herself had been "jumped" and "choked." Marlene's stitches from some recent surgery to remove tattoos came loose in the scuffle and she began to bleed profusely. Ambulance attendants called to the scene tried to convince her to let them take her to the hospital, but she refused. Screaming hysterically and hurling obscenities at police, she was charged and taken off to court.

A lawyer from Martin's office, in court on another matter, spotted Marlene and her police escorts. One of Marlene's eyes was blackened and the police officers were strangely outfitted in protective gloves and masks. Marlene had apparently told them she was a hepatitis-B carrier, a lie she had employed more than once to get her keepers to maintain their distance.

Martin rushed to the courthouse as soon as she heard about the incident. She found the judge wouldn't give her client bail "because she was the dreadful Marlene Moore." Martin quickly called for a bail review. She says, "Marlene was naturally very upset about being back in jail again, and I became quite convinced early on that this was yet another example, worse than many, of Marlene's reputation producing results that wouldn't have happened to anyone else." At the bail review the presiding judge expressed outrage to match Martin's that Marlene had been denied bail. He set her free pending trial – on the condition that she stay temporarily at one of Toronto's drug and alcohol rehabilitation centres.

At a pre-trial hearing the Crown's key witness was a young bouncer who claimed to have observed the incident through a glass door at the bar. The defence produced photos showing that the door was covered in posters, totally undermining the case against Marlene. Marlene pleaded guilty to the lesser offence of causing a disturbance. The charge of assault with a weapon was withdrawn, and she was placed on two years' probation.

Martin was dismayed at how vulnerable Marlene had become as a result of her reputation and "how easily she was getting trapped" into compromising situations. Marlene herself was frequently becoming despondent about her notoriety – the lingering fallout from the dangerous-offender hearing. One time Martin promised to give her client a legal name-change if she would stay out of trouble for six months.

Marlene's legal troubles weren't far behind when she became embroiled in a serious conflict with the Wellesley Street house over her relationship with one of the Elizabeth Fry staff workers. Given house rules that banned intimate relations between residents and house workers, it was not simply a private matter when Marlene and Sue Kemsley fell in love. Their relationship led directly to the agency's decision to fire Kemsley. That, in turn, caused Marlene to leave the halfway house abruptly in mid-March 1986 and move into the west-end apartment that the thirty-two-year-old Kemsley shared with her teenage daughter. As far as Marlene was concerned, Elizabeth Fry had turned its back on her. Callwood believes that Kemsley's firing was the beginning of Marlene's inexorable descent back to the Prison for Women. In Kemsley, Callwood later wrote, Marlene had found a "wonderful friend, a woman possessed of radiance and common sense. A troubled woman herself, tattooed and poor, she loved Marlene with her whole generous heart, and never stopped loving her."

The women paid a high price for their love. Forced to choose between emotional security and the support network co-ordinated by the Elizabeth Fry, Marlene took Sue Kemsley. The two of them found themselves in desperate financial straits. Marlene was employed for one week in an east-end sock factory, the first job she had landed in her adult life, until she had a seizure and collapsed over a hot machine. The company told her she was an insurance risk and fired her. She was devastated but determined not to revert to her old ways of coping with failure. During a newspaper interview a few days later, she proudly told a Toronto reporter that rather than slash herself she went for a walk and cried.

But she also spoke of mounting anxiety. "I am scared. I am afraid to be alone. I am afraid to even write my name because I know what it means. Marlene Moore means trouble. So call me Diane. Call me anything. But help me stay free. I don't ask for pity. All I ask is for a chance. All I want to do is make it."

As Marlene shifted her dependence to Kemsley her rapport with Graham Turrall began to break down. Turrall didn't like what he was seeing. He says the more difficulties Marlene and Sue Kemsley started to have, the more Marlene would drink – and "the more she would abuse drugs, the more she would slash and the more she would go out and carry on in the community and make a fool of herself." Turrall's sense was that Marlene's relationship with Kemsley, "although initially positive, ultimately became destructive."

In the summer of 1986 Marlene had been on the outside for one day short of a full year, the longest stretch of freedom in her adult life, when trouble came once again. By that time her safety net was in tatters. Marlene herself was falling apart. "Her physical condition was deteriorating and that frightened her very much," Martin says.

Graham Turrall saw Marlene covered in bruises and abrasions a few days after she had jumped out of a moving car in the midst of a dispute with the driver. Convinced that Marlene had suffered some type of brain injury, Turrall urged her to seek medical attention. "She came to see me, and she was twitching and quivering and having these minor seizures," Turrall says. He told her, "Marlene, I really can't deal with you any more. You're beyond what I can do for you. You need to see a neurologist." (Tests performed at Queen Street Mental Health Centre later showed "slight seizure activity in EEG" and staff there concluded Marlene's seizures were drug- or alcohol-induced.)

In the early morning of July 3, 1986, Marlene and her younger sister Audrey were arrested at an Islington Avenue apartment for possession of stolen credit cards. On the night of the arrest, Marlene overdosed on drugs and was rushed to Credit Valley Hospital in Willowdale, where she remained for several days. Her bail hearing was postponed until July 9. At that time Marlene was released with conditions, including orders to stay away from her sister and to "be amenable to" the rules and regulations of the Elizabeth Fry Society. Marlene would eventually plead guilty to the charges, though she had never attempted to use the cards, which had already expired. Martin says it wasn't easy to convince Marlene that she should keep her distance from certain members of her family. "Any of them who were thoroughly into the criminal subculture were trouble to her because she loved them so much, and they were the calls she could never turn down," the lawyer says.

The court's good intentions had little practical application: Marlene's relations with the Elizabeth Fry had broken down over her involvement with Kemsley. The agency made clear that its mandate did not include supervision of bail orders.

Marlene went back to Kemsley's apartment – and her probation officer, Suzanne Boothby, turned her mind to the nuts-and-bolts issues of money and housing, as well as counselling options to meet her client's urgent need for mental health care. Boothby, in her mid-twenties, took over Marlene's file when a colleague at the Ontario corrections ministry, Debbie Gibson, went on maternity leave. She had worked as a probation officer for less than a year when Marlene was added to her caseload on

June 30. She had met Marlene before that and knew that she demanded far more time and attention than other clients. More than once she had cautioned Debbie Gibson about becoming too involved. "I said to Debbie, 'You've got to learn to draw the line, there's only so much you can do.' And then I found myself in the same situation four or five months later."

Like others before her, Boothby was won over by Marlene's warmth, wit, and desperate needs. Over the next twenty-one months Boothby became an integral part of the small and informal coalition of friends and professionals who were Marlene's lifeline.

Away from the strict rules of the halfway house, Marlene became even more drawn into her old, self-destructive ways, turning to drugs and alcohol to dull her pain. Her fragile health, already under siege by chronic insomnia and a noxious junk-food diet, periodically collapsed. Now and then she went into seizure on the street and was picked up by ambulance and admitted to hospital for hours or days, each time returning contritely to Kemsley's apartment. Her friends grew more anxious about Marlene's erratic behaviour, but no one had a solution.

There was nothing demonstrably criminal in her abuse of alcohol or prescription drugs. Dianne Martin had taken pains to ensure that Marlene's probation order did not contain specific prohibitions on the use of drugs or alcohol, because she was afraid that her client might be shipped back to prison for a minor infraction if the stipulations on her behaviour were too strict. Marlene lurched through the summer on an emotional roller-coaster, making promises she could not keep and hoping for a better future that never arrived. By September her relationship with Kemsley had become strained. Probation officer Boothby redoubled her efforts to find suitable housing.

Because of Marlene's criminal record, social service agencies refused to give her a bed in any of the city's group homes. Her scarred, emaciated appearance caused most private landlords to reject her at first glance. To make matters worse, Marlene had little money and an inordinate fear of being alone. She was terrified by the loose security of rundown boarding houses, and her friends were concerned that moving to such a house would invite disaster. Marlene's pervasive fear of men brought an element of risk to any chance encounter. "That was something we were looking at," Boothby says. "If we put Marlene into a place like that when she was so afraid, someone could knock on the door – it could be the wrong apartment – and she could do something to them."

On September 15 Marlene didn't turn up for a scheduled meeting at the probation office, but Boothby felt no cause for serious concern. It wasn't the first time Marlene had missed an appointment, and she had always checked in later by phone. Sure enough, Marlene called – only this time, she was dialling long-distance from the home of her brother's girlfriend in Guelph. Within a few days Curry Moore arrived on the scene, and there was talk about Marlene moving in permanently with the couple.

One night after a bout of drinking at a Guelph hotel Marlene slashed her wrists. The next day she returned to Toronto and walked into the Queen Street Mental Health Centre. She asked to be admitted but was told no bed was available. She reluctantly made her way back to Guelph and a few days later poured acid on her bandages – a dramatic plea for help.

On October 6, 1986, Marlene boarded a bus and returned to Toronto, where word of her disturbed behaviour had spread to her circle of friends. This time Boothby accompanied her to the Queen Street Mental Health Centre – still commonly known as 999 Queen although its address has been officially changed to 1001 Queen Street West. The psychiatric hospital is a sprawling complex that dominates the surrounding neighbourhood of Parkdale, where ex-residents migrate between the out-patient clinic and tumbledown rooming houses. The largest psychiatric hospital in Ontario, it serves a city of 2.1 million people with about six hundred beds and two thousand admissions a year. About 50 per cent of its patients are diagnosed as schizophrenics. Another 12 to 15 per cent are manically depressed. The rest have organic disorders or have been labelled with personality disorders.

Boothby, Callwood, Kemsley, and lawyer Michael Lomer, who stepped in as legal troubleshooter when Dianne Martin took an office sabbatical to complete post-graduate studies in Britain, were adamant that 999 Queen accept Marlene. But Boothby says it was Marlene who settled the issue: "She had a piece of glass in her pocket, and she told them, 'If you don't take me, I'm going to slash.' "

Marlene was admitted to a locked ward as an emergency patient. Over the next several days her friends, joined by Lomer, would use all their influence to focus attention on her plight. Lomer says, "We were looking for Ministry of Health help because I guess we didn't really know how to deal with her, in the sense of a place where she could grow, or grow up, or live without getting into trouble. . . . It doesn't take a rocket scientist or a psychiatrist to tell you that when someone is into self-mutilation all the time, they are a disturbed person and need mental health care."

It was one thing to recognize that Marlene needed professional help and quite another to find someone willing and able to work with an angry young ex-prisoner, especially one saddled with the notoriety of being labelled the nation's "most dangerous" woman. At a meeting on October 17, 1986, the five people who made up Marlene's informal support team sat down with seven medical professionals from the Queen Street psychiatric facility to discuss long-term treatment options.

Psychiatrist-in-chief Dr. Sam Malcolmson remembers a palpable tension in the room as they discussed Marlene's case. When June Callwood attempted to explain the conditions under which Marlene would best respond, stressing the need for staff to be honest, caring, and flexible, hospital officials became defensive. Malcolmson made it clear that there were limits on how far the institution would be able to go in attempting to accommodate Marlene's needs. He says he tried to warn the group that there would be times that 999 Queen would fall short of their – and Marlene's – wishes and expectations, despite the hospital's best intentions. He says, "They were very understanding, and I think that helped because things didn't always run well."

Ultimately, what materialized from that round-table talk was only an interim solution. Hospital officials made clear that they could not provide the kind of long-term therapeutic environment Marlene needed. They agreed to keep her for a month and try to stabilize her. As it turned out, Marlene would remain in hospital for more than five months, initially resisting all overtures by psychiatric staff.

For a while Marlene lived on the hospital's crisis unit, a fourteen-bed ward where patients are observed and assessed for possible referral to a community agency. Confrontations with staff became regular occurrences. "She would push authority any time, any day, as far as it would go," Dianne Martin says. The lawyer heard about an incident that started with Marlene refusing to eat her toast. The refusal took hold and escalated. Finally the staff membes were pushed to the limit of their patience, and Marlene "would be proven right in not trusting them," Martin says. When Marlene's slashing continued and she began making physical threats to staff, she was transferred to a sixteen-bed secure unit. This part of the institution, where Marlene lived for close to three months, is as much a prison as a hospital. Security is tight: Visitors and staff must identify themselves on an intercom in the hallway before passing through a double set of locked doors. In the lounge area, televisions are enclosed in unbreakable cases and located high on the walls, out of reach. Surveillance mirrors hang over doorways, dining tables are bolted to the floor, and staff members have access to emergency buzzers. Outside, at one corner of the building there's a small exercise yard enclosed by a high chain-link fence and lined with astro turf.

Viewed by staff as threatening and self-destructive, Marlene also spent an inordinate amount of time in one of the unit's four "seclusion rooms" – locked five-by-ten-foot compartments with small unbreakable windows, pacifying pink walls, and nothing but a mattress and a bedpan on the floor. There, patients are kept under twenty-four-hour observation via camera monitor and a nurse stationed directly outside the door.

Marlene had entered Queen Street knowing she was out of control on the street and in desperate need of help. Once again, however, the help she was offered took the form of isolation and control. And once again Marlene fought back against the institutional rigidity and brutal indifference of her surroundings. At times Marlene was strapped to a bed in four-point restraints, arms and legs pinned. Curry Moore says he once telephoned the hospital posing as a lawyer and threatened to bring legal action against the institution if Marlene wasn't immediately released from the shackles.

Malcolmson was sometimes called to examine Marlene while she was in seclusion. "I would tend to see her when there was trouble," he says. "It wasn't a treatment issue, but a brief assessment to find out whether the level of seclusion was necessary, for how long. The question was, can we negotiate our way out of this thing?"

The main goal that Queen Street staff had for Marlene was equipping her to live safely, and productively, on the street. According to Malcolmson, "The severity of the problem with Marlene focused on the issue of self-harm, the issues of ongoing relationships, self-esteem, and employment. We had to try to get those in place and then have others on the community side maintain them."

Malcolmson says he saw many appealing qualities in Marlene. "I recall a kind of spunky, mischievous quality and some dimension of neediness. She was also appreciative and very, very much alive and bright . . . quite electric. There were other times when she was turning people aside and being rejecting, but again the energy of that was still very intense. It wasn't indifference or a message of 'get out of my life.' "

The staff tended to like Marlene and felt mainly frustration at their inability to reach her, Malcolmson says. "The difficulty is the same that occurs with any individual where it feels like you're not getting anywhere. People didn't view her as someone who was essentially nasty or negative or hurtful. People felt some empathy and, of course, if you like somebody and you want them to do well and they don't do well you feel unhelpful, kind of therapeutically impotent." Marlene once told Callwood how much she appreciated the efforts of staff to keep her from injuring herself. "They were sneaky," she said. "When they thought I was building up to slash, three staff would sit me down for a game of euchre. After a while, without being aware of it, I'd calm down."

Her dedicated coterie made regular visits, with Kemsley and Callwood stopping by almost daily. Kemsley spent hours and hours doing crossword puzzles with Marlene. One day Callwood presented Marlene with a gift – a bouquet of flowers in a glass vase. Given Marlene's slashing history, it was a naive gesture that didn't escape her black humour. It was an extremely painful time, Callwood says. "I tried to get her to co-operate but she hated her psychiatrist." For a time Marlene wore a string tied around her wrist, a symbol of hope that Callwood described as typical of her "delicious humour of basing faith on something so flimsy." But her despair was obvious. "One bleak afternoon," wrote Callwood, "sitting in a stripped cell under 24-hour supervision, she printed in a child's block lettering, 'THERE IS NO PLACE FOR ME IN THIS WORLD.'"

Boothby continued her methodical search for someone able to help repair the damage, some place where Marlene might begin to heal. Her office appealed to the bureaucracy, telling and retelling Marlene's sad story to ministry officials with links to health care, corrections, and social services. Marlene herself gradually began to emerge from the black hole of depression. In mid-December she was allowed out of hospital to spend the day with Callwood. They had lunch at a chic French restaurant where Marlene exulted in the novelty of a chicken and pasta concoction.

At 999 Queen, during the weeks leading up to Christmas, Marlene spent hours making felt bunnies and stockings to give as gifts to friends and the nursing staff. She asked Kemsley to make homemade jam, which Marlene later handed out to fellow patients. "It was a good example of basically how she felt about other people and people at the hospital were very touched and in a sense not suprised," Malcolmson says.

On December 24, Janis Cole and Holly Dale dropped by to visit Marlene on their way to a Christmas Eve party. "We were sitting there, all three of us holding hands, and she was in pretty good spirits, and when it came time to end the visit, I really didn't want to go," Cole says. "In a place like that Marlene had no escape."

Cole never did accept the idea that Marlene was better off in an institution during that period. While Marlene may have needed intense psychological counselling, the last thing she needed was more confinement. "Not St. Thomas. Not Queen Street. I didn't like visiting her in either one of those locations and she hated being in either of them," Cole says.

The next day Marlene spent a boisterous Christmas Day at the home of the close-knit Callwood clan. Overcome by the hubbub of generosity and kindness, she sat on the back steps and wept.

According to Malcolmson, Queen Street eventually geared its efforts to trying to find suitable housing and employment for Marlene but routinely faced rejection from community agencies put off by her criminal record. "If the individual has a history of arson or assaulting someone, the receiving end says what about the other people under this same roof?"

In mid-January 1987 a breakthrough came when officials from a drug-abuse program known as Portage agreed to accept Marlene at their treatment facility. The rehabilitation program, financed by the Quebec government and private donations, includes a hundred-bed facility for adult addicts at Lac Echo north of Montreal and a centre for adolescents outside Elora, Ontario. But Marlene could not decide whether to go. She was worried about the conditions: a promise not to slash or otherwise act up. Even more daunting was the prospect of moving to Quebec, where the program's adult treatment centre was located. She could not bear the thought of leaving behind the few close friends and family who were her only security.

In case the Portage proposal fell apart, the first steps were taken to set up support services for Marlene in the community.

When she was still at 999 Queen she resumed seeing the Elizabeth Fry social worker Billee Laskin, under a special contract arrangement approved by the Ontario corrections ministry. Hospital staff also agreed to refer Marlene to Archway, a 999 Queen satellite clinic where she could go as an outpatient for psychiatric treatment. They promised to contact the Community Occupational Therapists Association, which helps with everyday problems such as banking and grocery shopping.

An obstacle to planning for Marlene's release was removed on January 23 when she pleaded guilty to the July credit card charges, taking the rap for her younger sister. She got a two-year probation with the stipulation that her residence be approved by Boothby, her probation officer.

But as Marlene inched toward release from the psychiatric hospital, her behaviour began to deteriorate. It was an old pattern, an echo of her fear of being abandoned to her own resources once out of crisis. On February 9 she somehow got her hands on a sharpened edge and cut herself badly enough to require treatment at an outside hospital. The day after her return to 999 Queen, Boothby dropped by and found Marlene in a state of near panic. Marlene reluctantly confided her fear that attackers lurked behind closet doors. She was hesitant to name her paranoid imaginings for fear her probation officer would brush her aside as a crazy, hopeless case.

"I tried to show her that these feelings are normal, maybe not the most normal, but that other people do go through this," Boothby says. Afterwards Boothby sadly scribbled a few terse comments on Marlene's state of mind in her notebook: "She wants to end it, tired of trying, knows that she can't make it out there and doesn't want to let anyone down further."

Although Marlene was certain that she was ready to try living on her own, she accepted her pending release warily and began to go out on day passes, mainly with Callwood or Kemsley, who drove for miles through the city while Marlene searched ineptly for an apartment. By early March she had decided against the Portage program and had been designated a voluntary patient at 999 Queen. Callwood patiently coached her on the rudiments of house-hunting, showing her how to read the classified ads and cajoling her into using the phone. "It was just hell for Marlene to pick up the phone and ask whether the room was still available," Callwood recalls.

Nothing turned up for a few weeks, until finally Callwood drove Marlene to a rental agency, signed the papers, and paid the deposit on a one-bedroom apartment in the heart of Parkdale. The place rented for $395 a month. Marlene, who wore a black leather jacket and a ravaged look, wanted to concoct an elaborate story about where she'd been. Callwood insisted that she simply say she had been in the hospital, although it was quite clear what kind of hospital she'd been in. Her friends scrounged odds and ends to furnish the small apartment, which was within walking distance of both the Queen Street hospital and a community drop-in centre frequented by ex-psychiatric patients.

Boothby's housewarming gift was a deadbolt. Security was paramount for Marlene, who dreaded being alone at home and seldom went outdoors unaccompanied. "She needed a lot of locks and a sense of safety," Callwood says. "The quiet and the dark scared her. She kept that place so clean, and she was so proud of it. But she had sheets over the windows, double locks on the doors. She felt tremendous panic over being raped." Still, says Janis Cole, "Marlene had this desire to be alone, to prove to herself and to others that she could do that. But she had too many paranoias, too many insecurities."

On March 18, 1987, Marlene picked up her medication and the $200 discharge allowance provided on release from 999 Queen and moved into her new apartment. Boothby contacted welfare officials, who came up with $1,164 to cover the first and last months' rent and the cost of groceries and a phone hook-up.

Not long after she'd moved into her apartment Marlene dined with judges, cabinet ministers, and other members of Toronto's social elite. She was Callwood's guest at a $200-a-plate gala in Callwood's honour, held at the Inn on the Park. "I do admit to a certain nervousness," Callwood says, recalling that when Marlene accepted her invitation she promptly asked whether it would be all right if she whistled instead of applauding her appreciation during after-dinner speeches. When Callwood stepped up to the podium that evening, a broad grin heralded her private anticipation of the ear-piercing whistle she had heard before – a sound she knew was guaranteed to turn heads in a crowd. But it never came. In an unfamiliar social setting, Marlene opted for decorum.

"Her idea about herself was that everybody knew she was the 'most-dangerous' woman. She picked up all kinds of messages from that," Callwood says. "But what a blotter she was. Her table manners became the table manners of everyone around her. She just picked it up so fast that it was one of the most optimistic times I had with her."

But her friends could not always be at her side. Marlene spent hours alone and adrift with unfamiliar responsibilities. She had to learn to budget her money, to shop, to cook, and – even more difficult – to make critical decisions about her lifestyle, from her choice of friends to her use of drugs and alcohol. The challenge proved too much.

"She had a lot of motivation," Boothby says. "I often said to myself if half my clients had half her motivation but half her problems, we'd be much more successful. There were so many problems. It was almost too much for Marlene to handle." With something always appearing to block the next step, Boothby says, Marlene couldn't hold it together.

Bureaucratic inertia made matters worse. Although pre-release plans first discussed in January had dealt with the need to get Marlene involved in a life-skills program and out-patient psychiatric treatment, 999 Queen officials did not send the referral forms until Marlene had checked out of the hospital in mid-March. Subsequent foul-ups in a paper chase through the corridors of corrections, health, and social services extended the delay into late June.

Within a few weeks Marlene was hanging out at neighbourhood taverns, drinking alone. Sometime on the weekend of April 11 to 12 she was taken by police to St. Joseph's Health

Centre, after being picked up on the street bleeding profusely from a self-inflicted wound that took scores of stitches to close. Within a few days of that she was drinking again, but she refused to admit to an alcohol problem when Boothby confronted her. Marlene's friends grew more anxious, fearing that she was locked onto a collision course with disaster.

When that disaster came, it took the form of her worst nightmare. Late one night Marlene fended off a man in her apartment building and cut him with a broken bottle, inflicting a serious throat injury requiring thirty stitches. Police found Marlene convulsed in a seizure, the man bleeding in the hallway, and both high as kites. Marlene maintained steadfastly that she had lashed out in self-defence against a sexual assault. Michael Lomer, her lawyer, says he believes that the man's failure to come forward "lent credence to what she said happened." She was never charged. But, Lomer says, the incident had a traumatic effect on Marlene. "She had been attacked in her own home, which was like her first and only home." Her friends wasted little time in getting her back into 999 Queen.

On April 28 Marlene was readmitted to the psychiatric hospital. Once again she began to talk aloud about killing herself. Inexplicably, she was released after eight days.

This time Marlene huddled inside her apartment, drowning her despair in alcohol, "not wanting to go out because she always got into trouble," Boothby says. She had lost most of her support, except for Boothby, Sue Kemsley, and June Callwood. The institutions had still not decided who would work with Marlene. An apparent mix-up in communication between 999 Queen and the Community Occupational Therapists Association meant that Marlene did not meet her first support worker until May 29, nearly ten weeks after her initial release from hospital. Archway, which had been identified five months earlier as the best source of out-patient psychiatric care, had still not decided whether to accept her into a treatment program.

Callwood looked to other medical professionals for specialized treatment for Marlene, but without success. Marlene had serious physical problems, as well as mental-health problems: She suffered from a chronic bladder disorder. Callwood found an incontinence clinic at one hospital but was told that Marlene was too young to qualify for treatment. At another hospital she tracked down a physician doing research on self-mutilation, and she used her personal influence to get Marlene an appointment. But after a brief discussion the doctor sent Marlene away, saying he could offer no help. Callwood says Marlene's badly scarred body settled the matter at the outset. "He took a look at her and decided she was too dangerous. He believed that since she had cut herself so much she would just as easily turn on him. He saw Marlene as too sick to help. Marlene saw it as nobody cares."

As summer approached Boothby sensed that Marlene had resolved to sever her ties with those who cared about her, that she no longer believed she could survive outside institutional care. "I think she had concerns that she was falling down but didn't want to admit it." Marlene would often say to her friends, "You're doing so much," which to Boothby meant, "You're asking too much of me." Boothby was really concerned that Marlene was giving up. She says Marlene would say, "I don't want to have anything more to do with you," because of her sense of guilt about letting people down.

Marlene sank deeper into aimlessness and depression, finding temporary relief in the self-destructive therapy of alcohol and drugs. She suffered periodic seizures and blackouts. On the morning of June 17 Marlene phoned the probation office in a panic and told Boothby she had just awakened and discovered the acrid ravages of fire in her kitchen. She had set her kettle to boil and fallen asleep. The countertops were charred, the kettle was ruined, and everything was covered in black soot. It was more than she could bear.

Late that evening police officers in a passing cruiser spotted Marlene wandering along the railway tracks near the grounds of the Canadian National Exhibition. They talked her out of her suicidal meandering and into the cruiser and drove to the psychiatric hospital. From 999 Queen she phoned Kemsley, who alerted Boothby. Police then took Marlene back to her own apartment.

The sad episode stretched on through the night. Boothby reached Marlene by phone after midnight. Marlene seemed intent on going back to the tracks to cut off her arms. "There was no focus," Boothby says, "but she was very angry, angry at everybody." Marlene had called the police, who told her to call the crisis line. When she called the crisis line it was always busy. In the end Marlene returned to the empty tracks but fell asleep before dawn on a park bench. Within twenty-four hours she turned up at St. Joseph's Health Centre for repairs after being involved in a tussle outside a hotel. Boothby pleaded unsuccessfully with hospital officials to keep Marlene. Over the next few days she bounced between home and hospitals, intoxicated and combative and slashing.

That same month, only barely recovered from the kitchen fire, Marlene became involved in another set of bizarre circumstances. Someone from another apartment in her building overdosed on drugs while in her apartment. Marlene called 911, an ambulance arrived, and the man, not wanting to get caught with a weapon in his possession, passed Marlene a knife before being carried off to the hospital. When the ambulance attendants arrived, a hysterical Marlene was waving the knife in the air saying, "Get this dead body out of my apartment." She was charged with possession of a weapon but released on her own recognizance without a bail hearing. When Dianne Martin heard about the incident, she wasn't overly worried: "We didn't like it sitting there as an outstanding charge, but it was one that she had a defence for, for sure."

On June 24 Archway finally delivered its decision: the outpatient clinic could not meet Marlene's needs. Clinic officials recommended that she apply for admission to the group therapy program at St. Thomas Psychiatric Hospital as an inpatient for a minimum of one year. Marlene was furious. She couldn't understand the bureaucracy. She couldn't understand why no one was helping her.

She flatly refused to go back to St. Thomas but she did agree to reopen talks with Portage officials about their Quebec treatment facility. On July 2 Marlene went with Boothby to take a first-hand look at the program's youth centre outside Guelph. At the end of that visit Marlene agreed to enter the adult program, though not until the fall. She needed time, she said, to get ready for the move. Meanwhile she vowed to abide by the revised probation order that Boothby had secured, requiring her to abstain from drugs and alcohol. "It was not that I wanted to charge her," Boothby says, "but I would rather Marlene faced a charge of breach of probation than a charge of killing somebody or assaulting somebody – or killing herself."

The next evening, the night of July 3, the dilemma was taken out of Boothby's hands. Around 7 p.m. a shouting match erupted between Sue Kemsley and several men over a disputed parking space in front of Marlene's apartment building. The commotion brought Marlene out from her first-floor apartment. She joined the verbal uproar, exchanging profanities and insults with the male driver and his five passengers from the safety of the top step of an exterior flight of stairs. After a few minutes of heated argument, the six friends, including a couple who occupied a sixth-floor apartment in Marlene's building, headed up the steps toward Marlene. The man at the front of the procession scuffled with her on the top step.

At the preliminary hearing two weeks later, the man testified that he had spotted a steak knife in Marlene's hand and had lunged for her arm, ending up with a four-stitch cut in his leg. Marlene, who was knocked to the ground, scrambled to her feet and raced inside with the injured man and his friends in pursuit. She slammed her apartment door in their faces. Within a half-hour Marlene opened the door to two uniformed constables from the Metropolitan Toronto Police Force who arrested her and charged her with assault with a weapon. She was taken into custody, held briefly at 14 Division headquarters, then turned over to security staff at the Metro Toronto West Detention Centre.

Marlene had already fired two lawyers – Michael Lomer and a woman named Janet Howard who had taken over from him – by the time Dianne Martin returned from England and agreed to take over the case. She soon discovered that Marlene, who no longer trusted any lawyer, was determined to defend herself and wanted Martin only as a back-up. Martin's job, it seemed, was only to go through the evidence and tell Marlene the correct things to say to the judge. Martin says, "She had a chart of where everybody was, and where the fence was and where she stood, and she had speeches to Your Honour all written out and she didn't want anything to do with a lawyer ever again." Martin abided by Marlene's wishes and, on the day of the trial, informed the judge that she was there merely as a friend of the court.

The judge quickly assessed the situation and requested that all parties, including Marlene, follow him into chambers. "Is this the Marlene Moore I've heard about and are there serious consequences if she is convicted of this offence?" he asked. When the Crown attorney responded that a conviction on an offence of violence could very well trigger the dangerous-offender application, the judge made a swift decision. Back in open court, he explained very kindly, trying not to be patronizing, that he would not proceed until Marlene officially hired Martin. Marlene was furious and, believing Martin had orchestrated the entire event, promptly fired her too.

Still in custody at Metro West, Marlene made a late-night telephone call to another Toronto criminal lawyer, Ed Schofield – the same lawyer who had defended the Jeep driver she'd accused of raping her back in 1975. Schofield could hardly believe that Marlene now wanted him on her side. He was almost equally astounded to learn that the trial was scheduled to open in only seventy-two hours and that Marlene strenuously objected to an adjournment.

More than a decade had passed since Schofield had set eyes on Marlene, though he was aware of her infamy through press reports. Before agreeing to represent her, Schofield first checked to be sure that Marlene knew exactly when and how their paths had once crossed. She did. "She still insisted she was raped, but I detected no sign of antagonism toward me," Schofield says. "We hit it off pretty well."

Fortunately for both Marlene and her new lawyer, Martin had no intention of abandoning her long-time client. Again, Martin was convinced that the story told by the alleged victim lacked credibility. She and Schofield's daughter, a lawyer then newly called to the bar, began some investigative legwork and were still checking witnesses as the trial began. Their efforts proved fruitful.

Martin discovered that the witnesses who had corroborated the victim's story had never been properly, individually interviewed by the police. An officer had simply talked to them briefly as a group without taking notes and then later created eight separate witness statements, all slightly different. At one point during the December jury trial, Martin says, it was corroborated that three or four of the victim's friends were "sitting on him" to keep him from going back at Marlene, "and, yes, he tried to kick her door in and was going to go back a third time."

No weapon was ever recovered, and – after being held in custody for more than five months – Marlene was acquitted of the assault charge. But she was held until two days later, when she was scheduled to make an appearance on the dangerous-weapon charge arising from the incident in June when police had found her in her apartment with a knife in her possession.

On December 9 Marlene was released on bail and she moved into Kemsley's apartment on Berry Road in Etobicoke. As she had the year before, Marlene spent Christmas with June Callwood, joining the grandchildren sprawled on the floor over Snakes and Ladders.

In early 1988 Boothby and Callwood were again immersed in the task of rebuilding a support system for Marlene. They found a psychiatrist for her but Marlene tended to treat psychiatrists, as she did most professionals, as if they were on twenty-four-hour call. One day she turned up at the psychiatrist's office without an appointment. When the psychiatrist wouldn't see her Marlene grabbed a cup, broke it, and right in the office, with the secretary looking on in horror, slashed her abdomen. It was "a terrible cut," Callwood says. "She was going out of control again. It was a steady decline. The slashing got worse. I saw that she just didn't have enough protection on the outside. She wasn't secure enough."

Marlene continued to retreat from friends. By early February Callwood felt herself losing touch. "Sometimes a week or more would go by and I had no contact with her. I didn't know what she was doing."

On February 20, 1988, Marlene was arrested, along with Kemsley, for stealing a carton of cigarettes. Callwood signed the bail papers. Two weeks later Marlene got a break, receiving a one-day jail sentence on the theft charge from provincial court Judge John D. Ord, the same judge who had presided at the trial that sent her to the Prison for Women in spring 1977 following the Vanier hostage-taking. But old legal troubles had caught up with Kemsley and she was taken into custody. Marlene would have to spend the coming weeks alone. "She stopped eating and was living on Diet Pepsi," Martin says. "She phoned and talked in a slurry, hypoglycemic, or drugged manner and cried about wetting the bed. June went over several times but never got let in."

She made a long-distance call to her friend Craig Townson in Guelph. It was the last time they spoke. "She was spinny, spacey," Townson says. "She was obviously drinking or using drugs. She was talking the way I expect manipulative inmates to talk. She had people to blame for everything – everyone but herself."

Marlene had still learned almost nothing about how to fend for herself outside prison. Left to her own resources, she ate badly and slept fitfully. Shortly after Kemsley's release from custody, Marlene turned to robbery and bungled that, stealing women's purses at knifepoint without making any effort to hide her distinctive scars or to venture beyond her own neighbourhood. It was a behaviour totally out of character. She had never initiated crime before, ever. And her fear of men, of rape, became full-blown paranoia. Marlene obtained a gun for self-protection, buying the weapon illegally and in breach of her probation order. Within days Metro Toronto police received a phone call warning them that Marlene had a gun. Acting on the tip, police secured a search warrant for her apartment.

On the evening of March 30, 1988, Marlene was arrested at home. She faced a weapons' charge and three counts of armed robbery. Although Sue Kemsley had tried to stop Marlene, she also was charged with robbery. Martin succeeded in having those charges dropped. Marlene insisted that Martin represent Sue. She told Martin, "I'm bad. I'm hopeless. But you promise me she'll get off."

As for Marlene, it was obvious, according to Ed Schofield, her lawyer, that his client was "done like dinner." He struck a deal with the Crown. Marlene pleaded guilty to the charges in exchange for a five-year sentence and a promise that the dangerous-offender application would not be revived, regardless of the outcome of the as yet-unresolved knife-possession charge from the previous summer.

On April 13, 1988, Marlene returned to the Prison for Women for the last time.

10

Some day I
will die by my own hand

In Marlene's five-year absence there had been a few changes at the Prison for Women in Kingston. Women on the ranges now had hot water in their cells, although there was still none in segregation. Prisoners could purchase stereos and televisions, including cable service, for use in their cells.

The prison had expanded training programs and educational opportunities. Instructors taught woodworking, industrial sewing, food services, offset printing, upholstery, and carpentry. A small number of inmates commuted to the nearby Collins Bay penitentiary for men for courses in auto-body and small-engine repair, and microfilming. Prisoners could take university courses through correspondence and some on-site classroom instruction.

The prison now also featured what inmates referred to as the Little House, a two-bedroom bungalow where women could go for extended visits with family and friends. If scheduling allowed, prisoners could also apply for two or three days of "quiet time" in the Little House. Surrounded by a chain-link fence, it had a well-equipped kitchen, a dining room, and a recreation room in the basement along with a washer and dryer. There was a ping-pong table and a crib. Outside there was a barbecue, a picnic table, and attractive shrubbery.

The prison also had a new warden. In the fall of 1987 Mary Cassidy took over from George Caron. During the previous three years she had served as head of Kingston Penitentiary, becoming the first female warden of a maximum-security men's prison in Canada. Her rise through the ranks, from her first corrections job in 1967 as a secretary at Warkworth Institution, an hour's drive west of Kingston, has been dissected by the media, corrections staff, and prisoners alike. She came under heavy criticism from the guards union at Kingston Penitentiary, being accused of everything from spending too much time away from the prison to spending too much money on a flower pot. Relations with front-line staff became especially strained in the spring of 1986, when she came down hard on three guards for their involvement in an assault on a prisoner. She fired one of them and handed out $6,000 in fines to the others.

Controversy followed Cassidy when she moved across the street to the women's prison. The legacy of being a woman in authority in the pervasively male penitentiary system creates its own tensions. Now Cassidy found herself responsible for implementing a decision by the national headquarters of the Correctional Service of Canada to bring a small number of women formerly housed in protective custody back into the general prison population. Protective custody was a self-contained unit that had long been reserved for inmates deemed outcasts because their crimes involved abuse of children.

When Marlene arrived back at P4W, authorities had yet to resolve the protective-custody issue. Hostility was mounting among inmates, between prisoners and guards, and between unionized staff and management. The month before Marlene's return sixty-eight prisoners had filed a group grievance, expressing concerns about an escalation in the number of severe slashings and the use of punitive segregation as a response.

Inmates demanded changes in the treatment of self-mutilators, including better medical care and access to "outside crisis intervention volunteers." Their grievance ran into a bureaucratic brick wall. Cassidy returned the complaint and, in a memorandum dated March 25, 1988, quoted internal prison regulations known as Commissioner's Directives to support her position that their grievance was out of line because they were only indirectly affected by slashings.

The slashings continued. On April 23 a young native prisoner – the woman whose self-mutilation had sparked the group petition – cut her own throat for the second time in six weeks. Cassidy summoned psychologist Marsha Lomis from the Vanier Centre to take a closer look at the disturbing phenomenon. Lomis interviewed six prisoners whose identities are thinly veiled by the use of initials only. Among the prisoners was Marlene.

On their first meeting, Cassidy found the new prisoner "very, very thin, and very badly scarred but still with lots of spunk and spirit. She was kind of an enchanting little woman, especially on her good days, with a delightful wit and personality." Marlene, who knew of the warden from her days as head of Joyceville Institution when Curry Moore was incarcerated there, mischievously informed Cassidy that she would be calling her "Dawson," rather than by her new married name.

It was clear from the beginning, though, that Marlene was in physical and emotional distress. On her first day back she dropped by the inmate committee office and spoke briefly with Gayle Horii, the elected chairperson. "She was very weak and nearly incoherent," Horii recorded in her diary. Horii also remarked on how very thin Marlene was and noted that "though her mind energy was high she would lose her train of thought." Horii wrote that Marlene was bumping into furniture and that she said she needed glasses. The next day Marlene caused a scene by butting her cigarette in another prisoner's salad dish, a dish made of the same black plastic as the dining room ashtrays. Guards moved in to break up an angry shoving match between Marlene and the woman whose meal she had sullied. In less than twenty-four hours the destructive misconduct and punishment that had marked Marlene's earlier imprisonment at Kingston resumed. Both women were temporarily locked up in segregation cells.

A few days later the prisoners' committee filed an official complaint about excessive use of segregation by the prison administration. The committee referred to an inmate named Dianne who had been moved to the unit after slashing her arms, neck, and stomach. "This is the sixth incident of slashing that I'm aware of and the third where the person required an ambulance to outside hospital this year," Gayle Horii wrote. "The tension at P4W is high. Without a sense of order and confidence that emergency situations will be attended to in a professional, humane fashion, the tension promises to escalate." Horii was worried that other inmates, including Marlene, would be unable to withstand the pressure and also begin slashing. "Women cannot shut out the pain of their neighbors, and each incident threatens to become a contagious epidemic," she wrote. Her report also contained a description of the unit: "Segregation at P4W still has no hot water, cells have no flooring, only concrete, toilets are rusted out and putrid, bars are painted black in keeping with the punishment theme. The psychological damage done to the women in segregation is beyond the punishment of the prison sentence, the separation from one's family. It is straight torture for any human person to be subject to cages such as these."

While the administration studied options designed to stem the flow of blood behind the limestone walls, the turmoil at the prison intensified Marlene's anger and pain. Her frustration was aggravated by her physical condition. She experienced chronic pain from her bladder problems and was humiliated because of her incontinence, which forced her to seek relief through a catheter. Horii recalls a day in April when Marlene, suffering because she couldn't urinate on her own, became extremely agitated by a delay in response to her demand to see a nurse. Marlene climbed a painter's scaffold that had been erected inside the cell block and, in Horii's words, "began ranting and jumping up and down."

On April 26 prison guards returned Marlene to the segregation unit, where she spent most, if not all, of the next eight weeks. There she became involved in an altercation with a male guard and slashed herself. Afterwards she filed a grievance against the prison employee, alleging he had punched her in the head and thrown her to the floor. Three months later the federal government's correctional investigator, Ron Stewart, replied: "There is no doubt that the description of events provided by staff differed with that of the inmates. However, without any concrete evidence substantiating one version over the other, we are not in a position to accurately determine if the force used was excessive."

In May Marlene wrote a series of letters from her segregation cell to her friends in the general population. In a scrawling, four-page letter to Horii, she complained that nine guards had been dispatched to take her to segregation, and she described another slashing:

"This time Gayle, I went under [lost consciousness] & the hospital gave the guards shit & ast how long was she bleeding & I had oxigen on, but coming threw, I had no blood pressure. & they ast why'd you bring her here after bleeding since 1/4 to 5 & the ambulance was called at 10 2 11 . . . ."

She sent a second brief, plaintive note on May 10: "Gayle. The night I slashed I went to the hospital under. When I came back at 3 a.m. I put my mattress under the bed & my cell was cleaned out, but they left the thing I slashed with inside my cell. What are they trying to tell me. Keep doing it."

A few weeks later the inmate committee raised the issue of Marlene's treatment at a meeting with prison staff. Horii's notes on the discussion are terse: "Why continue to segregate when [it] doesn't stop her from slashing? We asked for a chance to help her in the population. Denied."

One respite from this bleak period was the spring powwow organized by the prison's Native Sisterhood. Marlene, given permission to attend, joined scores of inmates and their guests for a day of tribal dances, songs, and traditional foods that embody the sacred beliefs and ceremonies of native spirituality.

Fran Sugar, a young Saskatchewan native who headed the Sisterhood for several years until her release from prison in late 1988, believes that native culture held special appeal for Marlene after the death of Isabella Ogima, her partner in the 1977 hostage-taking at the Vanier Centre, and the 1980 suicide of Arlene Cote, also a native prisoner. Marlene shyly participated in native rituals while she was in segregation, including chants and the burning of sweetgrass. Sugar says that Marlene was "very forgiving of native women," that she gently and genuinely tried to mix with the native community. "That was really nice, and I found that to be probably the most humble part of her personality."

But Marlene's encounter with native spirituality brought only fleeting release from her consuming anger, Sugar says. "It was a nightmare doing time with her. Her anger would be totally directed at the screws. She could go for days, literally for days, without sleeping. She'd maybe be quiet for ten or fifteen minutes." Otherwise, Sugar says, she'd rock. "Sometimes she'd sing or laugh hysterically."

Marlene's physical health continued to deteriorate. Terri-Lee Seeley, the Elizabeth Fry social worker, remembers catching a glimpse of Marlene in a hallway at the Kingston prison sometime in the late spring or early summer of 1988. "It was like seeing a ghost," she says. "We saw each other and both looked in recognition, but it wasn't until she walked away that I really knew who she was. She was pale and stooped over. She was just a mess."

Others were also shaken by Marlene's appearance. The last time Allan Manson saw her "she was almost gaunt. My mind flashed back to seeing her standing there in the witness stand in 1978. She was a pretty woman and self-conscious about a few scars on her arms. The physical change over the ten years was dramatic." Mary Morissette, the senior guard who remembered Marlene from her earlier stretch at the women's prison, said Marlene had deteriorated so badly that she looked almost skeletal.

By mid-June Marlene was confined to the prison hospital, where she remained throughout the summer. Her close friend and fellow prisoner Barb Dennis was allowed to make regular visits. Security staff would summon Dennis from the range at odd hours, when Marlene was flipping out from loneliness and depression and from the debilitating pain and the embarrassment caused by her lack of bladder control. One holiday weekend prison authorities gave Dennis permission to stay in hospital with Marlene when the prison was short-staffed. "We talked for hours. She was in a lot of pain. She was sick and she did a lot of crying." When she was able to work, Marlene kept busy by painting and doing repairs in the hospital area. She proudly showed Dennis the tools that the warden had authorized for her use.

Over the summer Marlene also began to press Dennis for details of her sessions with prison psychologist Julie Darke, a contract employee and a specialist in working with incest survivors. Dennis says it was like Marlene was fishing for information. "She was happy for me. She didn't want to see me hurt myself. She kept asking me a lot about getting help, but then this wall would go up." Marlene listened attentively to her friend's description of a book about incest, but she repeatedly refused Dennis's offers to lend her the book. She didn't want people to know about her past. "I don't want the nurses to see the book," Marlene told Dennis.

For two months, in June and July, Marlene also went for counselling from the psychologist. Darke found her to be a complex woman who felt betrayed by her past dealings with mental health professionals. "Her level of trust was very low. I knew I had to move carefully. She needed to feel safe in her sessions with me." But suddenly Marlene decided to end the sessions, too frightened by the depth of her emotional pain. When it got to the point where it started to really hurt, she would pull away. "She didn't want the pain of dealing with whatever it was in her past," Mary Cassidy says. "She would say that it hurt too much." Julie Darke didn't forget about Marlene, though. Later that summer she received a flyer about a book that was being published in the United States containing stories written by women who had self-mutilated. "I sent it up to her, simply for her information, to let her know that she wasn't alone," Darke says.

At one point during the summer when Cassidy knew she was going to be away from the institution for three weeks, she extracted a promise from Marlene not to slash or "do foolish things to cause problems" during her absence. "She gave me her word and she kept it," the warden says. "It didn't last long after I got back. It used to be one day at a time. But we knew that if she gave us her word it was golden. I'm not aware that she ever welshed on a promise."

In the fall of 1988 lawyers Ed Schofield and Dianne Martin teamed up for an unusual legal manoeuvre that closed the books on Marlene's outstanding weapons-possession charge. The trial had been postponed repeatedly because prison officials failed to turn up with Marlene as scheduled. Finally the two lawyers took matters into their own hands. Martin donned her gown and Schofield took the witness stand, testifying about the delays. Their double-barrelled appeal to the bench resulted in the case being tossed out of court. Marlene greeted the news with delight and gratitude, but the phone call from Schofield brought only momentary relief.

By October Marlene was back in the general population. Warden Cassidy went out of her way to spend time with Marlene, going to her cell on the range for quiet talks and urging her to return to the hospital. She also tried to launch Marlene on a journal-writing project, suggesting that during times when she was lonely or couldn't sleep she try to write down her thoughts. "I told her early on if she got really upset about things, instead of slashing herself or acting out against staff she should try to sit down and write what she was thinking and feeling and that might help get rid of some of the frustrations. She did a lot of that. I didn't get a lot of what she wrote. Sometimes she would tell me that she wrote a lot of really rotten stuff but that she had ripped it up before sending anything to me."

Marlene also seemed to become more open, disclosing her feelings during long, private conversations in her cell with the warden. "Slashing was her way of punishing herself," Cassidy says. "If she did something that she thought was bad and we didn't do something to her, she felt that she should have sanctions." Marlene's slashing was also her way of alleviating the frustration and anger she felt toward others. By hurting herself, she was less likely to hurt others she really didn't want to hurt.

Cassidy and some guards and prisoners who had known Marlene over the years pleaded with her to admit herself to the hospital. Friends and keepers spoke openly about their concerns for Marlene's failing physical and mental health. In mid-fall, prison health-care staff arranged for Marlene to see an urologist, who recommended that she begin using an indwelling catheter and launched a series of tests, including an ultrasound, in an attempt to discover the source of her severe pain. Marlene's condition had been diagnosed as tonic enlarged bladder, but health-care staff had been unable to determine why she was in such pain. Desperate for some relief and frustrated that no one could find a cure to her problem, Marlene became increasingly despondent.

Marlene had to wear a urine bag, which meant constant attention to keep it clean and functioning properly, Dennis says. "She was getting blood clots they had to watch, and out on A range they couldn't do that. The nurses couldn't spend time on the range." Dennis says she tried to talk her into going back to the hospital, but Marlene wouldn't budge. Dennis was worried because she could see that Marlene just didn't have the physical stamina to exert herself or to recover from the blood she lost when she slashed. "Marlene was in pain and mad at everybody, at the world, the doctors, everybody."

Predictably, Marlene's pain spilled out in torrents of verbal abuse of staff. In early October she was sentenced to forty days in segregation after a confrontation with a nurse. She spent her thirty-first birthday, October 29, in segregation.

Two weeks later, around noon on November 10, Marlene tied a rope around her neck and tried to hang herself in her cell. Linda Cowan, the guard on duty, was alerted by an inmate yelling from the upper tier of cells that something was wrong with Marlene, who was locked in one of four camera-monitored cells on the lower level. When she saw Marlene hanging in the cell, Cowan ran to the guard station, hit an emergency button, and grabbed some scissors. She then saw, on camera, Marlene lift herself out of the noose, retreat to her bed, and begin rocking violently, alone in her misery.

Late in the afternoon that day, prison nurse Lorraine Quinton went to segregation to distribute medication. By then Marlene was taking several different types of medication for her bladder condition and for pain. Quinton saw that the prisoner had tied a blue blanket across her cell bars to obscure the view inside. When the nurse announced herself, Marlene stuck her arm out to retrieve her pills. Quinton told her she had to see her face before she could hand over the medication. When Marlene co-operated by pulling the blanket back a few inches, Quinton saw bruises, burns, and abrasions in her neck area. She watched as Marlene swallowed with a wince.

In a letter written four days after her attempted suicide to a long-time friend and former P4W inmate, Hasholina O'Keefe, Marlene confided her anguish: "I'm wetting all over the place. I dont feel good at all. Im sorry you guys I dont mean to wet – I cant stop. Bag or no bag. Im reelly embarrest. ashamed. hurt. I began to hate myself, ya no. Cuz I think whod want a person like me around. You no what I mean. I isolate myself cuz of this. Im juss so mad at myself cuz I cant stop."

The letter described a late-night slashing that brought a dozen guards to segregation to move her to another cell in the unit. Staff "threatened to get the men over from KP [Kingston Penitentiary] to handcuff me to the bars," she wrote, adding that she faced "another charge of throwing blood" at a guard.

Curry Moore waited anxiously for a reply to a letter he had mailed to Marlene soon after she returned to the federal prison. "She never replied, and that wasn't like Marlene," he says.

Moore became worried and phoned the institution, asking for information about his sister. The institution refused to let him speak with her. He phoned a second time, making up a story about pending heart surgery, and learned that Marlene was unavailable because she was confined to segregation.

November unleashed extraordinary tension: a double stabbing and a rash of assaults and suicide attempts. On November 23 all prisoners were locked in their cells after two women suffered stab wounds that required treatment at hospital. Security staff rounded up more than a dozen women over the next forty-eight hours, plucking from the general population those prisoners who were suspected of involvement in the violence or alleged to have used contraband drugs. The eleven cells in punitive segregation were filled, then the adjoining eight-cell "quiet" side was pressed into service. Marlene occupied a camera-monitored cell on the lower tier of the eleven-cell unit.

Guards blamed Mary Cassidy for the turmoil at the prison, saying she had undermined security by being too soft on inmates. The Elizabeth Fry Society cited constant delays in parole hearings as a source of extreme frustration among inmates. For their part, prison administrators said a sudden influx of illegal drugs into the institution had led to havoc in the population. Whatever the reason, relations between prisoners and guards had become especially strained, with many staff strenuously protesting the working conditions in segregation. Mary Morissette said arguments broke out among guards as well as between guards and the administration about how Marlene's demanding and disruptive behaviour should be handled.

"It had to be yes all the time," Morissette says. "She would want things that other inmates didn't normally have and she'd send word down that if the guard didn't give it to her she was going to slash. She held slashing over our heads and she would invariably get her way. I would get very angry because I never thought we were teaching her anything, except that was a method she could use all the time. And I worried what was going to happen when we finally did have to say no. A lot of other inmates resented that Marlene got away with a lot more than anybody else."

One morning Marlene refused to get out of bed when coffee was served at 7 a.m., and a half-hour later she asked Morissette for a cup of instant. The guard informed her that she wasn't getting any special treatment from her. Marlene, who frequently kept a cup of urine in reserve in case she needed it, doused Morissette.

By then Marlene was overwhelmed by rage and despair. Weak and plagued with crippling pain, desperately lonely for Sue Kemsley and her other Toronto friends, she had no one to comfort her, no one to listen to her side of the story. Her feelings of powerlessness and hostility toward her keepers escalated day by day, and she began to use her slashing both as a means of attracting attention and as a weapon.

Unlike segregation in the male institutions, where cells have solid doors, the women's unit is open-barred. At times guards resort to carrying portable shields for protection against body fluids thrown by inmates. "Can you imagine the ludicrousness of that?" Morissette asks. "Trying to hold a shield while carrying a tray of food for some inmate. Usually the stuff would come down over you anyway, and go all over your face and hair. I've seen officers whose scalps were burned by urine." Some staff also had concerns for their own health, afraid because they'd heard Marlene was a hepatitis-B carrier.

In an attempt to address some of the inconsistency in the staff's treatment of Marlene, Warden Cassidy posted a memorandum outlining how the prisoner's medical needs were to be handled. Still, Morissette and other staff members implored the administration to transfer Marlene from the segregation unit to the hospital. "She was too ill," Morissette says. "I thought she was punishing us by staying in segregation where no one wanted her to be. It was just not the place for someone who had the medical illness that Marlene had." But the wilful prisoner clung to her precious prison code – the unspoken rules that bond inmates – and insisted on doing her segregation time. "She thought it was not macho to do otherwise," Cassidy said later. Marlene was existing on sheer determination, as if giving in to the wishes of the administration meant giving up everything.

There were times, Morissette says, when Marlene's physical pain was so intense she could barely stand up. "When it got bad, she wanted somebody there helping her. And I'm sure it was very real because Marlene could take an awful lot of pain." Morissette began to think that Marlene might be contemplating suicide. "I was believing that the illness was just too much for her to handle. Her bravado was all she had." Morissette could also see that the attention-seeking slashing was becoming far more serious, that this time there was a noticeable difference. "She had broken down so much more than she had ever broken down. The fight wasn't there as it had been there before."

Mary Cassidy began consultations with the prison psychiatrist about whether Marlene could be transferred to either the women's treatment centre at Kingston Penitentiary or committed to the psychiatric hospital in St. Thomas, even though she had never been diagnosed with a psychiatric disorder. By this point, Cassidy says, after the months of slashing and throwing urine and blood, she felt as a warden that the staff needed a break as much as Marlene. But after talking to the doctor, Marlene told Cassidy that if they did anything to ship her out she would do something right away to strike back – "so forget about it." Cassidy told Marlene that she was trying to find things that would be of benefit to her, and that she wasn't trying to get rid of her. But Marlene had made her point. She didn't want to go to a psychiatric facility.

Prisoners diagnosed as schizophrenic, severely depressed, or psychotic were transferred to a secure unit at the St. Thomas psychiatric hospital. The only alternative for women like Marlene who haven't been officially classified mentally ill is the women's treatment centre in the penitentiary across the street. The ten-bed unit there is a component of the Regional Treatment Centre, housed in an east block of the maximum-security men's prison. The small, ground-level range of cells, looking out over a noisy prison compound, is dungeon-like. In its narrow corridors the women sit in small groups sipping coffee or playing cards or just staring at the cement walls and ceilings, which are cluttered with the steel entrails of the building's plumbing and heating system.

But it's not the physical austerity that deters many women from seeking treatment at the centre. Transfer to the women's unit means prisoners lose access to the educational and employment programs available at the women's prison. There is also a certain stigma attached to the unit because of the large number of protective-custody inmates who end up there: Many women don't care to associate with these prison untouchables. But even more repugnant for the women prisoners, most of whom have been physically and sexually assaulted by men, is the idea of being housed in the same building as rapists. Close to one-third of the ninety-two beds in the Regional Treatment Centre are filled by men undergoing treatment for sex offences. To try to make women there feel as safe as possible, the prison sees that they are escorted at all times by a staff member. But limited staffing resources means that women have to join groups dominated by male inmates if they want to participate in vocational programs. The prospect of being transferred to the treatment centre horrified Marlene.

Given the prison's limited repertoire of responses to emotional suffering, Marlene's self-destructive acts presented P4W staff with a clear dilemma. Morissette says that one choice was to gather together enough staff to go into Marlene's cell and forcibly take her blade away – which, given Marlene's medical condition, meant possible injury for the prisoner in the physical confrontation that would inevitably ensue. The other alternative, as staff saw it, was to keep her under twenty-four-hour observation by camera monitor, an invasion of privacy that Marlene detested. Guards often opted for outright manipulation, telling Marlene that as long as she was threatening to hurt herself they would have to put her cell on camera.

Still, this was an uneasy solution. Guards were loathe to

provoke Marlene with the camera light but were terrified of the risk that she might manage to seriously harm herself given an opportunity. Most often, the compromise solution was to make frequent rounds of the unit to check on her. "Sometimes, she would sit there in a corner and think and think and think. And sometimes she'd rock. You learned to watch her," Morissette says.

For the most part Morissette and other security staff stoically carried out their duties as prescribed, knowing that the prison couldn't offer Marlene what she really needed more than anything else: comfort. "Inside the institution, there was no one to really hold her at this point," Morissette says. Morissette was one guard who sensed the vulnerability beneath Marlene's tough demeanour. "She had the ability to draw you into her. She could do that. There was always something of the lost little girl quality about her."

On the evening of November 25, hysteria swept through segregation as a phalanx of guards struggled to cut down Brenda Blondell, who hanged herself in her cell on the upper tier. The unconscious prisoner was rushed by ambulance to Kingston General Hospital, where she remained in serious condition for several days before being moved to the prison hospital. Before dawn there would be two more attempted suicides in the unit.

Marlene responded to the chaotic scene in the only way she knew. She draped a blanket over the bars of her cell and began to slash, ignoring the screams of other prisoners begging her to stop. She methodically squeezed her blood into a paper cup and flung the contents onto the concrete floor outside her cell. Just before midnight two guards donned protective coveralls and moved a Plexiglas barrier into position across the front of her cell. It was a portable shield that had been specially constructed the first week of October, following a similar bloody assault on the staff by Marlene. A prison nurse entered her cell and applied cold towels to the cuts on the inside of her thigh. Later Morissette escorted Marlene to the institution hospital for medical treatment. "She had so much scar tissue on her arms that she was beginning to go to other parts of her body," the guard says. A few hours later guards returned Marlene to segregation.

Gayle Horii, who was summoned to segregation in the middle of the frenetic outbreak, wrote in her diary: "It is 1:45. I am unbelieving of the scene. I will never forget it. The suffering must stop. It must stop."

About eighty prisoners – almost every woman not locked in segregation – assembled in the exercise yard the next afternoon. The Native Sisterhood offered the ceremonial songs and prayers of a healing circle. Individual women stepped forward and pledged to restore peace and set aside past wrongs. Fran Sugar says, "It was an act of coming together by the population to make sure the administration knew we would keep the peace."

During the next week, the final days of Marlene's life, the inmate committee lobbied the administration for the release of the women in segregation.

On December 2 Marlene asked the assistant warden of security, Therese Decaire, to check on the status of seven new disciplinary charges related to spitting and throwing body fluids at staff. Because of these charges Marlene had been sentenced to another forty-five days of punitive segregation. As a matter of prison policy, a sentence of more than thirty days requires the approval of the region's deputy commissioner. Decaire found that the deputy commissioner had recommended that the time Marlene had already spent in segregation be counted against her new sentence. He also directed that she be allowed to spend the fifteen days still outstanding in the prison hospital. When Decaire gave her the news, Marlene immediately stated that she wanted to go to the hospital, and Decaire took her there later that afternoon. "She was moving very slowly," Decaire says. "She was very thin and very pale. . . . By the time we got to the hospital, she was totally exhausted."

The next day Marlene was dead.

Minutes after nurse Marsha Brown found Marlene's body,

shortly before 5:30 p.m. on December 3, normal prison routine was suspended. The prison postponed evening medical rounds and locked inmates on the ranges. Even before security staff summoned inmate-committee members throughout the prison and told them of Marlene's death, the prisoners knew something was horribly wrong. "A matron was crying hysterically," Sugar recalled. "That's the first time I've ever seen a screw cry."

Within a few hours guards had returned the women in segregation to the ranges, and off-duty staff and community volunteers began arriving at the prison. The prison postponed its normal 11 p.m. lock-up. At midnight about thirty prisoners on A range formed a circle and sang "A Strong Woman's Song" – an honour song for the spirit among native peoples.

Three days after Marlene's death, on Tuesday, December 6, prisoners and staff attended a memorial service at the penitentiary. On Friday, December 9, family members and friends gathered at the Ward Funeral Home in Toronto for the funeral service, an event that attracted an inordinate number of Toronto police cruisers. Barb Dennis was there, under prison escort. Curry Moore was absent: he was recovering from self-inflicted injuries. The previous night he had been found outside his cell at the Hamilton-Wentworth Detention Centre, bleeding from cuts to his wrists, ankles, and neck. Marlene's brother had slashed himself because prison officials had refused to let him wear a suit to the funeral home. Jail policy requires that prisoners dress in regulation-issue clothes on visits to funeral homes.

Marlene was cremated. Much later, on the second Saturday of October 1989, members of her family gathered for a wake in Toronto. That day they headed north to Lake Wilcox, where they scattered her ashes to the wind.

11

The worse thing I ever did
was to live

On the morning of Sunday, December 4, 1988, members of the board of the Canadian Association of Elizabeth Fry Societies (CAEFS) gathered at the advocacy group's sixth-floor Bank Street office in downtown Ottawa for an executive meeting. They had just settled back in their chairs for a short break when executive director Bonnie Diamond was called to the phone. On the other end of the line was a reporter from the Kingston *Whig-Standard*, breaking the news of Marlene's death the previous afternoon.

"It was a real shot of reality into a board setting, where you sometimes get away from the brutality of what you're dealing with," Diamond recalled more than a year later. "A very complicated process set in after that, but what we felt immediately was helplessness. And as we spread the word among the membership the next day, that was the overwhelming response. Marlene was a profound symbol of what can go wrong with women in conflict with the law."

Elizabeth Fry representatives, soon inundated with calls from the media, told reporters that the prison system had failed to provide Marlene with the help she desperately needed. Board member Beth Stacey, a former executive director of the Elizabeth Fry Society of Kingston, said she didn't know what would have been the proper place to offer treatment for Marlene – but locking her up at the Prison for Women was "like trying to make an ice sculpture in a furnace room." CAEFS national president Felicity Hawthorn described Marlene's experience with the criminal justice system as "a very sad comment on how we deal with people," asserting that her death was "a tragedy that should not have occurred."

Marlene's friends were grief-stricken and appalled that someone with so much promise had been unable to get the help she needed to survive. "She was a wonderful person," Janice Cole said. "People were attracted to the idea of helping her. She was a gifted person with a lot of loyalty. People like that are hard to find. . . . A lot of people would go to the end of the line to give her whatever they could and she always responded. You weren't hitting your head against a brick wall."

June Callwood expressed despair over her own inability, and that of others, to save Marlene. "I think we could have helped. I always thought we could have done something, right up until that last summer when I didn't know what to do any more – I just watched it play out."

After Marlene died probation officer Suzanne Boothby got four or five phone calls from people working in corrections, but she says it wasn't until one of Marlene's lawyers, Michael Lomer, called – someone who had also tried to help Marlene – that she broke down and cried. "In one way I wasn't surprised. I knew that Marlene wouldn't make it out of the Prison for Women alive."

Dianne Martin said Marlene was a prime example of how inept the justice and corrections system is at responding to human suffering. "In many ways she highlighted the inadequacies and inconsistencies of the system because there was a real person in that damaged shell. You could not, as comfortably as the system does with others, either blame her or leave her to sort it out herself."

Even though many people agreed that Marlene could be helped, Martin said, the awful reality was that there was nothing there for her. "That reality kills you. We provide help so badly and we continue to do it badly."

It was now paramount, Martin said, for an in-depth investigation into how the prison system contributed to Marlene's death. "Whom did they ask for help in dealing with troubled women like Marlene?" Martin asked. "Jails and jail officials use the damn Nuremburg Defence. They say these are our instructions and we followed them the best we could, and we saw people deteriorate and die right before our eyes but we can't be held responsible. But who did they complain to about their resources? That's the main question."

In the days and weeks following Marlene's death, Elizabeth Fry staff and volunteers went into the Prison for Women, supporting Marlene's bereaved friends with "a kind of grief counselling" that mirrored their own anger and sorrow. Beyond that concrete step, the association began to consider a more formal response to the much-publicized tragedy. Workers debated about what to do with the flood of media requests for information on Marlene. "It was certainly a story that caught the imagination of the public but not in a way that seemed very meaningful to us," Diamond says. "Nobody wanted to deal with it in the depth that we thought would do anything but declare Marlene – one last time – the most dangerous woman in Canada."

CAEFS members were torn by conflicting demands. Women who had worked closely with Marlene felt protective of her privacy and bound to respect her oft-repeated pleas that she be left alone by reporters. At the same time, the Elizabeth Fry felt a deep obligation to contribute somehow to public awareness of the desperate need for resources to help countless girls and women repair their damaged lives and escape the destructive cycle of abuse and imprisonment.

Within days of the discovery of Marlene's body, pressure

began to mount to broaden the scope of the coroner's inquest. In Kingston a citizens' coalition was formed, drawing members from prisoners' support groups and Queen's University students and professors. Dubbing themselves the Prison for Women Watch, the coalition announced plans for a public vigil with a dual purpose: to serve as a memorial for Marlene, and to launch a campaign for more public accountability on the part of the Correctional Service of Canada. In a press release the organizing committee urged that both former and current prisoners be granted standing at the coroner's inquest, "without limitations on numbers."

Just before dusk on a bitterly cold Sunday afternoon, twelve days after Marlene's funeral, some forty people gathered in a parking lot across the street from the federal penitentiary for the candlelight vigil. They stood silently as speakers denounced the Prison for Women: Marlene's suicide, they said, was the tragic consequence of "evil" conditions inside the walls. "There's a good deal of public concern that Marlene's death is not an isolated incident but that her death was the culmination of the violence and repression that have scarred the prison in the preceding month," Ronnie Leah, a Queen's sociology professor, told the assembled mourners. "We are very concerned . . . that prisoners are being incited and then unduly punished within the institution."

After the main group had retreated into the warmth of a nearby building, a half-dozen men and women clustered on the sidewalk in front of the prison's main entrance. Prison staff summoned Kingston city police and the group dispersed quietly under the watchful eye of uniformed constables. Although the citizen's coalition vanished as quickly as it sprung into existence, the ninety-minute demonstration had signalled unprecedented public concern over the death of a prisoner. The mood was ripe, it seemed, for a coroner's inquest that would put the administration of the Prison for Women on trial.

Felicity Hawthorn, who acted as lawyer for the CAEFS during the inquest, met with prisoners shortly after Marlene's death and advised them to consider carefully the possible ramifications of seeking an official role at the inquest. She was convinced that some guards might not take too kindly to any prisoner who had played a part in having them subpoenaed as a witness. She says, "I didn't consciously try to do scaremongering with them, but I was honest in telling them that when any prisoner considers any form of litigation, they have to be aware there are consequences to that, even if the warden says there won't be." Members of the inmate committee asked Hawthorn whether the CAEFS would consider applying for "standing," and for the first time members of the organization found themselves taking a long, hard look at whether they could make a difference in the outcome of Marlene's inquest.

By Ontario law it has been mandatory since 1887 for a coroner's inquest to be held whenever a death occurs inside a prison. "Standing" – a designation a coroner can grant to individuals or groups who apply at the outset of public proceedings – confers the right to call and cross-examine witnesses and make submissions to the jury. At the time no prisoners committee had ever secured standing at an Ontario inquest, although at least a half-dozen applications from elected inmate representatives had gone before Kingston-area coroners since the mid-1970s. All were denied.

There would be no break with tradition when lawyer Allan Manson, acting for the national Elizabeth Fry, made application for standing before Coroner Clifford Meyer on the morning of June 21, 1989. Less than two weeks earlier the CAEFS board had voted unanimously at its annual meeting in Kamloops, B.C., to go ahead with its unprecedented bid for an official role at the inquest. The organization was still waiting for a response from Legal Aid on its funding request. "One of the biggest problems we faced was gaining the courage to use money we didn't have," Diamond admits. "Our sum total set aside for legal fees was $1,500."

Even with pledges from lawyers Allan Manson and Felicity Hawthorn to work for expenses only in the event that grant money was not obtained, the CAEFS decision represented an act of faith, a tenuous hope that individual Canadians would rescue the already financially strapped organization from a potentially crippling debt. "We believed that if we could help people to understand the reality of Marlene's life, and how scarce the resources in society were to help somebody like Marlene, that her life would become meaningful in terms of getting more resources," Diamond says. The stakes were too high not to proceed. With standing, CAEFS believed it could convince jurors of the need for radical reform "to avoid some of the mistakes that the criminal justice system had made in the administration of Marlene's case."

When the inquest opened at 9 a.m. on June 21 before a packed courtroom at the Frontenac County Court House, a massive limestone edifice overlooking the city's largest park, Elizabeth Fry members from Toronto, Ottawa, and Hamilton were seated alongside their Kingston colleagues in the first two rows. The CAEFS's application for standing – and Marlene's notorious legacy as the "most dangerous woman" in Canada – had ensured the inquest of public and press attention. As it turned out, the association's determination that the inquest examine Marlene's death "not as an event but a process," in the words of Allan Manson, would derail the proceedings abruptly in the late afternoon, cutting off chilling testimony about Marlene's final hours.

But first, in the morning session, Coroner Meyer rejected Manson's arguments for full rights of participation for CAEFS, saying that he remained unconvinced the advocacy group had specific knowledge related to the direct circumstances of Marlene's death. Felicity Hawthorn had expected to take over from Manson once standing had been secured but instead soon found herself, along with Bonnie Diamond, in a car en route to Ottawa where they hoped to get a court injunction to halt the inquest proceedings.

Desperate to make their 4 p.m. appointment with a Supreme Court of Ontario judge, the two "drove like maniacs" through torrential rains that scared most other drivers off the road. In Ottawa Hawthorn succeeded in persuading Mr. Justice James Chadwick to issue a restraining order, pending judicial review of the standing application. Within minutes the order was transmitted by telephone from the court office in Ottawa to the Kingston registrar, who delivered it to Manson in the court-room. By then the sun had broken out in the nation's capital, and CBC cameras were waiting outside the Ottawa Supreme Court building to capture a jubilant embrace between Haw-thorn and Diamond.

In Kingston Manson burst into the courtroom at 4:35 p.m., holding aloft the court order. Two witnesses had already completed their testimony and prison nurse Marsha Brown was on the stand. The nurse had just described her dealings with Marlene throughout the Saturday afternoon of December 3, 1988. Before she could explain why she had ordered the death scene cleaned up before police were called, the hastily secured judicial order adjourned the inquest.

The high court had agreed to hear the Elizabeth Fry argu-ments for standing on July 4. Circumstances intervened, how-ever, in the form of a long-awaited split-decision by the divisional court of the Supreme Court of Ontario, which granted standing to twenty inmates of the super-protective custody unit at Kingston Penitentiary. The judicial review had been initiated in the summer of 1988 when the applicants, represented by Toronto lawyer Dianne Martin, were denied standing by regional coroner Dr. Walter Harris at an inquest into the suicide of protective-custody inmate Michael Zu-bresky. In the majority ruling released on June 28, 1989, Justice Archie Campbell said the coroner had erred by relying on too narrow a test for standing.

The judiciary's advocacy of a broader approach to standing did not go unheeded by key players in the unresolved contro-versy that had shut down the inquest into Marlene's death. At the request of the Ontario Attorney General's office the Su-preme Court hearing was delayed, and in late July the Chief Coroner's office announced its acceptance of the CAEFS's appli-cation for standing.

More than four months would pass before the public inquiry got back on track. In the meantime Elizabeth Fry began to map out its strategy for the inquest during long hours of consultation between Hawthorn and an advisory committee made up of the heads of the three Ontario chapters that had worked directly with Marlene over the years, along with Diamond and CAEFS board member Beth Stacey, who had frequently visited Marlene at P4W. Meanwhile, the financial burden had been eased considerably by Legal Aid's decision to pick up the tab for lawyers' fees and other expenses.

Strategy discussions covered the whole spectrum of concerns about how and why women come into conflict with the law and what happens to them afterwards. Diamond says that as the group explored the wider and the narrower approaches to the issue, "It became obvious that what really concerned us was not so much the death of Marlene but the deterioration process. . . . We felt that if you could prevent a young girl who was sexually abused from being incarcerated – and if you could bring to her a type of healing help at that time – that would be the biggest contribution we could make."

The inquest began anew in early December, a year after Marlene died in the prison hospital. CAEFS now had its chance to influence the recommendations of a coroner's jury.

Early on Wednesday morning, December 6, 1989, close to fifty spectators filed into the five double rows of public benches in the imposing, high-ceiling courtroom at the Frontenac County Court House. The sombre event attracted people from every corner of the corrections system, along with television, radio, and newspaper reporters from Ottawa, Toronto, and Kingston.

Elizabeth Fry representatives again filled two front benches. Two former wardens of the Prison for Women, Douglas Chinnery and Don Clark, sat at the rear of the court. The current warden Mary Cassidy also looked on from a back bench. Beside her, for much of the proceedings, sat Adrienne Brown, chairperson of the prison's Citizens' Advisory Committee, a group of ordinary people appointed by the Ontario regional headquarters to advise the prison's top administrator. Daryl Dollan, Marlene's close friend from P4W, was there, along with scores of prison staff, some of them sitting nervously as they waited to be called to the stand as witnesses. Noticeable by her absence was Sue Kemsley, the woman who had lived with Marlene for two years before Marlene's return to prison.

Also conspicuously missing were members of Marlene's family, five of whom had attended the June hearing. The reasons became clear at the outset when Coroner Clifford Meyer began hearing submissions from those seeking standing. Arlene Dickinson, Marlene's younger sister from Toronto, who had been granted standing on behalf of the family in June, had informed the coroner by letter that she was dropping her application for an official role at the new inquest. No reason was indicated, Meyer told the courtroom. Kingston lawyer Fergus O'Connor, who had secured standing in June for Kemsley when she travelled from Toronto to attend, submitted a letter from his client, announcing that she too had decided to withdraw her application.

The letter, revealing Kemsley's bitterness over media coverage of her personal relationship with Marlene and her disillusionment with Elizabeth Fry, was read into the record on the instructions of the coroner: "In learning that the Elizabeth Fry will be allowed to continue their political bullshit, I no longer want to be involved with this public arena," Kemsley wrote. "I have had to continue on with my life such as it is without Marlene. What I shared with this woman was very special and real to me. I have taken great pains to avoid 'cashing in' on my relationship with her. Unfortunately, I feel others are using her in death as they did when she was alive, and strongly feel Elizabeth Fry is one party that is very guilty in this respect. If anything, I owe Marlene this one last dignity."

The sting of Kemsley's words showed on the faces of Elizabeth Fry officials and piqued the interest of the jurors. "All of a sudden you get this absolutely damning letter, and you wondered, Where is this coming from? What is she referring to? What did she mean?" juror Esther Dalrymple later commented.

The coroner granted standing to the Correctional Service, represented at the inquest by lawyers Charlene Brenzall and

Paul Evraire, who both worked for the federal justice department in Toronto. He also approved an application for standing
for the inquest's three medical witnesses, represented by lawyer Domenic Crolla. And as he had in June, Meyer granted
standing to Brenda Blondell, the P4W inmate who had been
alone in the hospital with Marlene when she died and who
would become a target of suspicion during the inquest. Blondell was represented by Allan Manson – the same lawyer who
had argued CAEFS's historic application for standing before the
Kingston coroner six months earlier. By now there was no
question that Meyer would accept the application. The organization was poised to bring a new, broader perspective to the
inquest. And now that the Moore family and Sue Kemsley had
dropped out of the proceedings, it was even more critical that
Elizabeth Fry bring the perspective of those with a close,
personal relationship to Marlene. ✓

A new five-member jury composed of four women and one
man was sworn in. The first witness was Constable Robert
Carr, a seasoned officer who had served on the Kingston police
force since April 1968 and who was identified as a specialist in
technical services. Most of Carr's ninety minutes on the stand
were devoted to painstaking identification of twenty-eight
colour photographs of different parts of Marlene's body that he
had taken at the scene and in the morgue at Kingston General
Hospital. In what took on the appearance of a gruesome ritual,
each photo was methodically handed from Crown Attorney
John Bett to Carr and back again, passed hand to hand down
the line of jurors, retrieved by the Crown, and, finally turned
over to the lawyers. The jurors viewed the brutally stark,
disembodied images of Marlene's scarred remains with their
faces held frozen – belying the emotional impact. "The pictures
were shocking," juror Samuel Haggerty later said. "For nights
afterwards, I could still see her face." Esther Dalrymple had
thought her work as a psychiatric nurse would steel her against
whatever the inquest held in store. "It was just overwhelming.
I found it very hard to remove myself from it when the day was
over. When it was all over, the day after, when it was completely

done with, everything in life seemed to refer, to relate to it."

Dr. Allan Fletcher, an assistant pathologist at Kingston General Hospital and assistant professor of pathology at Queen's University, was unequivocal in his testimony on the cause of death in Marlene's case: "Asphyxia, secondary to compression of the neck, consistent with atypical hanging or strangulation." Jurors soon found out, however, that there would be no clear-cut assertions about the manner of death. The hospital room had been cleaned up before police even arrived at the prison, thwarting an effective criminal investigation into Marlene's death and denying the pathologist the evidence he said he needed to support a particular theory on the way she died. As a result, much of the inquest would be devoted to the question of how Marlene died.

When asked by the Crown whether he had looked for signs of a struggle, the pathologist responded that he did look specifically for such evidence and found none. Still, by the end of the cross-examination, considerable doubt had been raised about the manner of Marlene's death. "I'm unable with any degree of certainty to determine whether this death was the result of homicide, suicide or misadventure," the witness said.

Allan Manson attempted to set to rest the homicide theory when he queried Fletcher's observation that marks consistent with a typical hanging were made at least several days or weeks earlier before Marlene died. His unspoken question was, Why consider homicide?

By mid-afternoon, key witness Brenda Blondell was on the stand. Wearing blue jeans, a light blue cotton shirt, turquoise headband, and a small star-tattoo on her right cheek, the nervous prisoner was brought into the courtroom in handcuffs, escorted by two uniformed guards. Manson promptly requested that the handcuffs be removed from his client. The coroner responded that issues of security were in the hands of the penitentiary service. Corrections lawyer Charlene Brenzall stood to say that the warden of the Prison for Women wanted Blondell in cuffs.

Blondell had been sentenced in April 1986 to life imprisonment for second-degree murder with eligibility for parole after fourteen years. She testified that she remembered nothing of her own attempted suicide by hanging in segregation in late November. Beforehand, she said, she had taken anywhere from forty to one hundred Valiums, drugs illegally obtained within the institution.

Asked by the Crown whether she expected Marlene to kill herself, Blondell said that most of the inmates of the prison were "almost surprised that Marlene lasted as long as she did."

Under questioning by Crown Attorney Bett, Blondell would provide jurors with their first glimpse of the phenomenon of slashing. Struggling for words, the witness said she realized it would be hard for someone not in prison to understand what drove women to injure themselves. "It's a way of coping," she said. "You get angry and frustrated and you can't do anything and so you turn your anger inwards. It's common. You either hang yourself or you slash or hurt yourself in some other way." Blondell said she herself had slashed, sometimes to try and end her own life and other times as a form of release.

Asked how she would stop women from slashing if she were warden, her answer came quick and hard. With anger and frustration in her voice she said, "I would have more therapists. About 90 per cent of the population has been sexually assaulted but there's an eight-month waiting list to see therapists. I would educate staff. I wouldn't leave people bleeding in a goddamn cell while they did it."

When Blondell stepped down after forty minutes, none of the jurors even suspected that both the police investigator and the coroner still harboured strong suspicions that she had been more than an innocent bystander to Marlene's death.

Next on the stand was former Prison for Women nurse Marsha Brown. When the tall, slender nurse had stood in the witness box on the June afternoon that the court order abruptly quashed the inquest proceedings she had been anxious and fidgety, and with good reason: she was on the firing line. Brown had ordered the clean-up of the death scene, which had in turn thrown the police investigation into chaos. She was also the person directly responsible for Marlene's care on the afternoon she died.

The second time around Brown delivered her testimony with confidence and composure. She explained that Marlene had a chronic bladder problem and suffered bouts of incontinence that were "mentally and physically very disturbing to her." As an interim solution Marlene had been outfitted with a catheter. Although medical tests had revealed no specific cause for her condition, Marlene "had sharp pains and periods of dull pain," Brown said. Soon after the nurse came on duty that day Marlene complained of intense discomfort and sharp pains in her pubic area.

Although Marlene had told Brown that she would slash or hang herself if the pain kept on, the nurse hadn't considered her patient suicidal. "She'd said that so many times," Brown explained, adding that Marlene had slashed on her shift in the past. Later Brown added that many prisoners had slashed at least once, and she estimated that the population had ten women who slashed regularly.

When she was asked whether she felt Marlene should have been under a twenty-four-hour watch, Brown said Marlene hated surveillance. "If they put her in a monitored cell she lived under the bed. If she had been monitored in the hospital she probably would have lived under the bed. She hated being on camera."

The first witness who'd had a long-term relationship with Marlene was Patricia Farmer, a guard supervisor in her twenty-second year with the Correctional Service. Farmer told jurors that Marlene "seemed to have deteriorated mentally and phys-ically" by the time of her final jailing in 1988, but her testimony shed little light on how the prison had responded to Marlene over the years or on how she had changed. The Crown didn't even broach the issues and Hawthorn's cross-examination elicited little added information. Hawthorn asked what resources were there to help Marlene deal with her emotions?

"We'd try to talk to her," the witness replied. Asked about rules governing the use of segregation, Farmer said, "There are regulations, I suppose, but we just use common sense."

Carmine Tedesco was the acting head of security on the day Marlene died. When she was told about the crisis Tedesco had headed straight for the hospital area where she found Brown and another nurse working over Marlene. She said she didn't think to preserve the scene until after a 6 p.m. telephone call from the Kingston police. By then, it was too late.

Bett asked the security chief how guards respond to inmates who verbally abuse staff or act out in other ways. Tedesco briefly described the range of options, from verbal warning to the use of segregation and disciplinary charges. Asked how important it is that segregation be available to maintain order at the prison, the witness said it was critical, because "we don't have much recourse beyond it."

In her questioning Hawthorn focused attention on the resources available to distressed prisoners. Tedesco's vague response indicated how wide the chasm was between custody and care of the women. She said her own recent training as a senior officer had included no counselling experience or education about self-mutilation and she couldn't recall whether Marlene or others received counselling after slashing. The questions raised by Hawthorn simply went unanswered for the jurors.

Gladys Porter, the long-time sentence administrator at the women's prison, told jurors that at the time of her death Marlene was serving five years for three counts of robbery and a firearms charge. During cross-examination Manson attempted to get Porter to talk about the milestones in Marlene's criminal history. His disjointed effort failed, leaving the jurors with only a scattered chronology that gave no sense that 80 per cent of Marlene's adult life had been spent in prison, and no hint of the persistent efforts by the government to lock her up indefinitely. Hawthorn's cross-examination noted simply that Marlene had never been released on day parole or full parole.

The next three witnesses described two separate suicide

attempts by Marlene, spanning close to six years. Linda Cowan, an experienced guard who had worked at the prison for seventeen years, was on duty in the segregation area on November 10 when Marlene tried to hang herself. The guard made it clear that the suicide gesture was far from uncommon. "I was always finding strips [of linen] in her cell."

The next witness made it obvious that prison staff simply didn't take Marlene's suicide attempts seriously. Lorraine Quinton, the prison nurse who had dispensed medication to Marlene in segregation later on during the day of November 10, said that her shift changeover report contained nothing about the incident, despite Cowan's testimony that she had reported the hanging. Quinton only became aware of the suicide attempt when she saw for herself the bruises, burns, and skin abrasions on Marlene's neck. She left the stand leaving no clues as to why Marlene was in such despair that day.

Nurse Jane Einwechter, who'd known Marlene since the early 1980s, told jurors about another suicide attempt that had occurred at least six years earlier. Guards in the segregation area had been worried that Marlene had a piece of glass in her cell and had asked Einwechter to check on the prisoner. She had found Marlene on a mattress under her bed with a ligature knotted around her neck and a bluish cast to her skin. The nurse said, "The tissue had swelled around [the ligature] so much that I couldn't get my fingers under it," and she was forced to cut away the noose. She added that Marlene had been "quite angry that I had yanked the mattress because she was just nicely drifting off."

Sometime during her final stretch at the women's prison, Marlene asked Einwechter whether she remembered her from her previous time in P4W, and what specifically she recalled. Einwechter testified that when she told Marlene about finding her under the bed, the prisoner said she had forgotten about the incident. But her ominous response was, "Now I know how to do it if I want to do it."

As the chief of correctional operations at the Prison for Women, Therese Decaire was the most senior staff member called to testify at the inquest. She was also the woman who had taken Marlene to the hospital the day before she died. On the stand for almost an hour, Decaire said she had known Marlene since she was first admitted to the institution at age nineteen, and that she had personally encouraged her to stay in the hospital through the summer of 1988. When Marlene ended up in segregation, first for twenty-five and then forty-five-day sentences on disciplinary charges, it was Decaire who brought her the news that she had the permission of the Ontario regional deputy commissioner to return to the hospital. "She really needed and really wanted to leave segregation and go to the hospital," the witness said. By then Marlene was in such a weakened state that she could scarcely manage the short walk along a hallway and down a flight of stairs. "We moved very slowly and we had to stop to rest." Decaire later said, "I could see the pain in the eyes but she didn't complain about it much that day."

When the Crown asked the same question he put to all the prison witnesses – did she consider Marlene suicidal? – Decaire's answer was by then predictable: "Marlene would always stop at a certain point. Even when she slashed she seemed to know where to do it and how deep she could go. When she tried to hang herself she did it when an officer was there or when she could lift herself out." Yet when asked under cross-examination by Manson about the suicide attempt that took place several years earlier, Decaire said, "I heard of it for the first time today."

It was the next witness who would capture the media headlines from the inquest. Sergeant Paul Lorenz of the Kingston police force, the officer in charge of the criminal investigation into the death, volunteered no hint at the outset of his grave misgivings about the role inmate Brenda Blondell played in Marlene's death. Ironically, he began his testimony with an account of an experiment he had conducted that gave weight to the theory of suicide. He explained how he had tied a strip of bedsheet around the calf of his leg using one knot – "similar to tying one knot in a shoelace" – and had given it a hard yank. The knot had held tight, supporting the idea that Marlene could have strangled herself by manually tightening a knotted bedsheet around her neck.

Crown Attorney Bett had just finished his examination of the officer when the coroner dropped a bombshell on the jurors. Meyer asked, "Isn't it true that you offered Brenda Blondell a lie detector test?" The officer replied that he had, and that she had originally agreed but later declined the polygraph on the advice of her solicitor. Blondell's lawyer was infuriated by the disclosure. Manson jumped to his feet to exonerate Blondell, saying he had advised her against taking the lie detector test because evidence obtained in such a manner is inadmissible according to the Supreme Court. Manson also admonished Lorenz, insisting they had an agreement that the polygraph wasn't an issue. "It was just between you and me. You and I resolved the lie detector test," he said angrily.

The jurors were visibly stunned by the clear insinuation of criminal intent in connection with Marlene's death. "Why was Blondell asked to take a lie detector test?" one juror asked. "I had certain doubts myself about the events as she told them to me," Lorenz replied. "I still have those doubts." With that, leaving questions unanswered, the officer stepped down.

When John McCann, the cordial police officer who served as the coroner's constable, approached jurors with a tray of coffee during their afternoon break, he found them in a state of bewilderment. Still reeling from Lorenz's startling testimony, they began plying the constable with questions. McCann told them he couldn't speak for Lorenz but that they had every right to recall any witness they wished.

The jurors asked that Blondell's statement to police be filed as an exhibit. Lawyer Manson said he had no objection but expressed concern that the jury "not be distracted by a non-issue." The coroner countered, "I'm not as content as you are that it's a non-issue." Interestingly, Blondell was elected chairperson of the prison's inmate committee shortly after Marlene's death, an event that may have been partly a show of support by the general population at P4W for the woman who had fallen under a cloud of suspicion during the police investigation.

During the hearing attention was also turned toward the state of Marlene's physical health during her final days at the prison. Dr. Veronica Mohr, a family practitioner who began contract work with the Correctional Service of Canada in 1987, estimated that she had seen Marlene about twenty times in the prison's weekly half-day clinic. Mohr said when Marlene was referred to an urologist for her bladder disorder, the specialist at first recommended an intermittent catheter to drain the bladder but later decided on a permanent "indwelling" catheter. Mohr described Marlene's condition as a "tonic enlarged bladder" but said health-care staff remained baffled about the source of the chronic pain. Normally there is not that much pain associated with the condition, Mohr said.

Early on the second day of the inquest Marlene's mother and her sister, Maureen Sutton, had slipped quietly into the public benches. After a brief, whispered conversation with the two family members, Hawthorn had asked the coroner if she could be allowed to pose questions on their behalf and was granted permission. Hawthorn now rose to query Veronica Mohr on the one issue raised by Edith Moore: If her daughter was so ill, why wasn't she in a regular hospital? The witness responded that Marlene would probably have refused to go. "She was deathly afraid of outside hospital. We referred her numerous times. We were very concerned because her haemogoblin was so low from slashing."

In the late afternoon of that day Dr. Julie Darke – the person that CAEFS executive director Bonnie Diamond later rated as the single most important witness to their case – took the stand. Darke, a clinical psychologist who had graduated from Queen's University in 1986, was working three days a week at the women's prison. A feminist therapist, she has the unenviable task of working to empower women, by increasing their sense of control of themselves and the world around them, in a system antithetical to individual freedom. She had met with

Marlene on a weekly basis through June and July in 1988, and had resumed seeing her in November, just three weeks before the death. A striking witness with her unorthodox razor haircut and intense manner, Darke clearly impressed jurors with the commitment and genuine concern she displayed for her clients. "You got the very distinct feeling that she gave everything she had to give, and then some, for these women," Esther Dalrymple said.

Darke had seen Marlene on each of the three days leading up to December 3 and testified that she was "shocked" by her death. She said that after her session with Marlene the day before the death, she considered her to be a lower risk of suicide than at other times. She said, "I saw her move to the hospital as Marlene actually making a move to take care of herself."

Bolstering earlier testimony by Blondell, Darke painted a bleak picture of mental health resources at the prison. As one of three part-time therapists she had a caseload of thirty-five women, and it was normal for a prisoner to sit from eight months to a year on a waiting list. She said, "It's a problem and it has been for a long time."

When the Crown asked her whether monitored cells "made sense" as a means of attempting to prevent suicides, Darke replied: "No. You also need to look at someone's quality of life. To keep someone in a monitored room, day after day, year after year, who are we protecting? I think we are protecting ourselves." It was a provocative ending to a long, gruelling day of testimony.

On the third and final day of the inquest Dr. Roy Brown, a self-employed psychiatrist whose practice since 1985 had included nine hours a week at the Prison for Women, took the witness stand. His assessment of Marlene, delivered in a soft-spoken Scottish brogue, was based on twelve half-hour consultations between April 20 and November 29, 1988, as well as his review of the observations of "ten to twelve psychiatrists" who had dealt with her at the women's prison, St. Thomas Psychiatric Hospital, and the Queen Street Mental Health Centre.

Brown told jurors that Marlene was a "very, very difficult" client, who would often cancel appointments or arrive at his office in an angry and hostile frame of mind. Though not mentally ill in the strict sense of diagnostic illness, Marlene represented "an extreme case" of combined antisocial and borderline personality disorders – behavioural problems for which therapists had met with very limited success, he said.

There was no mistaking his message to jurors throughout his fifty-minute testimony: Psychiatric resources were made available to Marlene but she had refused to co-operate with those seeking to help her. Brown told the inquest that his placement options for inmates who have "difficulty getting along" in the prison environment include St. Thomas Psychiatric Hospital and the ten-bed women's unit at the Regional Treatment Centre, the facility on the grounds of Kingston Penitentiary, used primarily for treatment of sex offenders. The psychiatrist didn't volunteer to the jury the information that Marlene had twice been committed to St. Thomas for the minimum thirty-day period, and under crosss-examination by Hawthorn he later admitted that he had never been inside St. Thomas and couldn't describe the hospital's treatment programs. Brown did offer testimony about Marlene's steadfast refusal to go to the Regional Treatment Centre. The prison had considered her transfer to the centre but staff reached a consensus that it would not have been in Marlene's best interest, he said. Because the facility housed men convicted of sexual assault, "The idea was horrendous to Marlene," he explained.

Brown also testified that when he spoke with Marlene on November 16, just three weeks before her death, about her aborted hanging in segregation, she told him she had no intention of ending her life. He portrayed the incident as one of "numerous suicidal gestures" she had made over the years, saying he believed Marlene had never at any time made a genuine attempt at suicide. As for her death, he characterized it as simply a tragic miscalculation on her part: "I have to think that she made another gesture and it went further than she had planned, but that's only speculation."

Unlike witness Julie Darke, who had described the prison's team of three women psychologists as severely overburdened, Brown said he had no concerns about his ability to handle a caseload of "about 50 per cent" of the prison population. Brown was seeing, on average, sixty-five to seventy women on a schedule that ranged from weekly consultation, in a small number of cases, to sessions once every two months. Brown said that he felt "no need to see anyone more often than I'm able."

But the next three witnesses – each called by the CAEFS – presented neither a picture of complacency about the therapeutic resources at the Prison for Women nor the faintest echo of the psychiatrist's bleak assessment of Marlene's potential for positive change.

Jan Heney, as an expert in self-abusive behaviours and a founder of an innovative treatment model, led the jury into unsettling foreign territory. She described new research findings about direct links between childhood sexual abuse and women's self-mutilation. As CAEFS had intended, her testimony shifted the focus of the inquest away from the circumstances of Marlene's death and into an exploration of both the impetus for slashing and the inappropriateness of the punitive response of segregating women in emotional distress. She testified that the longstanding practice of transferring women to segregation cells for slashing did more harm than good. She said when inmates have been abused and feel bad, locking them in segregation "will only reinforce the feelings that they are bad and worthless."

The final two witnesses, both of them close friends of Marlene's, focused on the lack of community resources available to help her make the difficult adjustment to freedom on her release from prison. Darlene Lawson, the executive director of the Toronto Elizabeth Fry Society, had known Marlene since 1976 and described the progress she had made during six months at the group's halfway house in 1985–86. Lawson stressed, however, that the residence did not have the staff resources to provide the intensive therapy and life-skills training that Marlene – and others like her – must have to repair their badly damaged lives. Lawson told jurors that locking up Marlene and punishing her since childhood for "behaviour that was a manifestation of her pain" had reinforced her feelings of being a bad person. Marlene's life, she said, was "a challenge to us," and we had failed her.

Until the last half-hour of testimony, witnesses had spoken only in generalities about survivors of sexual assault. It wasn't until June Callwood took the stand that jurors heard about Marlene's personal history of incest and rape and her ensuing battle with rage and and self-loathing.

Callwood, a prolific author and one of the nation's few journalists with celebrity status, has devoted the past twenty-five years of her life to helping society's downtrodden. Sorrow and anger merged in her voice as she outlined her unsuccessful quest for help for Marlene. She told jurors that psychiatric staff at the Queen Street Mental Health Centre felt the hospital was the wrong place for Marlene, that a specialist in self-mutilation saw her but decided he couldn't be of any assistance, that an incontinence clinic rejected her because she was too young. "Nobody wanted her. They took a look at her arms and didn't want her," Callwood said. "That's not what they said. They said that what they had [to offer] wasn't appropriate. . . . I'm pretty skilled in what the community has to offer and I found nothing."

Callwood described Marlene with open affection, drawing a portrait of a deeply troubled woman with a generous heart and a survivor's courage, "spunky and funny, wise in the way street people are wise." Callwood also related her revulsion and despair over Marlene's gruesome self-mutilations. "She would sit in a bathtub and slash inside her vagina so the blood would go down the drain." It was a stunning bit of testimony that caused Hawthorn to lose her composure briefly. One of the jurors later questioned the lawyer's motives, saying he was put off by the emotional display. "I thought it was a bit of play-acting," he said.

During a short break the inquest lawyers collected their

thoughts in preparation for final arguments and recommendations to the jury.

When Hawthorn approached the coroner's jury in midafternoon on December 8 to make her final submissions, she was painfully aware that she hadn't even come close – during three days of testimony – to bridging the immeasurable distance between the relatively orderly, peaceful lives of the jurors and Marlene's brutal existence. But the Elizabeth Fry lawyer was unaware of the extent of the scepticism felt by the five citizens on the bench facing her.

In her closing remarks Hawthorn spoke of the need to consider "the context of women's lives" when determining sentences and, in keeping with the organization's stance on abolishing prisons for women, stressed that "sentencing should take place in the community." She appealed for a more compassionate justice system that takes responsibility for "people who've been damaged and who've been hurt" and urged the jurors to use their intelligence and creativity to improve conditions for women prisoners.

But it was Crown attorney John Bett who struck a chord with the jurors. In a meandering, ponderous speech, the Crown attorney distanced himself from the reform-minded goals of the prisoners' rights organization. He bristled at the suggestion that society should feel culpable for Marlene's premature death. In a society of limited financial resources, he said, it was necessary to make "ugly decisions" about "those on the periphery." Surely, when confronted with someone like Marlene, society has a right to decide to "set that person aside and go on with something else." Bett's bottom line was: "Are we structured to provide the greatest good for the greatest number, or is society structured to provide the greatest good to its dissenters? . . . It almost boils down to whether the earth should rotate around the sun or the sun around the earth."

Somehow, the public investigation into Marlene's tragic death had taken the shape of the perennial, polarized debate that had long underlain the criminal justice system. The

Elizabeth Fry appeal that Marlene be seen as a product of her total experience further provoked Bett into defending a system of justice "predicated on individual responsibility." People are prosecuted on the basis that they have free will and are responsible for their acts, Bett said. "If you want to throw out that premise, I don't know where you look to find justice." Bett showed himself unaware that free will was meaningless for a woman who had long ago lost control of her life as a result of incest and rape.

The Crown attorney dismissed as unreasonable and impractical the key recommendation of CAEFS that the prison abandon its practice of isolating women who slash to a segregation cell. Such a move would strip prison employees of the one measure they have for quelling potentially disruptive events, he said. "If a woman in emotional crisis is generating crises in other people by upsetting other inmates, is it wrong to isolate them?"

Reiterating a theme advanced by both the lawyer for corrections and the lawyer for the doctors, Bett urged the jurors to be "practical" when formulating recommendations. That message was hammered home again by the coroner in his final comments to the jurors. If the recommendations are "foolish or cost a fortune," they will be disregarded, Meyer said.

As to the manner of Marlene's death, the Crown attorney advised the jurors that while misadventure and suicide were the stronger possibilities, homicide simply couldn't be ruled out. That directive, too, was underscored by Meyer. "The only answer you can give is indeterminate," the coroner said.

Jury members retired in the late afternoon to ponder the testimony of the inquest's twenty-five witnesses. When they emerged almost two hours later they made six recommendations. But first they exonerated Brenda Blondell by describing the manner of Marlene's death as "probable misadventure by own hand" – concluding that she had unintentionally killed herself. In making that finding, the jurors had flatly rejected the advice of the coroner. "We all agreed," said Dalrymple, "that whether Marlene intended to or whether it just got beyond her and she couldn't save herself, who knows. We rather suspected it was another one of those cases where she was making a statement and had expected she would be brought back."

It wasn't until the coroner read aloud the juror's preamble to the recommendations, praising prison resources and staff, that Elizabeth Fry representatives got their first inkling of how miserably they had failed to impress upon jurors the grim reality of prison conditions. "Anybody who could start by commending the prison could not have been given a clear picture. They had quite a different idea of what was available to women in emotional crisis," Bonnie Diamond commented within minutes of the close of the inquest.

In general, the jurors' recommendations were predictable and cosmetic. They called for the installation of "some means of communication" between the hospital ward and other parts of the prison, and the introduction of "annual certification" of all security staff in basic first-aid procedures, including cardiopulmonary resuscitation. They asked prison officials to "maintain" two directives issued by Warden Mary Cassidy a year earlier. The first – implemented six days after Marlene's death – ended the practice of locking inmate-patients in hospital without staff supervision when the duty nurse left the health-care unit. The second instructed prison employees on required procedures for "protection and preservation of evidence and the scene," in the event of murder, suicide, or major assaults on staff or inmates. The jury also recommended that all security staff "continue to receive ongoing training" in suicide prevention and in working with victims of physical and sexual abuse and with inmates who slash themselves or engage in other forms of self-abusive behaviour. Its final recommendation stated that "in recognition of the stressful nature" of the work performed by guards and nurses, ongoing "support and counselling" should be made available to them.

Ironically, the inquest that had captured national attention and that some had predicted would continue for weeks was over in just three days – making it shorter than the average Ontario inquest in 1989 of 38.1 hours.

Elizabeth Fry members were stunned by the limited scope and vision of the recommendations and incensed that the jurors had refused to address the issue of segregation. "Our evidence made it abundantly clear that women cannot heal from sexual abuse if all control is removed from them," Diamond stated at the close of the inquest. "Segregation is the antithesis of what should happen when a woman is displaying self-abusive behaviour or any type of emotional trauma." Despite Elizabeth Fry's determination to broaden the inquiry beyond the last few hours of Marlene's life, jurors had resorted to what Diamond termed "apparatus-driven" recommendations – jurors spoke, for instance, of installing emergency buttons and providing sheets that don't rip. As too often remains true of coroners' inquests, the focus was simply on thwarting future suicide attempts rather than understanding how prisoners are driven to such despair. At least one juror made it clear in an interview with a reporter that he hadn't ever accepted CAEFS's basic premise that Marlene's death be examined in the context of her life experiences. "The issue was how did she die, not what drove her to die," remarked Sam Haggarty.

Diamond said, "I think we underplayed the journey that the jury was going to have to travel to deal with such complex and heavy emotional issues in such a short period of time. . . . It's such a leap in the context in which we all live to say that no young girl who is sexually abused should be incarcerated. It's asking people who have never even thought of alternatives to incarceration to go a very long distance."

Misgivings about CAEFS's motives had arisen in the minds of jurors with Sue Kemsley's embittered letter and then deepened as the inquest progressed. Hawthorn could have diminished the impact of Kemsley's statement by eliciting testimony from one of CAEFS's own witnesses about how the former Elizabeth Fry employee had been asked to resign when she became personally involved with Marlene. But the lawyer had decided to deliberately avoid impugning Sue in any way. However well-motivated, it turned out to be a costly mistake.

Jurors also saw the advocacy group as blinded to the practical realities of prison by its mission of helping prisoners, and naive in its criticisms. "Some of the Elizabeth Fry's recommendations were so ridiculous almost to the point of being laughable," Esther Dalrymple said.

Corrections officials were delighted with the outcome. Warden Mary Cassidy cited the jurors' commendation of staff as the most important outcome of the inquest. "People on the outside simply don't know the efforts staff put in or the abuse they take on doing the job," she said. But she also noted that programs to make prison guards sensitive to the family backgrounds of inmates were long overdue. "It's been lacking for fifty years and it's desperately needed," she said. Corrections spokesman Dennis Curtis unabashedly endorsed the jurors' recommendations for being "reasonable and not terribly expensive to implement."

Despite its unusual and difficult attempt to broaden the scope of the inquest, the prisoners rights organization had failed miserably to impress jurors with the need for profound changes. Despite the CAEFS's historic participation, the proceedings proved a missed opportunity.

CAEFS had asked the jurors to radically restructure the existing prison system into a therapeutic community – to come up with a blueprint for change that would transform a system built and operated for the past fifty years with security as its paramount concern. Lawyer Felicity Hawthorn had unveiled a thirteen-point program for change, which included a call to ban the use of segregation for women in emotional distress, more resources for women about to be released into the street, and an end to incarceration for girls and women who are "acting out" in response to childhood sexual or physical abuse. But three days of testimony had failed to give the jurors any inkling of the philosophic underpinnings of the Elizabeth Fry Societies' abolitionist position.

Time after time Hawthorn had had witnesses on the stand who could have enlightened jurors as to how the system had failed Marlene. But she hadn't pursued a line of questioning to bring out what prison officials did and didn't do for Marlene, and why. Jurors were given little or no understanding of Marlene's own history or of how the prison system itself had been a major contributor to Marlene's death. Jurors were never told, for example, that Marlene was committed to training school at age thirteen without ever having committed a crime. They were never told about the state's repeated, misconceived efforts to label her dangerous and lock her up indefinitely. Details of her sexual and physical abuse as a child, and her rape at age seventeen, were mentioned only in passing by one witness.

Also troubling was that CAEFS, with carte blanche to call any witness, didn't see fit to subpoena Warden Mary Cassidy, the woman who had spent many hours in conversation with Marlene and who was better informed than anyone else about what resources are, and aren't, available to women in her custody. Hawthorn later explained her decision not to call Cassidy by saying, "She was so opposed to being called that she would have been a crappy witness. She just hates publicity." Of the more than two dozen witnesses called, only two were inmates. Where were the prisoners who had become Marlene's friends and confidantes during the months after her return to the women's prison? Where were the prisoners who witnessed her treatment by prison staff while locked in the segregation wing?

To those who knew Marlene, the omissions and denials during the three days of testimony were more suprising than her self-inflicted death. The few glimpses of her tortured existence were buried beneath the inquest's preoccupation with the facts of her death. The CAEFS brought no new script and called only three witnesses, turning in a cameo performance that fell far short of the association's own goals.

Unfortunately, from the outset, CAEFS felt such gratitude at having been allowed entry into the official inquest process that it was reluctant to make any moves that might antagonize the coroner or the Crown attorney. CAEFS clearly felt under pressure by Coroner Meyer not to rock the boat – "once having got a toehold, not to abuse it," as Diamond put it. Diamond remembers her sense of trepidation when she spotted one juror "nodding off" during Julie Darke's critical testimony. "I couldn't have felt more desperate at that moment," she said. "We should have insisted, and others should have insisted, that we adjourn and come back fresh the next morning."

The Elizabeth Fry Society has traditionally trodden lightly when it comes to direct criticism of the Correctional Service of Canada and the administration at the Prison for Women. Despite its clear mandate as an advocate for women prisoners and its oft-stated abolitionist stance, the prisoners' rights organization shies away from open conflict with CSC. At the time of the inquest Hawthorn spoke of the need to "find a balance between questioning enough of CSC and their policies and their institutions without alienating ourselves." Elizabeth Fry's reticence may be attributed partly to the fact that the organization receives significant funding from CSC. Whatever the reason, there is no place for timidity in an organization whose role is to protect and expand the rights of women prisoners.

Hawthorn admits, as well, that CAEFS simply wasn't prepared. The problem arose partly because the inquest collided with a government task force on female offenders. As co-chair of the task force working group, Hawthorn devoted all her time during the weeks leading up to the inquest to writing the report. "I had my mind on other things," she says. "I had allowed myself ten days to really focus on the inquest, but things kept coming up that I had to deal with." As well, Hawthorn had counted on the inquest extending well beyond the initial three days scheduled by the coroner. "I assumed that the Crown would present his case in the first three days and that the inquest would then be put over until after Christmas. I had sort of banked on basically being able to have all their material and then work out our strategy as to exactly what we were going to do and on the basis of that call our witnesses." As it turned out, Hawthorn sat at her portable computer in her Kingston hotel room until 3 a.m. on the last day of the inquest, writing her recommendations to the jury. Then she woke up at 5 a.m. to prepare her submissions.

The frustration expressed by Marlene's lawyer Dianne

Martin was felt by many who followed the inquest proceedings. "I was appalled and depressed by the outcome," Martin says. "It was shocking, patently ridiculous. The authorities, who definitely wanted a lid on Marlene's death and the general conditions at the Prison for Women, succeeded in limiting the scope of the inquiry so drastically that the jury had no idea what was going on."

Although reluctant to criticize anyone in particular, Martin makes a veiled reference to Elizabeth Fry's failure to stand up to the dictates of the coroner. "Presumably, decisions were made about not challenging the coroner's rulings as they were happening and not forcing him to expand the length of time assigned. He ran it with a goal in mind, which was to utterly limit what came out. So not surprisingly, nothing came out. It's a tremendously false document about Marlene and about the Prison for Women."

Martin was incensed that no one at the inquest even challenged the testimony of the prison psychiatrist that someone with a personality disorder is not considered to be mentally ill. "It's been classified as a mental illness for the last ten years, but if she were mentally ill then they couldn't [justify] treating her that way," Martin says. "This was a beautifully orchestrated statement that the prison did everything correctly, and what a pity that this woman who was going to off herself anyway did it in this messy way."

The results could have been different if either the family or Kemsley had pursued standing, Martin says. "There was no one at that inquest asking questions or pressing issues in a way designed to expose either what the system had done to Marlene or what individuals had done to Marlene or both – and that's why it was such a distorted result."

12

If I were in charge
I'd change the correctional system

Marlene Moore's death continued to haunt many who knew her and the community at large. Within weeks of the inquest, spray-painted pro-women graffiti appeared on seventy buildings in the city of Kingston. One slogan read "Justice for Marlene." A year or more after her body was found in the prison hospital, some distraught members of the prison staff were still insisting that Marlene's spirit lingered in certain areas of the building. "A few staff still talk about a certain presence in the hospital area," Mary Morissette says. "I know staff members who have dreamed of her. In fact, I had a dream of her one night myself and I hadn't been in the institution for months. I dreamed that she was alive again, and it was a strange, eerie dream."

Despite the inquest's failure to produce substantial recommendations, Marlene's tragic life and violent death left an indelible imprint on the prison system and intensified existing pressure on the Correctional Service of Canada to bring about dramatic reforms. In early 1989 the Canadian Association of

Elizabeth Fry Societies became engaged in intense discussions with the csc over the launching of a national task force on federally sentenced women. The publicity and external scrutiny of the women's prison sparked by Marlene's death would not go away.

The problems plaguing the correctional system for women aren't novel to anyone who has followed the debate over the Prison for Women in recent years: Many women are locked up far from their families and home communities. About 60 per cent of inmates come from across the province of Ontario; 24 per cent from the western Canada; 10 per cent from Quebec; and 7 per cent from the Atlantic provinces.

About half of the 280 female offenders serving sentences of two years or more in Canada live in the Kingston prison. Since the government introduced the Exchange of Service Agreements in the mid-1970s, allowing some women to serve their federal sentences in a provincial institution, female offenders have been faced with a difficult dilemma that male inmates don't have. A woman must choose between remaining close to her family or having access to the enhanced education and work programs geared for long-term offenders – programs available only at the women's penitentiary.

Another discriminatory feature of the system is that the fortresslike Kingston prison, designed as maximum-security, subjects all its women to the same rules and constraints on work and recreational programs. In fact, only a handful of the 130 women inside are designated maximum-security inmates.

Women inmates have had fewer opportunities to help cushion their release back into the community. In the male system, inmates are "cascaded" from maximum- or medium-security into minimum-security facilities as a means of easing them gradually back into the community. Because there is only one federal prison for women, female offenders haven't had the same opportunity. Also, women who become eligible for community passes usually end up spending their time in the Kingston area rather than in their home communities because of the great distance and the expense of going home.

A 1990 CSC task force report provides the latest statistical profile of female offenders. A majority of inmates are poor, unemployed, and undereducated. Some two-thirds of the women serving federal sentences either haven't completed high school or have no training or educational qualifications beyond high school. Many native women are grade-school drop-outs. Some have never attended school. In the majority of cases, drugs or alcohol have played a major part in the commission of offences.

Close to two-thirds of Canada's female federal inmates are mothers. About a quarter of them have a child or children younger than five years. "There is nothing harder than facing kids that don't know you. Doing time is easy compared to that," a P4W inmate once stated.

Native women make up 15 per cent of the federal prison population. According to the 1988 annual report of the Canadian Human Rights Commission, an aboriginal woman is more likely to go to prison than to university. Behind walls, native women are the most disadvantaged. Too often, prison rules take no notice of their cultural and religious beliefs. Too often, parole boards are insensitive to the systemic discrimination they have faced. In the words of one aboriginal parolee: "P4W and the National Parole Board separate [our families], stipulate that we stay away from known criminals. . . . Please, my grandfather, uncles, aunts, cousins, brothers, sisters, the whole Indian Nation would be known criminals."

During the past two decades, first-time female offenders have been getting younger and their crimes more serious. Gone are the days when the female prison population was made up mainly of drug offenders and prostitutes. Now, 39 per cent of female offenders are serving time for murder or manslaughter. Some 41 per cent are first-time offenders with no previous convictions. Still, most are serving heavy sentences. Over half of them are doing more than five years; 29 per cent are serving ten years or more; and 20 per cent are on life sentences.

The one thing most women in prison have in common is a history of being abused as children. Of the women in P4W, 82 per cent report having been physically or sexually abused at some time in their lives. The rate was highest among native women: 90 per cent of native women and 61 per cent of non-aboriginal women said they had been physically abused; 61 per cent of native women and 50 per cent of non-aboriginal women said they had been sexually abused.

Few women have been lucky enough to receive substantial psychological counselling while inside. A small handful of dedicated therapists have fought burnout while they grapple with unwieldy waiting lists and the limitations imposed on treatment by unbending prison rules. Left to their own resources in coping with overwhelming feelings of despair and powerlessness, many women seek release by slashing.

Emotional pain confounds the prison system. Said one prisoner recently: "Why have I witnessed over one hundred slashings . . . wiped up pints of blood from floors and walls and carried blood-soaked mattresses outside to the garbage . . . held women in my arms as they bled . . . and as they cried? Why?" Locked in rigid and archaic traditions that dehumanize both the imprisoned and their keepers, prisons have been unable to respond to human misery. The standard response has been to move women who slash and are believed desperate enough to try to kill themselves to a segregation cell where guards can observe them through closed-circuit television monitors. The end result is hardly surprising. The slashing has continued, even escalated.

Only recently has P4W's administration turned to outsiders for advice. Psychologist Marsha Lomis, who works in the Ontario corrections system, interviewed prisoners identified as slashers and found that most of them have long histories of self-injurious behaviour. She concluded that the prison system had failed to meet the women's special needs. In her report, submitted in May 1988, Lomis urged the Correctional Service to develop a long-term treatment unit with up to twelve beds. Such a unit, she said, would help "meet the needs that these women have for a highly structured environment with special provisions for mental health services and physical safety measures." While prison officials pondered Lomis's report, tension at the prison and the incidence of self-mutilation – particularly after Marlene's final return to the institution on April 1988 – spiralled and prison authorities felt renewed pressure to find solutions.

In January 1989 the warden turned to Jan Heney, whose success in treating women who self-injure outside of prison had come to the attention of Correctional Service officials. Marlene's death a month earlier was a catalyst for the investigation that followed. Heney was asked to investigate the feasibility of introducing her treatment methods inside the penitentiary. She spent many hours interviewing guards, administrative staff, and prisoners, searching for answers to why women slash in prison and how they could be helped.

Although Heney found that it was difficult to determine the extent of self-mutilation at P4W, her discussions with inmates and the physical evidence – the number of women bearing scars – convinced her that a large percentage of the population had a history of self-injury. While most women reported slashing as their primary method of wounding, many also cited headbanging, starvation, burning, and tattooing.

Heney found that guards held widely divergent views on the prevalence of inmate self-injury. Some staff were virtually oblivious to the problem. Guards reported the rate of slashing at anywhere from 2 to 3 per cent to 70 per cent of the prison population. Heney believes that the discrepancy was most likely explained by differences in definition of self-mutilation. For some "only deep wounds" would count, she said. Some staff routinely dismissed more superficial injuries as a form of manipulative or attention-seeking behaviour. The fact that prisoners' estimates of the rate of self-injury were much higher than staff's was easier to explain. Many women who injure themselves do not report their actions to staff for fear of ending up in segregation, Heney said. Prisoners refer to these cases as "quiet slashings."

Given a free hand to explore all aspects of life at P4W, Heney witnessed firsthand how security took priority over the mental health needs of prisoners. A troubled young prisoner who couldn't get in to see a prison psychologist approached Heney and asked to meet with her. A guard interrupted their talk by knocking on the interview room to announce that the daily population count was about to begin. "This woman needed to finish her conversation with me but the rules of the institution took precedence," Heney wrote in her report. That same night, the prisoner slashed.

Heney also began to see how the harsh conditions of confinement gradually eroded a women's ability to cope with day-to-day life inside: The longer a woman's stretch in prison the more likely she was to resort eventually to self-mutilation. It wasn't the fact of imprisonment alone that drove women to slash, Heney reported, but a pervasive sense of injustice that triggered feelings of frustration and powerlessness.

She found a direct link between periods of severe stress inside the walls and the rate of self-mutilation. In September and October 1989, when tension peaked over a plan by the administration to integrate protective-custody inmates into the general population, there were slashings by women who had not engaged in such acts for years. Heney also documented what she described as "outbreaks of self-injury." Many prisoners reported that when a sister inmate slashes, the act sharpens their own pain and increases the likelihood that they will self-injure. One woman said: "Friendships are intensified in the prison. When someone you care about slashes, it upsets you because you are already upset about the same shit she is. So you're dealing with the shit and now you're dealing with your friend's pain and it's just too much."

The most common complaint voiced by inmates was the prison's protocol of transferring women who slash to segregation cells and locking them up for at least twenty-three hours a day without work or education programs. Prisoners perceived these transfers to segregation as punishment. "You are treated the same [when taken to segregation] whether you hurt someone else or yourself," one inmate told Heney. But the prison staff, who still viewed slashing as a suicide attempt, defended the practice, saying that women who are a danger to themselves belong in one of the segregation area's camera-monitored cells.

As the prison's front-line workers, guards are ultimately responsible for a prisoner's safety. They feel an enormous emotional burden and many of them spoke openly to Heney about the "stress and feelings of helplessness" they experience when a woman self-injures. Some guards confided that the frequency of self-injury had caused them to become hardened just to cope.

The overriding concern of the inmates was that the harsh, isolating conditions of segregation can drive women who are already in emotional distress to attempt suicide. Heney agreed: "Whether intentional or not, isolation and punishment may overwhelm the individual, leading to more drastic measures to stop the pain."

In early 1990, a year and one month after Marlene's death, Heney presented Warden Mary Cassidy with a set of bold recommendations aimed at reducing and treating self-injury at the women's prison. Her forty-two-page report was a tactful, politically sensitive document that took pains not to aim any direct criticism at prison guards or administrators. But Heney's general assessment was blunt: Longstanding prison practices and policies have fostered the kind of tension and desperation that provoke self-mutilation; more than that, the institution's manner of responding to women who slash is likely to escalate rather than reduce the rate of self-mutilation and suicide among prisoners.

Heney, calling for sweeping changes, said that self-injurious behaviour should be seen as a mental health issue rather than a security matter. She said the prison must move quickly to develop new ways of responding to emotional pain caused by childhood physical and sexual abuse. She recommended an immediate end to the use of segregation for women who slash, saying isolation increases rather than decreases suicidal tendencies. It was an unequivocal message that underscored how devastating the prison's long-time policy of segregating women had been for Marlene and others like her.

Heney said women who self-injure should be taken to the prison hospital, where a psychiatrist, psychologist, or properly trained nurse can assess whether they are high suicide risks and then decide whether they should remain in the hospital or be returned to the general population.

She also called for a realignment in the balance between security and treatment, urging an enhanced role for psychology, psychiatry, and health-care services in the shaping and implementing of prison policy. For too long, she said, security matters have held priority, often at great cost to the mental health of prisoners. "Psychologists must have equal if not greater power than security in the policy process," Heney said.

She recommended the establishment of a "time-out room" where a women could express emotions privately without fear of negative sanctions from security. She also called on the prison to hire more therapists to better reflect the number of prisoners with a history of sexual and physical abuse.

A key component of her therapeutic approach was her recommendation for the establishment of a formal program to train select inmates in the principles of peer counselling. She envisioned a crisis/support team composed of inmate counsellors and staff professionals that would be able to respond to women in emotional crisis on a twenty-four-hour basis. The report also called for sexual assault "survival" groups and special services for native women. As well, she said, prison nurses should be trained in "intervention" techniques and guards should be educated in the dynamics of childhood sexual abuse.

Although Warden Mary Cassidy wasn't without reservations, she was determined to find a better way of coping with self-injury. She endorsed Heney's report and, by spring 1990, had gradually begun implementing most of her recommendations. The future looked both scary and exciting, the warden said. For her it would be "frightening" to take women out of the controlled environment of a camera-monitored cell but she also believed that it might help. As it turned out, the administration's preoccupation with surveillance later led it to install camera monitors in the hospital.

The changes would come all too late for Marlene Moore. But prisoners still living at P4W enthusiastically embraced Heney's vision for a humane, treatment-oriented approach to self-injury. Brenda Blondell was one of the prisoners trained as a peer counsellor. For a while she had secreted a medical kit, complete with sterile strips and bandages, in her cell so she could tend to the slash wounds of women afraid to seek official medical help. "That's the way it had to be unless you wanted to go to seg," Blondell says. "If they found out, you went to seg."

Some people both inside and outside the prison remain sceptical that Cassidy, despite her good intentions, will be able to create a therapeutic environment behind the walls. For a woman who has been sexually abused, the healing process is extremely painful and can take months, even years. The success of treatment hinges on building trust between therapist and client. In a prison setting, where personal survival often depends on suppressing feelings, developing trust and letting down defences do not come easily.

Heney doesn't downplay the difficulty of attempting to introduce a treatment model that emphasizes the need for personal control in a prison environment. But what may at first glance seem like an insurmountable contradiction is possible to overcome, she believes. "There are ways to personally empower women, even in a situation where some control has been taken from them." But Heney stressed that her recommendations were intended simply as interim "Band-Aid" measures. Ultimately, offenders who have experienced childhood abuse must be given an opportunity to serve their sentences in facilities directed solely toward treatment. "In an ideal world, I'd like to see women get help from the first time they run into conflict with the law," she says. "I'd like to see us working with adolescents because I believe that a lot of what eventually happens to them in life is based on the fact that they were abused. Our goal is treatment and providing women with a place where they can do their healing."

Within two months of the release of Heney's report, the Correctional Service of Canada and the Canadian Association of Elizabeth Fry Societies held a national press conference to trumpet their own long-awaited task force report. The collaborative effort by the volunteer organization and the corrections ministry, which got underway in March 1989 – three months after Marlene's death – had been fraught with tension. CAEFS and most of the other non-CSC personnel involved in the task force consider themselves prison abolitionists. Diamond admits, "It really tried our souls to be designing a prison system when we don't believe women should be in prison."

The radical vision contained in the 156-page document, *Creating Choices: The Report of the Task Force on Federally-Sentenced Women*, represented a breakthrough for the treatment of female offenders, recognizing the importance of restoring the women's control over their lives and offering them opportunities to heal from devastating childhood abuse. The recommendations were urgent in tone, calling for the country's only penitentiary for women to be closed by 1994 and replaced by five regional "cottage-like" facilities, with room for up to ten women in each. The report recommended the establishment of a native "healing lodge" in one of the Prairie provinces, where aboriginal women prisoners could serve their time without being cut off from native customs and elders. It said there should be an increase in halfway houses and addiction treatment centres across Canada to help women move back into the community as quickly as possible.

One highly controversial recommendation highlighted the issue of prison mothers. Since 1985 four studies had been commissioned by the Canadian government to examine the impact of separation on women and their families, the social costs of incarcerating mothers, and the possibility of institutional nurseries. But no action had ever been taken to address the critical problems. The task force report stressed that new facilities for women offenders must include "live-in programs" for children.

The task force recommendations followed a long chorus of voices condemning the Kingston prison. In 1938, just four years after the prison opened, the Archambeault Committee investigating the penal system had recommended that the women's prison be shut down. Since 1968 no less than thirteen government studies and private sector reports have reaffirmed that P4W should be closed and that decentralized facilities should be established closer to women's homes. In 1978 Solicitor General Jean-Jacques Blais announced that the prison would be closed within a year. Instead, a new eighteen-foot-high concrete wall was erected around the prison in the early 1980s, at a cost of $1.4 million. A later 1985 target date announced by the federal government for dispersing the women also passed without any action being taken.

Several women have launched court actions alleging that P4W violates equality guarantees in the Charter of Rights and Freedoms. The first such action was initiated in April 1987 by former prisoner Daryl Dollan along with Jo-Ann Mayhew, who was still serving time at the Kingston prison. Later that same year the Women's Legal Education and Action Fund (LEAF) in Toronto formed a national working group to build the framework for a court challenge representing what the group describes as "the first full-blown systemic discrimination" action submitted to the courts on behalf of female offenders. The lawsuits contend that the Correctional Service of Canada discriminates against women in its charge, based on evidence of widespread disparities between facilities and services available to women and those available to men sentenced to federal prisons.

None of the Charter challenges has yet reached the courts. However, the protestations of the CSC that it simply can't afford equality for female offenders because of their small numbers have worn thin. And it appears that the reputation of the federal women's penitentiary has penetrated the consciousness of the country's judiciary. In July 1990 an indignant Saskatchewan judge handed down a life sentence for second-degree murder in the case of a woman found guilty in a stabbing incident; but the judge stipulated that Carol Daniels should not be banished to the Kingston prison, nearly 3,200 kilometres from her home. Judge Marion Wedge went even further in her ruling, stating that no native women from the West should be sent to P4W. It was a violation of the Charter of Rights and Freedoms to force a woman to serve her sentence in a prison so far away from her home compared to the distance a man would have to go, she said.

Women's groups have not been the only source of pressure on the Correctional Service of Canada to improve the lot of female offenders. In September 1988 the Canadian Bar Association released a 300-page report, *Justice Behind the Walls*, calling for closure of the Prison for Women. "In the case of P4W, we are of the view that the time has now passed when another royal commission or another committee report is required to urge its closure," the report states. "We recommend that legislation be introduced to compel closure of the Prison for Women in a timely way."

Finally, in September 1990, federal Solicitor General Pierre Cadieux announced that the fifty-six-year-old Prison for Women would be closed in four years and replaced by five regional centres to enable women offenders to live closer to their families and friends. He said the initiative would cost $50 million. The new centres, one of them a healing lodge for aboriginal women under federal sentence, would stress counselling, education, and treatment for drug and alcohol abuse. Cadieux said, "We recognize that many of the women sentenced to our care have needs similar to those of disadvantaged women in the larger community. Most of them have been physically, sexually or emotionally abused, many have related substance abuse problems, low self-esteem and heavy responsibility for parenting children on their own."

Contrary to expectations, the announcement that the prison will close has caused considerable uneasiness among many of the women inside. An often-expressed fear is that the government will shut down the prison without first investing in new, improved facilities. Prisoners worry that they will be transferred to overcrowded provincial jails where educational and social programs are limited. They fear that few advantages of the federal prison that make long sentences bearable, such as being allowed to wear their own clothing and being able to form close relationships, will be lost. Prisoner Terry Brewer, who has been in the corrections system for the past twenty years, since she was a juvenile, said she's worried about the future. "I just can't perceive them building new federal jails for women. They haven't done it for how many years, and I just can't see it happening in the near future." Some prisoners also believe they will become more vulnerable if dispersed. "We have developed a certain political voice here in Kingston," says Jo-Ann Mayhew, an Antigonish woman serving a life sentence at P4W. "If you take women and put them in small pockets across the country, we will lose that." Prisoner Mary Sibley, from Hamilton, expresses it another way: "We're being subdivided into little black holes in Canada. It's frightening."

The Correctional Service has taken some emergency measures to try to make conditions more tolerable as long as the Kingston prison remains open. The federal penitentiary has stopped accepting transfers from provincial institutions of women serving two years less a day – a practice that only perpetuated the disadvantages faced by women offenders. The women's prison has hired a second full-time psychologist and renewed a sexual-abuse education program for inmates and staff. Prison authorities have recruited part-time an aboriginal elder from the Dakotas as a spiritual resource for the native population, a full-time native counsellor, and an instructor for native studies. The administration has also signed contracts for a native parenting program and a native "grief resolution" program. It has started to expand the prison's program for drug and alcohol abuse, including one-on-one counselling, education programs, and a therapeutic unit for substance abuse.

The prison has also increased opportunities for women to

have contact with family members through long-distance phone calls and family visits, and cost is no longer to be a consideration in determining who is allowed to attend funerals of close family members. The administration has promised to install lights in the exercise yard to enable women to participate in more organized sports and outdoor leisure activities.

The Correctional Service of Canada took another modest step in March 1990, when it opened a minimum-security institution for women in Kingston – the first of its kind in Canada. The renovated limestone house, without bars on the windows or doors, can accommodate eleven women. Solicitor General Pierre Cadieux, shuffled into the portfolio only two weeks earlier, said the new facility was designed to offer inmates easier access to community programs and counselling in substance abuse, sexual abuse, and psychiatric problems. The more relaxed surroundings combined with intense programs are supposed to provide a "prescription for developing individual responsibility and confidence" to help ease the women's transition from prison to the street.

Despite these changes there is no room for complacency as long as women remain confined at P4W. Since Marlene Moore took her life, five other women from the Kingston prison have died by their own hand:

• In March 1989, Patricia Yvette Bear hanged herself from a tree in a Kingston city park, only two months after being released from P4W on mandatory supervision. The twenty-five-year-old Sioux woman was just a teenager when she was first shipped to the Kingston prison.

• On October 12, 1989, Sandra Bernice Sayer was found hanging from a bedsheet in her cell during a routine hourly patrol of prison cells. A medical coroner pronounced the twenty-five-year-old native woman from Calgary dead at the scene.

• On February 26, 1990, Marie Helen Ledouxe was found hanging in the basement of the bungalow used for family visits in the prison. Her father was visiting her overnight in the special unit and called security when he woke up that morning and couldn't find his daughter. Efforts to revive her failed. She was twenty-seven years old.

• On September 15, 1990, Careen Daigneault of Prince Albert, Saskatchewan, hanged herself in her cell. The thirty-one-year-old was one of fifteen native women participating in a spiritual fast in P4W in support of the Mohawks at Oka. She was taken to hospital and pronounced dead on arrival.

• On November 16, 1990, Janice Neudorf (Bear) was found hanging in her cell on A range. The twenty-three-year-old Métis from Saskatoon still hadn't gained consciousness two months later.

• Lorna Claira Jones, aged twenty-three, was found hanging in her cell from a television cable at about 6:15 p.m. on February 4, 1991. She was pronounced dead at Kingston General Hospital. The young prisoner, from Dawson Creek, B.C., was serving a two-year sentence. She was expected to have been released on mandatory supervision in six months.

Whether the latest government commitment to close the prison amounts to more than smoke and mirrors remains to be seen. The government has made and broken promises so many times that it's hard not to remain sceptical. In any case, new buildings are not the whole answer. Once a new decentralized system is put in place, it must be accompanied by new attitudes and new staff who are capable of seeing women prisoners in the context of their life experiences. But the pressure for change is coming from many different directions and continues to mount. "I'm exceedingly optimistic about the prospects for radical change," Bonnie Diamond says. "I won't be confident until the Prison for Women is closed but this is as close as we've come."

Ultimately, significant reform depends on widespread public understanding. Can society accept that female offenders, with few exceptions, aren't dangerous? Is society ready to transcend its desire to punish and instead provide opportunities for healing and rehabilitation? Are we ready to acknowledge just how much imprisoned women have suffered – and continue to suffer – because of their small numbers?

A few weeks after Marlene Moore's death, Gayle Horii and other women in P4W expressed their grief in writing: "Marlene had a smile that would light up the sky, a heart with lots of love and a mind with much intelligence. The system and society failed her terribly. We never thought of her as 'the most dangerous woman in Canada.' We always thought of her as a child never given a fair chance in life."